AF661745

Dynamics of Industrial Development in India

Dynamics of Industrial Development in India

Harish Tyagi

CYBER TECH PUBLICATIONS
4264/3, Ansari Road, Daryaganj, New Delhi-110002 (India)
Ph.: 011-23244078, Fax: 011-23280028
E-Mail: cyberpublicationsdelhi@yahoo.com

DYNAMICS OF INDUSTRIAL DEVELOPMENT IN INDIA

Harish Tyagi

© Reserved

First Edition 2009

All rights reserved. No part of this publication may be reproduced, stored in a retrieval system or transmitted, in any form or by any means, electronic, mechanical, photo copying, recording or otherwise, without the prior permission of the publisher.

Published by :

G.S. Rawat for **Cyber Tech Publications**
4264/3, Ansari Road, Daryaganj, New Delhi-110002 (India)
Ph.: 011-23244078. Fax: 011-23280028
E-Mail: cyberpublicationsdelhi@yahoo.com

Printed at : **Amit Enterprises**, Maujpur, Delhi, (9810878184)

Preface

The system of Industrial Development Banking being a global issue is the basic approach in the global business. Hence, in this book the authors' presents a comprehensive and an analytical picture of the development banking in India in industrializing the country. The text contains objectives of the study with review of researches in development banking, new vistas in development finance, operational policies and practices of development banks in general and a case study of IDBI in particular. Keeping in view, the research norms a brief chapter end-summary and suggestions and number of figures and tables have been designed in order to make the script more informative illuminating and insightful.

This book will make a significant contribution to the existing literature on development banking sector in the changing business scenario. The book is intended to be useful for business professionals, researchers, financial executives and business educators of the world."

—Author

CONTENTS

1

Indian Agriculture

Agriculture — across the expanse of India — is heralding the country's second Green Revolution. A progressively larger number of states have been amending their Agricultural Produce Marketing Committee (APMC) Act, along the lines of the Model APMC Act, to allow farmers to directly sell their produce to the buyers.

Significantly, several agricultural sectors like horticulture, floriculture, development of seeds, animal husbandry, pisciculture, aqua culture, cultivation of vegetables, mushroom under cultivated conditions and services related to agro and allied sectors have been thrown open to 100 per cent foreign direct investment (FDI) through the automatic route.

Consequently, a number of corporate players have entered into agreement with the farmers with major investment plans to tap the huge potential in this sector.

- PepsiCo after introducing farmers to high-yielding basmati rice, mangoes, potatoes, chillies, peanuts and barley, has launched a five-year program with the Punjab Government to provide four million sweet-orange trees.
- Cadbury India Ltd has entered into an agreement with the Tamil Nadu Horticulture Department to promote cocoa farming in 50,000 acres.
- Reliance Retail plans to establish links with farms in Punjab, West Bengal and Maharashtra with an US$ 5.6 billion investment.
- Skol Breweries India Ltd, the wholly owned subsidiary of SABMiller India, has entered into a contract farming agreement with barley farmers in Haryana.

- Himalaya Drugs plans to associate with farmers across southern Indian states for sourcing at least 70 per cent of its herbs.

Already agriculture is one of the most important sectors of the economy contributing 18.5 per cent of national income, about 15 per cent of total exports and supporting two-thirds of the work force. And with recent developments, it is set to play a more dynamic role in the economy.

PRODUCTION

India with its favorable agro-climatic conditions and rich natural resource base has become the world's largest producer across a range of commodities.

- India is the largest producer of coconuts, mango, banana, milk and dairy products, cashew nuts, pulses, ginger, turmeric and black pepper.
- It is also the second largest producer of rice, wheat, sugar, cotton, fruits and vegetables.

The year 2007-08 promises to be a bumper year for Indian agriculture, with a host of crops clocking record output levels. Some of the highlights of the third advance estimates of the production of major crops, released by the Agriculture Ministry for 2007-08, are:

- Food grain production is estimated to be at an all time record level of 227.32 million tonnes (MT).
- Wheat production is projected to be at a record 76.78 MT.
- Rice production likewise is estimated at an all time record of 95.68 MT.
- Coarse Cereals are also estimated to produce an all time record 39.67 MT.
- Cotton production is estimated to be 23.19 million bales of 170 kg, the best ever production level.
- Pulses production is estimated at the highest ever production level of 15.19 MT.

Apart from these, other crops which are likely to record highest ever production levels in 2007-08 include Maize (18.54 MT), Tur (3.03 MT), Urad (1.56 MT), Oilseeds (28.21 MT) and Soyabean (9.43 MT).

In fact, the estimated growth in food grains output by 4.6 per cent in 2007-08 is nearly four times the average annual growth of 1.2 per cent during 1990-2007.

Also, according to the US Department of Agriculture, India will register the highest increase in rice production (16.3 million tonne) globally in the next 10 years.

Simultaneously, with the changing lifestyle and dietary pattern of the consumers along with the increasing brand and variety consciousness of farmers, the demand for certified high quality seeds has been growing rapidly. Already, a billion-dollar industry, the Indian seed industry is the eight largest in the world and has been growing annually at 12 per cent growth rate. Consequently, several transnational players like Bayer, DuPont, Monsanto, Syngenta and Advanta among others have been stepping up their operations in the country.

EXPORTS

Along with the impressive production growth rates, exports of agriculture and allied products have been increasing steadily. For example, India's share in the world cotton trade has increased from 8 per cent in 2005-06 to 12 per cent in 2006-07. Further the government has prepared a plan to increase India's share in processed food trade from the current 1.6 per cent to 3 per cent in 2015.

Agriculture and allied product exports increased by 20.5 per cent during April-October 2007 to total US$ 11.9 billion as against US$ 9.87 billion in the corresponding period in 2006.

- Spice exports registered a 16 per cent growth in volume and 19 per cent growth in value terms to US$ 940.47 million during April-February 2007.
- Coir exports rose sharply by 20.47 per cent to 118,158 tonnes during April-November.
- Indian sugar exports are expected to more than double in 2007-08, on the back of 1.1 million tonnes exports in 2006-07.
- Cotton exports stood at 6 million bales during the 2007-08 fiscal year.
- Rice exports grew by a whopping 61 per cent during April-October 2007 over the corresponding period in 2006.

ORGANIC FARMING

With the global demand for organic food rising at a feverish pace, India is well placed to raise its share in the US$ 30 billion global market of organic products, given its wealth of natural resources Currently, India ranks 33 in the world in terms of total land under organic cultivation and 88 in terms of the ratio of agricultural land under organic crops to total farming area. But this is set to improve with increasing interest shown by many states.

Nine state including Haryana, Maharashtra and Tamil Nadu among others have already submitted proposals for accreditation to APEDA, which will allow them to certify produce of their farmers as organic. In fact, Kerala is set to turn "organically" green, with the government plans to convert 20 per cent of agricultural land to organic farming each year, with total conversion in five years.

With the accelerating interest shown in organic cultivation, the area under such crops is estimated grow almost four-fold to cross the 2 million mark, says National Centre for Organic Farming (NCOF). Currently, land under organic cultivation is 528,000 (including 312,000 hectares of certified land). Already, India is the second largest producer of organic cotton in the world with a production of 10,365 tonnes a year.

Simultaneously, exports from organic farm produce have been growing at a frenetic pace to total US$ 83.08 million in 2006-07 against US$ 26.4 million in 2005-06, and are well on way to surpass US$ 125.88 million this year. In 2002, exports were US$ 15.5 million.

AGRI-BIOTECH

India has also been making rapid strides to fully utilise the advances in the biotechnology industry for accelerating the growth of its agricultural sector. According to a report by Rabobank, the Indian agri-biotech sector has been growing at a blistering 30 per cent growth rate in the last five years and is likely to maintain this growth well into the future.

In fact, since 2002, when India made its entry in the agri-biotech segment, this segment has been the fastest growing segment among all the biotech industries in the country. The agri-botech industry's sales have been growing at a tremendous growth: from US$ 82.37 million in 2004-05 to US$ 149.14 million in 2005-06 and US$ 230.9 million in 2006-07. It accounted for about 10.84 per cent of total biotech industry's sales in 2006-07.

The growth of this segment can also be seen in the continuous increase in the area under cultivation of such crops. For example, within six years, area grown under genetically modified (GM) cotton variety, Bt cotton, rose sharply to account for 70 per cent of the total area under cotton cultivation.

According to Rabobank, India has the potential to emerge as the major producer of transgenic rice and several GM vegetables by 2010. Already research work is being carried in 19 crops like rice, wheat, cotton, potato, banana, tomato, rapeseed, mustard and coffee among others.

GOVERNMENT INITIATIVES

Government has been taking various progressive measures to accelerate the growth of this sector. Some of the recent initiatives taken by the government include:

- Allowing private sector companies engaged in business of warehousing or transport of food grains in procurement operations on behalf of the Food Corporation of India (FCI)
- A weather-based agricultural insurance scheme is to be rolled out across select districts in 12 states for the forthcoming rabi season.
- Construction of seven Modern Terminal Markets with modern infrastructure facilities that will help farmers realize maximum returns for their produce, remove middlemen and ensure lower prices for end-consumer.

In addition, the government has already approved 60 agricultural export zones (AEZs). Besides, four zones have been identified to provide US$ 12.1 million worth of funds under a scheme called Assistance to States for Infrastructure Development of Exports. Further the Government will provide an additional US$ 6.17 billion for new farm initiatives launched by states to double the growth rate in agriculture to 4 per cent over the 11th Plan period.

MEDIUM AND LARGE INDUSTRIES

India started her quest for industrial development after independence in 1947. The Industrial Policy Resolution of 1948 marked the beginning of evolution of the Indian Industrial Policy. The Resolution not only defined the broad contours of the policy, it delineated the role of the State in industrial development both as an entrepreneur and as an authority. Successive policy resolutions also reiterated this basic tilt in favour of the public sector. The Industrial Policy Resolution of 1956 gave the public sector strategic role in the economy. It categorised industries which would be the exclusive responsibility of the State or would progressively come under State control and others. Earmarking the pre-eminent position of the public sector, it envisaged private sector co-existing with the State and thus attempted to give the policy framework flexibility.

It was considered that the private sector does not have the resources to undertake huge infrastructure projects described by Pandit Jawaharlal Nehru as the temples of modern India. Without the basic infrastructure industries, the foundations of a modern industrial economy could not be laid.

In 1956, capital was scarce and the base of entrepreneurship not strong enough. Hence the 1956 Industrial Policy Resolution gave primacy to the role of the State to assume a predominant and direct responsibility for industrial development.

The Industrial Policy initiatives undertaken by the Government of India since July 1991 have been designed to build on the past industrial achievements and to accelerate the process of making Indian industry internationally competitive. It recognises the strength and maturity of the industry and attempts to provide the competitive stimulus for higher growth. The thrust of these initiatives has been to increase the domestic and external competition through extensive application of market mechanisms and facilitating forging of dynamic relationships with foreign investors and suppliers of technology. The process of reform has been continuous. While, as a result of policies pursued since Independence, a broad-based infrastructure (roads, power & transport) has been built up, basic industries established, a high degree of self-reliance achieved in a large number of items, new centres of industrial activity have emerged as well as a new generation of entrepreneurs and a large number of engineers, technicians and skilled workers also trained and overall a climate for rapid industrial growth created, the industrial licensing system had promoted inefficiency and resulted in a high cost economy. Major policy changes were therefore introduced in 1991 to provide competitive stimulus for accelerated economic growth.

With the introduction of the New Industrial Policy (NIP) in 1991, a substantial programme of deregulation has been undertaken. Industrial licensing has been abolished for all items except for a short list of six industries related to security, strategic or environmental concerns.

The number of industries reserved for the public sector were reduced to eight, where in Government's view, security and strategic concerns predominate. Recently, a decision has been taken to open defence industry sector to private sector with foreign direct investment permissible up to 26 per cent. Now, the areas reserved for the public sector would be: (a) atomic energy; (b) the substances specified in the schedule to the notification of the Government of India in the Department of Atomic Energy No. S.O.212(E), dated the 15 March 1995, and (c) railway transport. Even in these areas, private sector participation can be invited on a discretionary basis.

Foreign investment had earlier played only a minor role as a source of finance. Several developing and less advanced countries have received foreign capital several times more than India. This is mainly because they had simplified their investment procedures. In conjunction with industrial deregulation, the Government also liberalised substantially the process relating to foreign investment. Foreign Direct Investment (FDI) is seen as a means to support domestic investment for achieving a higher level of economic development. FDI benefits domestic industry as well as the Indian consumer by providing opportunities for technological upgradation, access to global managerial skills and practices, optimal utilisation of human and natural resources, making Indian industry internationally competitive, opening up export markets, providing backward and forward linkages and access to international quality goods and services.

In pursuance of Government's commitment to further facilitate Indian industry to engage unhindered in various activities, the Government has permitted, except for a negative list, access to the automatic route for Foreign Direct Investment.

Tamil Nadu Industrial Profile

Tamil Nadu is one of the well-developed States in terms of development and has carved for itself a place of pride in the Industrial Map of India. In the post liberalisation era, with gradual dismantling of licence restrictions, Tamil Nadu has emerged as one of the front-runners by attracting large number of investments. The State is the third largest economy in India and its current State Domestic Product is well over $19.6 Billion. Tamil Nadu has a diversified Industrial base ranging from automobiles, textile, leather, petro-chemicals and information technology.

Competitive Advantages of Tamil Nadu

- Availability of high quality of both industrial and social Infrastructure- Infrastructure status of Tamil Nadu rated as the best in the country.
- Availability of high density of transportation network facility both rail and road besides international airports and modern sea ports.
- Affordable skilled manpower, large English speaking population and harmonious industrial relations.
- Network of well developed Industrial Parks and Industrial Estates spread over the State with high quality Infrastructure.
- Diversified Industrial base with support services.
- Modern world class communication facilities offering value-added services - bandwith is no barrier for SW and IT enabled services.
- Adequate power supply.

The decision by the then English East India Company to set up a trading post at the fishing village of Madraspatnam can be said to have given Tamil Nadu areas an early start in industrial development and trade. Over a period of time, Madras became a significant port in the eastern coast and helped in the industrial development of the surrounding areas. By the time of Independence, Tamil Nadu had a strong presence in textile industry with a highly developed handloom sector with the largest concentration of looms in the country and a well established third largest mill sector around Coimbatore. It also had a reasonable base in the engineering industry. Post Independence, flow of public sector investment and setting up of import substitution industries in the private sector gave a strong fillip to the State, with major units such as the Integral Coach Factory, Bharat Heavy Electricals and Madras Refineries along with private sector initiatives taken by the TVS, Amalgamation, Murugappa and other groups coming up to take advantage of the potential.

Many multinational companies like Ford, Hyundai, Saint Gobain, Matsushita, etc., and International Financial institutions like World Bank, ABNAmro Bank, Standard & Chartered Bank, etc. have chosen Chennai for locating their back offices. At present the State accounts for over 11-12% of India's industrial output and has contributed a considerable share to the country's Industrial Production. The following data is the indicative of its traditional strengths:

Share of Industrial Production of Tamil Nadu

Industrial Category	Tamil Nadu's share in India's output (%)
Cars	21
Heavy Commercial Vehicle	33
Auto Components	35
Railway coaches	49
Motor Cycles & mopeds	46
Newsprint	17
Cotton Yarn	32
Power driven pumps	50
Leather products	70
Software	13

Source: CMIE & ASI Publications Centre

Tamil Nadu stands third among the States in the country in Industrial Output, Value Addition and Foreign Direct

Investment flow. The State has the highest number of factories and employs the largest number of workers in the country.

The Tamil Nadu State targeted a growth rate of 7 per cent per annum in GSDP for the Ninth Five Year Plan Period (1997-2002).

The State registered a growth rate of 8.03 per cent in 1997-98, 6.09 per cent in 1998-1999,5.78 per cent in 1999-2000, 4.36 per cent in 2000-2001, and 3.06 per cent in 2001-2002. The annual average growth rate of GSDP during the Ninth Plan was 5.46 per cent.

The following is the comparative statement on the growth of GSDP in Tamil Nadu and GDP in All India at constant prices. (Base:1993-94) during the Ninth Plan.

GSDP/GDP at constant (1993-94) prices-Tamil Nadu and All India

	GSDP/ GDP (Rs. in crores)		Tamil Nadu
Year	**Tamil Nadu**	**All India**	**Share**
1997-98	76097	1016399	7.5
1998-99	80728	1083047	7.5
1999-00	85391	1151991	7.4
2000-01	89110 Q.E	1193922	7.5
2001-2002	91841 A.E	1258231	7.3

Source: Economic Survey,2001-02 & CMIE Reports

The share of Tamil Nadu in India's GDP is about 7.3%. Given the current high growth rate, Tamil Nadu is expected to emerge as the second largest economy in the near future.

The share of manufacturing sector in SDP is 34.04 per cent. The composition of SDP is as follows:

Activities	**% share in SDP in 2001-02 (at 1993-94 constant prices)**
Agriculture & Allied activities	16.65
Manufacturing	34.04
Services	49.31
Total	100.00

Industrial Growth during Plan Periods

The manufacturing sector registered an average growth rate of 7.4% followed by the Mining and Electricity sector which registered an average growth rate of 6.7% and 5.8% respectively during the period 1982-83 to 1990- 91 (Base 1981-82 = 100). The annual average growth rate of overall industrial production stood at 9.1% during the period 1982-83 to 1985-86 which came down to 5.8% during the period 1986-87 to 1990-91 and further to 2.0% in the five year period 1991-92 to 1995-96 (Base : 1981-82=100). According to the new base (1993-94=100), the manufacturing sector registered a growth rate of 6.4% followed by 21.2% under mining sector and 17.0% under Electricity sector in the year 1994-95. The annual growth rate of overall industrial production which stood at 7.3% in 1994-95 came down to 2.3% in the five year period 1997-98 to 2001-02. The details of IIPs are as follows:

The table below shows the growth of GSDP at constant ('93-'94) prices by economic activity for the years from 1994-95 to 2001-02.

The following table shows the comparative sectoral contribution to the GSDP for the years 1993-94 and 2001-02.

Economic Activity	1993-94	2001-02
Agriculture & Allied, Forestry, Fishing	24.82	16.65
Manufacturing and Construction	33.72	34.04
Trade, Transport, etc.	20.40	23.83
Banking Insurance, etc.	11.01	13.63
Public Administration & Services	10.05	11.85

Source: Department of Economics and Statistics.

In respect of Manufacturing sector the State ranks second in terms of contribution to GSDP. The major industries contributing to the GSDP are the traditional industries like cotton textiles, rubber, food products, machinery, transport equipments, leather and leather products, etc. The secondary sector of the economy comprising the sub-sectors viz., manufacturing (both registered and unregistered), electricity and construction contributes roughly one-third to GSDP. The contribution of these sub-sectors to GSDP in 2000-01 was as follows:

	(Rs. in crores)
Manufacturing	21166
Electricity	2894
Construction	5931
Sub-total	29991
Total GSDP	90760
Percentage of GSDP	33.0%

The growth of the Manufacturing Sector, however, was inconsistent with growth rates of -1.41%, -3.73%, 14.09% and 1.02% in the first four years of the Ninth Plan due to the general recessionary trend in the industrial sector in the country which had its impact in Tamil Nadu also, though there were signs of gradual recovery in the year 2001-02. Within the sub-sectors there are wide variations in growth trends. Though the growth in manufacturing sector has been sluggish, the construction sector recorded a growth rate of 8.59%, to emerge as one of the fastest growing economic activities. Tamil Nadu has emerged as one of the favoured destinations of investors through its investor-friendly and transparent decision - making policies. The State is also one of the major recipients of foreign direct investment. Recent examples of FDI are Ford Motors of USA, Hyundai of Korea, Mitsubishi of Japan and St. Gobain of France.

The comparative details of FDI approvals accorded in the last ten years in some of the major States are as follows:

Foreign Direct Investment Flow

Sl. No.	States	Foreign Private Sector (Rs. crores (April 2002)
1.	Maharashtra	48534.19
2.	Delhi	33493.32
3.	Tamil Nadu	23209.54
4.	Karnataka	22447.05
5.	Gujarat	18352.30
6.	Andhra Pradesh	13037.72
7.	Kerala	1524.51

Source: SIA, GOI.

The current realisation rate (i.e.) percentage of investment under implementation however is low, at 34% as against the all-India average rate of 41.62%.

Exports

Tamil Nadu is the largest exporter from southern region constituting about 60% of the southern region exports. During 2000-01, the value of the State exports was Rs. 30636 crores which accounted for about 15% all India exports. The following table summarises the export performance during Ninth Plan period.

Year	Exports (Rs. in crores)
1997-98	19232
1998-99	21387
1999-00	23937
2000-01	30636

Source: Federation of Indian Exports' Organisation (FIEO)

Performance of Traditional Industries in Tamil Nadu

Leather Based Industries

Tamil Nadu has a dominant presence in the leather and leather based industries. The tanning industry in India has a total installed capacity of 225 million pieces of hide and skins of which Tamil Nadu alone contributes as much as 70%. Leather industry occupies a pride of place in the industrial map of Tamil Nadu.

Tamil Nadu enjoys a leadership position with 40% share in India's export. It currently employs in the country about 2.5 million persons in production of products such as shoe uppers, shoes, garments, and so on.

Leather exports from the country by the end of the year 2000-2001 was Rs. 900.43 crores. Government of Tamil Nadu offers a special capital subsidy to encourage leather industry. TALCO, a State government organisation was setting up common effluent treatment plants in leather industry clusters. The main features of the leather industry in India which has a massive potential of growth, export and employment opportunities are as follows:

- Employs 2.5 million persons

- A large part (nearly 60-65%) of the production comes from the Small and cottage sector.
- Annual export value poised to touch about 2 billion US dollars.
- Endowed with 10% of the world's raw material and export constitutes about 2% of the world trade.
- Has enormous potential for future growth.
- Very high value addition within the country.

Tanning Sector - The tanneries in the State enjoy a pre-eminent status not only in India but also in global leather trade in terms of the quality of finished leather manufactured. The tanneries in the State have increased their environmental preparedness and in complying with the economics imposed by many importing countries and lead to fashion forecasting of leather colours and textures with respect to their advanced preparedness in manufacturing colours forecast. The colour shade card for the world is now made in Chennai.

These developments open up a new opportunity for Tamil Nadu in leather sector. Recognizing the need and importance of modernization of tanneries in India, the Government of India has commissioned a Tannery Modernization Scheme. The enrolment of tanneries of Tamil Nadu in Tannery Modernization Scheme is yet to pick up momentum. A rational policy of the State for promoting additional investments into the tanning sector for modernization of existing units is needed. The Tannery Modernization Scheme of the Government of India provides investment grants for enabling the small and medium enterprises to readjust quickly to the changed circumstances of WTO regime.

Tanneries in China and other major competing countries have invested significant amounts of funds in large tanneries. The tannery sector in Tamil Nadu needs to modernize urgently. Footwear Sector - The footwear industry in Tamil Nadu is export driven. The installed capacity of the manufacture of closed shoes has been estimated at 71 million pairs only as of 1999. Of the installed capacity for the manufacture of closed shoes in India, nearly 50% is in Tamil Nadu. Some of high quality brands of shoes are made in the shoe factories in the state.

Technology absorption in footwear factories in Vellore district during 1985-95 periods has led to the generation of more than 50000 jobs for women in the district.

The unit-value realization from export footwear industry in Tamil Nadu is higher than in many other States in India. This leads also to a state of vulnerability in global leather trade. Since the non-leather footwear component industry is not developed adequately in the State or in South India, there is an excessive dependence on imports of components adding to inventory costs and time delays in supply.

The national policy of reservation of footwear industry of the Government of India for small-scale sector has led to the emergence of a large number of small footwear enterprises in the State. These units do not enjoy economy of scale for supplying to the large volume round the year markets. These are more suited to the markets where the economy of scope and small volume supply are advantageous. However, these markets demand that the supply of each consignment is effected quickly and three or four consignments are shipped within 3-4 months of a season. Since airfreight adds to the cost of the consignment to an extent, cost competitiveness is lost. Port facilities with an infrastructure for adjusting to the quick turn over and market response needs of the fashion oriented market can open up new opportunities for the state.

A proactive State policy for integrated development of footwear industry in the State will be valuable and such a step could lead to

- Leveraging of global strength of the state in manufacture of finished leather.
- Increased employment with a special focus on gender empowerment.
- Doubling of returns from leather industry in the State by way of export realization.

Leather Garments - Tamil Nadu enjoys a strong position in the export trade on leather garments. The State is strong in the manufacture of leathers from goat and sheepskins suited for the manufacture of leather garments.

Since the garment units in the State do not enjoy any longer cost competitive advantages with respect to the leather garment-manufacturing units in other States in the country, it is becoming necessary for the sector to specialize on some select markets. A careful strategy is required for promotion of leather garment sector in Tamil Nadu. The main markets for the leather products of Tamil Nadu have been in Western Europe. These markets are sensitive to the technical and non-trade barriers including environmental and social audit norms. The leather garment units in Tamil Nadu may need to prepare themselves for such exacting demands of the market.

Leather goods - The manufacture of small leather goods like wallets, dress gloves and bags has registered a significant increase in India during 1995-2000 periods. Tamil Nadu has kept up with the pace of national growth in leather goods sector so far. There are still untapped opportunities in global leather goods sector in Tamil Nadu.

The major recommendations for leather industry are:

1. Tamil Nadu may take measures to attract large FDIs and JVs in leather sector from potential investors in Europe and China.
2. Tamil Nadu may identify footwear as focus sector and attract large investments. This being an employment oriented industry without any pollution related problem, focus on footwear industry is advantageous to the State.
3. Footwear Component Park and a footwear complex with Special Economic Zone facilities may be established, possibly at Ennore.
4. Strengthening of road and utility infrastructure in existing leather complexes with support from Government of India may be accorded high priority.
5. Modernization of Common Effluent Treatment Plants may be supported. Grant of subsidy by the State Government need not be park, besides currently implementing a LNG handling terminal at Ennore Satellite Port. Based on LNG terminal, a number of down-stream petrochemical projects have been planned.

Apart from upcoming refinery at Cuddalore, two new refineries are proposed to be set up at Nagapattinam and Ennore. Petrochemical industry in Tamil Nadu is in the threshold of rapid expansion. At the end of October 2001, 28 major chemicals and related petrochemicals and rubber projects with an aggregate investment of Rs. 33,219 crores are proposed/ under implementation. This constitutes 20.5% of total investment proposed/under implementation in Tamil Nadu. The details of investments and number of projects are given below.

Product	Investment (Rs. in crores)	No. of Projects
Chemicals & Plastics	16,461	20
Drugs & Pharma	509	5
Plastics Products	15	1
Petroleum products	15,908	6

Auto Ancillaries

Tamil Nadu is the Detroit of India with mother automobile plants like Ashok Leyland, TAFE, Heavy Factory-Avadi, Integral Coach factory, Enfield, TVS, etc. supporting a large number of auto ancillaries in SME sector. With setting up of 3 car projects by Ford, Hyundai and HM-Mitsubishi and with expansion of TAFE & Ashok Leyland, Tamil Nadu's position got further consolidated as a major hub. A large number of new ancillaries with foreign collaborations also came up as the result of the three car projects. At present Tamil Nadu accounts for :

Biotechnology - the Emerging Industry

Bio-Resource endowments in Tamil Nadu - With 5,000 species of flowering plants, 22,500 sq.km of forest cover and a coastline of 1,000 km, Tamil Nadu is exceptionally rich in biodiversity. This kind of wealth, rarely occurring in a State, needs to be put to sustainable use, especially since the market for biotechnology products in the country is expected to double to Rs. 15,000 crores in the next five years.

The State Government has made a commitment to set up a Rs. 30 crore venture fund to provide the single-window clearance facility to obtain clearances from the various Central government agencies, such as the Recombinant DNA Advisory Committee, the Institutional Biosafety Committee, the Review Committee on Genetic Manipulation and the Genetic Engineering Approval Committee, to establish biotechnology enterprises. The policy document promises the creation of a

Biotechnology Board, under the chairmanship of an expert, and consisting of senior government officials, scientists and industrialists. The Board will form standing advisory committees to identify and attract investments, mobilise resources, and work out guidelines and set up a regulatory framework for the use of bioresources.

Schemes are being worked out to protect and develop various biosphere resources, such as the Gulf of Mannar off Rameswaram, the Pichavaram mangroves in Nagapattinam district & Muthupettai in Tiruvarur district. The Global Environmental facility has announced an assistance of $7.85 million to protect the Gulf of Mannar.

Industrial activity has so far been confined largely to first generation biotechnology enterprises such as fermentation of antibiotics. To broaden the industrial base, a large number of plant tissue culture units are being set up, besides promoting the production of food and industrial enzymes, classical fermentation products (antibiotics and immuno-modulators), bioenergy and bio-polymers, and other such activities.

According to the policy document, all efforts are directed towards the creation of a critical mass of industrial activity in biotechnology.

A two-pronged strategy would be evolved to encourage modern processes in the areas of agriculture, industry and medical and veterinary sciences at the same time focussing on traditional biotechnology products, especially industrial and food enzymes. There is also a move to encourage commercial enterprises to develop recombinant DNA (deoxyribonucleic acid)-based products and bioinformatics.

In the field of medical biotechnology (the State accounts for 11 per cent of the market in the country), the focus is on such areas as diagnostics, vaccines (Hepatitis-C and malaria), therapeutics (Interferon and insulin) and veterinary drugs.

In the field of agriculture, the Government would work with the germplasm data available with the Tamil Nadu Agricultural University and the M.S.Swaminathan Research Foundation to develop biopesticides and biofertilizers, natural health care products, animal feed, transgenics and diagnostics. The Government would also facilitate the creation of quarantine facilities and sanitary/phytosanitary measures as per the World Trade Organisation (WTO) agreements for biological items.

The Tamil Nadu Government has proposed the setting up of four biotechnology parks across the State. Apart from the Rs. 6.2 crore Women's Biotech Park at Kelambakkam near Chennai, which will commence operations shortly, the remaining three parks have been tentatively suggested at Mandapam (Marine Biotech Park), Madurai-Nilgiris (Hill Biotech Park) and Chennai (Biotech Incubator Park). According to the draft report, the HPC (chaired by Dr.M.S. Swaminathan), are planning for concerted effort between the research institutes, the industry and the Government and are developing professional approach.

Cornell University has evinced keen interest in setting up and managing these parks. The projects should be economically and commercially feasible with a strong networking of State and global research institutions so as to cross-utilise the facilities and to avoid "re-inventing the wheel" in a capital and knowledge intensive field like biotechnology.

Strengthening of Human Resources pool in Tamil Nadu - The Government will initiate measures to enhance the human resources pool for Biotechnology available within the State. Efforts will also be made to facilitate greater interaction between scientists at various universities and representatives of industries including occupants of the various Biotechnology Parks. An appropriate framework will be positioned for this. Human Resource Initiatives of the Government will consist of the following:

Suitably changing the procedures in existing State-supported universities and institutions to facilitate better interaction with the business community and encourage the creation of scientist/technologist entrepreneurs.

Initiating the creation of certain new, short duration technician oriented courses at appropriate universities in specific areas (post B.Sc./M.Sc.).

Increasing the intake of students in Biotechnology courses currently offered in various universities.

Evaluate and provide one-time grant to specific institutions for establishing appropriate training courses for creating

Bioinformatics professionals to exploit the emerging opportunities in this area.

The thrust areas in environmental biotechnology products would be those concerning leather and textiles. The idea is to develop apparatus/ techniques for biosensors, microbial strain development of cultures for waste management (bioremediation), and so on.

Thrust Areas in Biotechnology

- Diagnostics
- Therapeutics
- Pharmacogenomics
- Bioinformatics
- Agriculture biotechnology
- Industrial biotechnology
- Inputs to the industry (hardware suppliers-instrumentation and chemicals)
- Marine biotechnology
- Forest and Environment-focused biotechnology
- Contract research in all areas of biotechnology and related areas.

Overview of State Public Sector Enterprises

In the pre-liberalisation era when the State had to play a major role in achieving economic development, public sector undertakings were considered as engines of growth. Therefore, PSUs were promoted as instruments of public policy. PSUs were established with the objectives of achieving a combination of objectives like:

- Providing start of investments and initiatives
- Employment generation
- Production of goods and services for maximizing social benefit and to ensure unfair trade practices do not lead to shortages.
- Balanced regional development and backward area development.

The Public Sector Enterprises in Tamilnadu (not considering nine Statutory Boards) can be broadly categorised into ten groups as given below:

Sl.No.	Group	No. of PSEs
1.	Passenger Transport	19
2	Other Transport	1
3.	Mining	2
4	Manufacturing	11
5	Trading	2
6	Development (Finance)	10
7	Development - Others	9
8	Agriculture & Allied	5
9	Construction	3
10	Miscellaneous	5

Source : Bureau of Public Enterprises (BPE), Annual Report 1999-2000.

Going by the very poor rate of return on the investments by Government in the Public Sector and the present scale of private sector competition and activity, the role of many public sector entreprises, especially those manufacturing goods where there is a significant private sector presence now is being called into question. Burdened with surplus labour paid very well compared to the private sector, paucity of cash precluding timely technological upgradation, lack of strategic and competitive flexibility which the private sector has, many organisations are on the rapid decline path. In the case of public utilities, non revision of tariffs to match increasing costs is an additional handicap to viable functioning. Therefore, the following recommendations are made:

- In the industrial sector, the State Government may not enter into fields or spheres of activities unrelated to Governance. It may actively encourage the private sector to grow rapidly in various spheres of manufacturing.
- In respect of existing Public Sector Undertakings (PSUs) a case by case analysis has been undertaken. It may be the effort of the Government to restructure these Undertakings so that they stop making losses or to close them down.
- Government may augment the State Renewal fund - the safety net mechanism out of proceeds of disinvestment

and through additional means of resource mobilisation so as to minimize the problems of labour reduction.

- Improvement of management of Public Sector Undertakings may be given the highest attention. A pool of officers may be utilised to ensure continuity of management in these Public Sector Undertakings.
- In case of Public and Private organisations operating essential services, an independent regulatory body may be envisaged to monitor provision of quality essential services and fixing user charges.

Raghavan Committee on State PSEs

The State Government of Tamil Nadu, in January 1997 (vide Finance (BPE) Department G.O.Ms.No.26, dated 21.01.1997), constituted an Expert Committee under the Chairmanship of Thiru S.V.S. Raghavan to study the performance of the Tamil Nadu Public Sector Enterprises, specifically,

(1) to make a comprehensive review of the performance of the State Public Sector Undertakings,

(2) to identify the causative factors responsible for the poor performance of the loss making units and

(3) to recommend measures to improve the performance of the Public Sector Undertakings so that each PSU earns a reasonable rate of return on the investment.

The Committee, besides making its own study and evaluation, also took into account the recommendations of two earlier Committees appointed by the State Government to review the working of Public Sector Corporations - the Venkataraman Committee (1976-77) and the Ramanathan Committee (1988), and the Pattabiraman Committee on State Transport Undertakings.

The Report while giving an overview of performance of State PSEs, indicates an investment of over Rs. 5000 crores, a negative networth of Rs. 44.14 crores of the State PSEs with the result that there was an annual average cash outflow of over Rs. 250 crores every year from the State Government and with nothing else to show except an employment of approximately 1.61 lakhs of persons.

The State PSEs were constituted to give a fillip to the industrial growth in the State and develop into an important segment of the economy of Tamil Nadu. However, the performance of these enterprises, barring some exceptions, was below par. They either incurred huge losses or earned very meagre profits.

In the revised economic order, questions whether these PSEs have been able to fulfil their role as instruments of public policy, the rationale for the existence of these units, especially under the aegis of the Government, and the chances of survival of these enterprises in the long term, had arisen.

The study of the Committee brought into focus the following major areas of failures:

- The State Public Enterprises have not been functioning on business lines.
- The financial performance has been poor and no significant contribution has been made to the State. The profitability of these enterprises and their return on investment have been negative.
- The Government of Tamil Nadu had invested over Rs. 1,964.33 crores (excluding Tamil Nadu Newsprint and Papers Ltd.) in the State Public Enterprises as March 1977, and had not derived any significant returns over the years.
- The originally envisaged 'trickle-down' effect of economic growth did not materialize. For all the investment and efforts over the years, the PSEs have not had a great impact on the economy of the State except for direct employment of 1,61,000 (in 1996). There seems to be hardly any ripple effect in terms of industrial growth. In short, the State PSEs did not transform themselves into 'engines of growth'.

The Committee pointed out that the changing complexion of modern business warrants dynamic responses, which these enterprises do not seem to be capable of in the present form. Further, the role of Government itself is changing - from that of a provider to that of a facilitator, with focus on policy making and development of social infrastructure. The Committee endorsed the prescriptions laid down by Ramanathan Committee under which in future, a direct role for Government, particularly in industry, could be contemplated in three sets of circumstances, viz.,

i. Where the activity has been specifically reserved for the Public Sector under Government policy and it will not be possible for the private sector to undertake the activity at all.

ii. Where it is unlikely that the Private Sector will be willing to take up the activity, because of reasons such as large capital expenditure involved or the unlikelihood of immediate adequate return.

iii. Where the development of large areas of backwardness requires Government intervention as a result of the reluctance of private industry to venture into the area because of its very backward nature.

Out of the 66 Public Sector Enterprises and 18 Co-operative Spinning mills studied by this Committee, the Committee recommended:

- Retention of 14 Enterprises in the present form;
- Restructuring and Disinvestment of 34 Enterprises (including 19 State Transport Enterprises); and winding up of 18 Enterprises

  Out of the 18 Co-operative Spinning Mills studied by this Committee, the Committee recommended:
- Restructuring and Disinvestment of 8 Co-operative Spinning Mills; and · Winding up of 10 Co-operative Spinning mills.

The Committee recommended setting up of a Tamil Nadu Public Sector Disinvestment Commission to dispose off and to disinvest in the best interests of the State.

In regard to administration of the Public Sector Undertakings to be retained by the Government, the Committee recommended that the appointment of the Chief Executive should be by an autonomous Selection Board known as the Tamil Nadu Public Sector Selection Board. The Chief Executives should generally be professionals and with a proven track record of having worked in either Central or State Public Sector or in Private Sector of some repute, the Board should also have members drawn from different expertises and need not necessarily be Government employees, the Government nominees should not include nominees of the administrative ministry under which the public enterprise operates, and the Board should be given total autonomy to manage the company.

On the role of Government, the Committee set the long term perspective as follows:

Modern business has become very complex and competitive. Global markets, where there are no barriers, are the order of the day. The new business environment mandates professional management denoted by creating sustainable competitive advantage, modern and world class technology, economy of scale, operating efficiency and productivity, resource optimisation, flexibility in operations, accent on quality and cost, and customer focus through faster response. In the globalised scenario only those units that are market oriented, efficient and customer focused will survive.

World over, the contemporary wisdom is to confine governance to policy making, providing an investment climate, facilitate industrial and business growth and concentrate on development of social infrastructure such as Education, Health Care and setting up Research Institutions. Government and Public Sector investments concentrate in areas such as Defence and highly capital intensive industries where Private Sector is unable to contribute. In all other sectors, investment and management should be left to the Private Sector.

The Government still has a major role to play in the new and global scenario, in terms of setting appropriate goals and strategic directions and creating a competitive climate. Its role is to push and challenge its industries to advance and perform. The goal of Government policy towards economy should deploy the State's resources at high levels of productivity.

Government should function as the principal engine of factor creation and should endeavour to create competitive advantage in specialised industries such as automobiles, auto components, textiles, leather, food processing, etc.

In the long run, only those Enterprises that are characterised by high public purpose and efficient management will be accepted. They will be expected to perform like any other Private Sector company. Their performance will be measured on the same yardstick such as productivity, profitability, growth and accountability.

The recommendations of the Committee were examined in Government by the Secretaries' Committee headed by the Chief Secretary to Government and placed before the Cabinet. Orders have been issued from Government for winding up of the following six Corporations:

1. Tamil Nadu Steels Ltd.
2. Tamil Nadu Poultry Development Corporation Limited
3. Tamil Nadu Leather Development Corporation Limited
4. Dharmapuri District Development Corporation Limited
5. Cheran Engineering Corporation Limited
6. Tamil Nadu Agro Industries Limited

Further, it was decided to wind up the following two Corporations:

1. Southern Structurals Limited (Approval from BIFR is awaited for its closure)
2. Tamil Nadu Film Development Corporation Limited (Orders issued for closure)

The Secretaries' Committee has to consider the position in regard to the other PSUs.

Ninth Plan Outlay and Expenditure

An outlay of Rs. 700 crores was provided for Large and Medium Industries for the Ninth Plan which is inclusive of State Owned Corporations, viz., TIDCO (Rs. 130 crores), SIPCOT (Rs. 230 crores), TACID (Rs. 130 crores), ELCOT (Rs. 50 crores), Director of Sugar (Rs. 50 crores), TANCEM (Rs. 100 crores) and Tamil Nadu Minerals Ltd. (Rs. 10 crores). Against this outlay, the expenditure for the Large and Medium Industries during the Ninth Plan was of the order of Rs. 476.77 crores.

Tamil Nadu Industrial Investment Corporation Ltd. - TIIC

The Tamil Nadu Industrial Investment Corporation Ltd. (TIIC), the one stop finance shop for industries, was set up as a first state level financial institution in the country as early as in 1949. It provides term loans currently up to Rs. 800 lakhs for a single industrial project for acquiring fixed assets like land, building, plant and machinery and equipments for setting up of new industrial units a well as for expansion, modernizsation, diversification, etc. of existing units. Financial assistance is also extended for Small Road Transport Operators, Hotels, Hospitals and Nursing Homes, Doctors, etc.

The progress in vital operations of the Corporation namely sanctions, and disbursements during Ninth Plan are given below:

Performance during Ninth Plan

(Rs. in crores)

Year	Sanctions	Disbursement
1997-98	242.08	192.89
1998-99	154.69	117.74
1999-00	251.09	172.81
2000-01	286.52	200.20
2001-02	213.00	188.00

TIIC is mainly concentrating on the promotion and development of small scale industries (SSI) besides playing a significant role in the development of first generation entrepreneurs.

a. Employment generation during Ninth Plan - The units assisted by TIIC generate employment opportunities to a sizeable number of persons. Employment opportunities created by TIIC during the last five years are given below:

Year	No. of persons
1996-97	46404
1997-98	29972
1998-99	19630
1999-00	20930
2000-01	21512

b. Subsidy Disbursal during Ninth Plan- TIIC also sanctions and disburses the state capital subsidy for the units assisted by it as an implementing agent of the State Government. In order to help its assisted units to implement the project without any delay, subsidy is being sanctioned as bridge loan and disbursed to the assisted units along with term loans.

These bridge loans are being netted off after the subsidy is reimbursed by the Government.

The sanctions and disbursements made by the Corporation under the State Capital Subsidy Scheme during the past five years are as follows:

Year	Sanctions	Disbursement
1997-98	22.68	18.54
1998-99	11.98	6.94
1999-00	11.94	6.10
2000-01	10.34	6.98
2001-02	7.46	6.81

c. Special Schemes operated during Ninth Plan - The Corporation is operating a number of special schemes like Single Window Scheme. SEMFEX scheme for Ex-servicemen, Concessional Assistance for Women Entrepreneurs, Soft Loan scheme for first generation entrepreneurs, scheme for marketing assistance, short term loan for working capital purposes, Bill Discounting Scheme, Assistance for Technology Development and modernization (RTDM), Special Scheme for Textile Industry under Technology upgradation Fund (RTUF), Marriage Hall, Community Hall, Commercial Complex, Warehouse, etc. State Industries Promotion Corporation of Tamil Nadu (SIPCOT) State Industries Promotion Corporation of Tamil Nadu (SIPCOT) was established in the year 1971 under the Companies Act. The main objective of the Corporation is to promote medium and large scale industries in Tamil Nadu by

- Developing, marketing and maintaining Industrial Complexes
- Implementing infrastructure development schemes.
- Servicing the existing term loans.

Special Focus like Apparel Park etc.

A proposal to establish an Apparel Park in towns like Irungattukottai, Perundurai, Tiruppur is under consideration.

Progress in implementation of "Critical Infrastructure Balance" (CIB) schemes in Tamil Nadu.

Common Effluent Treatment Plant for Small Dyeing Units at Salem.

For setting up of a Common Effluent Treatment Plant (C.E.T.P.) for the Small Scale Dyeing Factories at Salem, SIPCOT has prepared a project through M/s.Industrial and Technical Consultancy Organisation of Tamil Nadu (ITCOT) and gave it to Erumaipalayam Bye-pass Small Scale Dyeing factory C.E.T.P. Ltd. for implementation under Critical Infrastructure Balance Scheme (C.I.B). The cost of the scheme is estimated at Rs. 1.90 crores. Since the Company is prepared to bring in 50% of the project cost, SIPCOT has forwarded the application to Government of India for financial assistance under C.I.B. scheme for the balance of 50% of the project cost. It is under consideration of the Government of India.

Proposals for availing central assistance

(i) Establishment of Food Parks at Nilakottai and Bargur by availing grant of Rs. 4 crores each from Government of India and

(ii) Establishment of Market Intelligence and product development center at Kancheepuram for Silk Industries at an estimated cost of Rs. 2 crores under C.I.B. Scheme.

Tamil Nadu Industrial Development Corporation Limited (TIDCO) TIDCO, a wholly owned by Government of Tamil Nadu enterprise, was formed in 1965 to promote Large and Medium Scale Industries in Tamil Nadu.

TIDCO plays a vital role in the industrial development of the State. It identifies medium and large scale investment opportunities and promotes such projects in partnership with private companies and individual entrepreneurs. Over the years, TIDCO has moved away from Public sector investments and currently focusses on equity partnership in Joint ventures especially in the infrastructure sector. TIDCO's joint/associate sector partners include reputed industrial houses of the country such as TATA, BIRLA, MAC Groups, JK Group, Lakshmi Machine Works, Sakthi Group, Nagarjuna Group and Mahindra Group.

TIDCO has so far promoted over 100 projects in various fields viz., iron & steel fertilizers, chemicals, petrochemicals, automobiles, food processing, leather, textiles, pharmaceuticals, floriculture and horticulture. TIDCO also carries out facilitation work (escort service) for overseas investors and multinationals such as Ford and Hyundai to launch their new ventures in Tamil Nadu. TIDCO also assists promoters in obtaining statutory clearances, acquisition of land, technology sourcing, loan tie-up, obtaining water supply, power connection for the joint ventures. TIDCO has completed and commissioned the following major projects during the year 2000-2001.

Infrastructure Projects

1. Golden Jubilee Biotechnology for Women.
2. Chennai Trade Centre.

Manufacturing Projects

1. Iron Castings Limited.
2. Optical Fibre Cable Project of Tamil Nadu Telecommunications Limited.
3. Blood Bags (Innvol Medical India) Limited
4. Southern Steel Company Limited (Steel Rolling Unit)

Knowledge Sector Project

1. TIDEL Park Limited

Tamil Nadu Explosives Limited (TEL)

Tamil Nadu Industrial Explosives Limited (TEL) is a subsidiary company of TIDCO manufacturing NG based explosives, slurry explosives, detonators and detonating fuses. These explosives are less hazardous, cheaper and safer for handling. Government of India has already issued orders to all public undertakings to reduce manufacturing NG explosives in view of internal security/ safety reasons. Therefore, the manufacture of emulsion explosives as per the market demand had become essential for the survival of this company. In this background, TEL has entered into an agreement with M/s Central Mining Research Institute, Dhanbad for developing the required formulations for manufacture of emulsion explosives for TEL. The total cost of the project is expected to be around Rs. 5.17 crores to be financed from TEL's internal sources and the project is likely to be completed in 2002-03. The following products are proposed to be manufactured under the diversification plans of TEL:

A. Non permitted packaged small dia emulsion explosives

B. Non permitted packaged large dia emulsion explosives

C. Permitted emulsion explosives

D. Emulsion based bulk explosives

E. Non electrical detonators

F. Low Grammage detonating fuses.

Tamil Nadu Cement Corporation Limited (TANCEM)

Tamil Nadu Cement Corporation Limited (TANCEM) is a multi product and multi locational organisation with an annual turnover of Rs. 210 crores. Cement (Alangulam & Ariyalur), Asbestos sheets (Alangulam), Asbestos pipes (Mayanur in Karur District) and stoneware pipes (at Virudachalam) are produced by the Company in its factories in the locations indicated.

The paid-up capital of the company is Rs. 18 crores. The net worth of the company stood at Rs. 49.41 crores as on 31.3.98. The withdrawal of purchase preference by the Government for the products w.e.f. April 1998 plunged the Company in severe losses since then wiping out the net worth which became Rs. (-) 17.76 crores as on 31.3.2001. The company became sick in terms of the Sick Industries Company's Act, 1985 and set to be referred to BIFR.

The Committee under the chairmanship of Thiru K.V. Ramanathan set up in April 1988 recommended for the gradual disinvestment of TANCEM, first by converting it into a Joint Sector enterprise by association with a suitable entrepreneur. In 1991/ 1994, the Government decided to convert TANCEM as an associate sector company and invited offers through open tender for the transfer of 89% shares held by TIDCO. This notification was challenged in the High Court which was dismissed as infructuous in 1997 as the Government decided not to pursue the disinvestment. An Expert Committee under the Chairmanship of Thiru S.V.S.Raghavan to study the performance of State PSUs, reiterated the earlier observations of the Ramanathan Committee that production of cement is not area of activity for Government and recommended outright sale of TANCEM. The Committee of Secretaries, which considered the recommendations of the Raghavan Committee observed that a phased disinvestment of the Government holdings in TANCEM would be a better option. Meanwhile, an announcement was made in May 2000 that Government would not privatise TANCEM.

The installed capacity of Alangulam plant was 4 lakh tonnes and that of Ariyalur plant 5 lakh tonnes per annum. In the present context of fierce competition, plants of capacities less than 10 lakh tonnes per annum are not commercially viable. The Alangulam cement plant was designed with prevalent wet process technology which is outmoded and very costly in the present context. No significant investment was made in the two cement plants either for enhancing the capacity or for modernising the plants during the last 30 years with the result, the consumption of power and coal of these two cement plants is much higher than the private sector plants, which have constantly upgraded their technology. The two cement plants with 9 lakh tonnes of capacity employ a work force of 1,774 as against a modern plant of similar capacity which employs 400 persons. Naturally, the manpower cost of TANCEM cement plants out prices private sector cement plants.

In June 1997, the project for modernisation of Alangulam Cement plant was approved at an estimated cost of Rs. 160 crores with the object of enhancing the capacity from 4 lakh tonnes to 5 lakh tonnes per annum and converting the wet process technology to modern dry process technology. The project was to be funded by contribution of Rs. 50 crores by TANCEM and Rs. 110 crores by loan from financial institutions. Since TANCEM did not have funds to finance the scheme, the modernisation could not materialise.

The project cost has now escalated to Rs. 200 crores. As regards Ariyalur Cement Plant, TANCEM commissioned a study by a reputed consultant to examine the scope of modernization. It is estimated that the modernization of Ariyalur cement plant would cost Rs. 120 crores. The modernization envisages capacity enhancement from 5 lakh tonnes to 8.8 lakh tonnes per annum and technology improvements in the plant. Thus, the total cost for modernization of the two cement plants works out to Rs. 320 crores. While about Rs. 220 crores can be raised as loan from financial institutions against Government guarantee, Rs. 100 crores would be required as equity infusion by the Government.

The asbestos pipe unit at Mayanur was established in 1984 primarily to cater to the requirements of TWAD and Metro Water Board. The cpacity utilisation which stood at 48% during

1997-98 declined sharply thereafter due to the introduction of G.O.Ms.No. 75, dt. 19.2.1997, the operation of the turn-key system by these organizations and switchover to PSC, CI & PVC pipes. The stoneware pipe unit at Virdhachalam, originally established by TANSI in 1962 and taken over later by TACEL was finally taken over by TANCEM in 1989. It was modernized in 1993 and it was doing well till March 1998. The introduction of G.O.Ms.No.75, dt.19.2.1997 affected the unit badly. The company suffered heavy losses of Rs. 66 crores from 1998 to 2001 and this was financed by borrowing from Tamil Nadu Urban Finance and Infrastructure Corporation Ltd. (TUFIDCO) to an extent of Rs. 11.5 crores, Rs. 2.5 crores from TIDCO, Rs. 20 crores from public deposits mobilised by TANCEM and S.T.loan of Rs. 39 crores. The loans outstanding as on 31.3.2001 is Rs. 126.77 crores. Yet another cause for deterioration in the finances of TANCEM is the default of Government Departments in settling the bills of TANCEM and as on 31.3.2001, Rs. 31 crores was due.

Measures warranted to revive the Company:

(1) Modernisation of the two cement plants and the asbestos sheet plant.

(2) Reduction of manpower through Voluntary Retirement Scheme.

Tenth Plan - Goals, Objectives, Strategy and Outlay

The goal is to make Tamil Nadu "Numero Uno" among the Indian States in all spheres including industrial development during the Tenth FiveYear Plan.

For the Tenth Plan, a target of achieving a minimum of 8% overall GSDP growth rate has been contemplated for Tamil Nadu. This overall GSDP growth rate of 8%, is arrived at on the basis of projected growth rates of 3.79 for primary, 7.12 for secondary and 9.77 for Tertiary sectors during the Tenth Plan period. However, given the vision of the State Government to double the Per Capita Income by the end of 2010, the required overall growth rate is 9.05 percent per year. This warrants the CAGR of marginally above 8% for secondary sector. At 8% CAGR in secondary sector, the sectoral GSDP works out to Rs. 45,941.24 crores (while at 7.12% CAGR it will be Rs. 44,100 crores).

Outlay - The outlay proposed for Medium & Large Industries is Rs. 200 crores and this is mainly for meeting the subsidy claims. In the process of liberalization of the economy, during the last 10 years, there has been substantial de-regulation and abolition of industrial licensing except for a few items. Several industries earlier reserved for public sector were opened to private sector. Access to automatic route for FDI has been permitted except for a negative list. FDI is seen as a means to support domestic investment for achieving a higher level of economic development. Thus, in this environment and other facilitating measures, the required investments (for achieving the targeted growth rate) will come from private sector including FDIs and Central investments. It may be noted that secondary sector includes mining & electricity which are capital intensive. Further, infrastructure investments have a high ICOR. In this setting, a reduction in ICOR warrants an environment that reduces transaction costs and improves the marginal efficiency of capital.

Measures for attracting private investment and FDI flows into the State have been outlined in Chapter 2.4.

The main elements of the strategy envisaged for the industrial development in the Tenth Plan will be as follows:

·Private-Public Partnership in upgrading infrastructure. Since the State is a Knowledge State with a strong base for technical education, the State can take a facilitator role for attracting industry to use the academic and professional competence available. Selective interaction with centres of learning abroad and MNCs to foster further industry-institution partnership is likely to prove rewarding.

Mahindra City - Project symbolising Public - Private Partnership

Mahindra City, an Integrated Industrial Park has been developed near Chengalpattu, on the emerging concept of Private and Public Partnership. Spread over 1450 acres, the Mahindra Industrial Park Limited (MIPL) has been promoted by the Mahindra Group in association with Infrastructure Leasing and Finance Services and the Tamil Nadu Industrial Development Corporation to offer specialised business zones with customised infrastructure. Such innovative Industrial ventures are aimed to provide the required cutting edge in industrialisation of the State and to make Tamil Nadu the most desired destination of choice for investors.

(Inaugurated by the Chief Minister on 20th September 2002.)

Introduction of infrastructure enabling policy and creation of infrastructure fund - enactment of an Infrastructure Development Enabling Act, with provisions for setting up of an Infrastructure Development Board. This Act will spell out clearly the policy and procedure for the involvement of private sector investment in various areas of infrastructure development, either in collaboration with a Government agency or entirely by itself.

A significant share of the investment required for the secondary sector will have to come from non-state resources. To enable this to happen, a special strategy for attracting private investments would be required, particularly for infrastructure. It may be worthwhile to consider infrastructure - enabling initiatives as in Andhra Pradesh and Gujarat.

Along with the development of a Golden quadrilateral, the feasibility of a Golden Pentagon connecting Chennai-Coimbatore-Tiruchi-Madurai-Tuticorin can be explored. It is likely that the Chennai-Coimbatore axis will provide the scope for growth of traditional industries and software. Coimbatore-Tiruchi-Madurai will help the growth of agricultural based food processing industries. Madurai-Tuticorin would aid hinterland development and Tuticorin-Chennai for marine bio industries. Entertainment industry with beach development would also take place.

General Infrastructure - Effort will be made in consultation with Government of India for development and upgradation of airports and seaports in the State. Development of Tuticorin port as a gateway for business with South East Asia and Australia and Colachel as a transhipment port would be very worthwhile objectives.

Major traffic corridors along high density will be widened into 2 or 4 lanes. Quality upgradation of the road links between Chennai-Coimbatore, Tiruchi-Madurai and Tuticorin will provide the base for the growth of traditional industries, s/w industries and agro-based food industry and also promote heritage tourism. Notifications under the Tamil Nadu Industrial Township Area Development Authority Act will be issued in line with the development of the Industrial Park or Estate concerned to enable better management with a provision for a revenue stream for the local body concerned.

A State-Level Investment Promotion Board with the Chief Minister as the chairperson and a Project Approvals Authority under the Chairmanship of the Chief Secretary have been put in place for sanction of projects with investment levels of over and below Rs. 100 crores respectively. An infrastructure Cell has been instituted in the Budget of 2002-03.

All the infrastructure assistance offered by Government of India will be availed of to the maximum extent.

- Disinvestment in State Public Sector Undertakings-Government has already formed a Cabinet Committee and some PSUs are being considered for disinvestment. While State Government is adopting overall the Government of India guidelines, the disinvestment route, however, varied from case to case. The role of PSEs needs to be looked at on a case to case basis to increase efficiency and cost saving and phasing out of non-core activities. Ways of privatisation of the unviable cooperative manufacturing units also needs to be looked into.
- Business deregulation and single window facilitation.
- Improving the current project germination rate from about 26% to 75% by facilitation.
- Strong support to liberalization: Empowering the different economic agents and freeing them from the concept of dependency inherent in a controlled regime.
- Launch and continue state level Reforms programme to make Tamil Nadu truly investor-friendly.
- Improving industrial competitiveness in export and domestic markets,including policies to enhance skills and knowledge.
- Policies to attract foreign investment and technology and simplify thelegal framework and codes governing investment.

The relevance of certain restrictive labour laws need to be reviewed and changed without compromising on the needs to pay labour a fair wage and to protect them against exploitation. At present, industries need to file a number of monthly/ quarterly/ annual returns under various Labour Laws. In summary, industrialists need to file 51 monthly/ quarterly/ annual returns under following major Labour Laws:

This results in considerable amount of paper work on the part of industrialists and failure to furnish returns in time attracts penalties. This is one of the major irritants to industries and not in consonance with the spirit of economic liberalization. As part of business deregulation, one of the methods of removing the above irritant is to simplify the procedures and to introduce a combined annual return to be filled and filed by industries. The Tamil Nadu Industrial Guidance Bureau therefore did an exercise to prepare a combined annual return to be filed by industries under various Labour Laws. This may be adopted.

Notifications where possible under the Industrial Township Act, steps to increase facilitation and furthering Business Deregulation are all important to attract investments and to ensure early germination.

Services sector exercises a pull effect on the secondary sector- these two sectors need to be synergised with some accent on retailing Venture Capital Funds to be set up in collaboration with financial agencies depending upon need.

Thrust Areas - During Tenth Plan, the following thrust areas have beenidentified based on the resource endowments and competitive advantages inthe State.

(1) Bio-technology

(2) Software & Electronics

(3) Drugs & Pharmaceuticals

(4) Processed Food Industries

(5) Leather Industries

(6) Textiles and Readymade Garments

(7) Gems and Jewellery

(8) Petrochemicals

(9) Automobiles & Auto Ancillaries

(10) Telecommunication

(11) Information Technology etc.

- In addition, it is proposed to establish 'Agricultural Export Promotion Zones', which would provide a strong support for Agricultural and Allied and other socio-economic activities in the State.

  A High Level Committee chaired by the Chief Minister with representatives from various chambers of industries will meet periodically to analyse the industrial scenario prevailing in the State and suggest corrective steps and also necessary policy initiatives. In addition, the Executive Committee under the Chairmanship of the Chief Secretary will co-ordinate the efforts of the Government and Confederation of Indian Industries (C.I.I.) and focus on specific steps needed to accelerate industrial development, simplification of procedures for approach and inspections etc.

- Traditional industries like textiles and readymade garments, leather, chemicals, auto ancillary would be under stress and require timely policy and infrastructure help. Tax effects of VAT particularly on chemicals and auto industries are likely to be significant and needs be studied. Textiles and leather industry would need support in cost cutting and environmental regulation compliance.

- Apart from support to traditional industries which are likely to be cast into a state of stress, the potential sunrise industries like IT and biotechnology need be fully exploited. The State has announced policies for the development of both the sectors and efforts to create high quality and IT and BT parks need to be continued.

- Export Promotion - Export Promotion is another vital area that will receive special attention of the Government during the Tenth Plan. The State has now 15% share of the country's exports. This can be raised to 20% by closer monitoring of exporters' needs and articulating them, timely use of infrastructural assistance provided by Government of India and the early operationability of the SEZ at Nanguneri. The location of SEZ at Ennore and AEZs wherever viably possible for floriculture/ agro processing foods should be done. A Committee formed in this regard will draw a shelf of infrastructure programmes to smoothen the flow of exports. Further, the NRI Cell created in the Guidance Bureau will network with NRI bases and sangams abroad for the sourcing of ideas and investments.

The Government will give focused attention to the development of Special Economic Zones. Already the Hi-tech Park at Nanguneri is proposed to be developed as a Special Economic Zone. The State Government's Policy in development of Special Economic Zone will be formalized shortly and backed with appropriate legislation on the lines of the Model Act of Government of India for SEZs. It would also endeavour to set up such Zones making use of the new port facilities available at Ennore, as well as the concentration of units in certain commodities like Leather, Garments etc. in Tamil Nadu.

One of the main objectives of the Government will be to create infrastructure facilities comparable to International Standards, as they exist in Southern East Asian countries so that investments from foreign countries could be easily attracted.

NEW INDUSTRIAL POLICY

Tamil Nadu is formulating a 'New Industrial Policy', with many innovative features to promote industrial growth with sustainable development and create industry-friendly environment to enable the State to achieve 'number one' position in the sphere of industrialization in India after taking cognizance of the prevailing competitive/market environment among the various States. The new industrial policy will concentrate on providing incentives to industries, promoting employment, creation of a minimum of one million jobs in industrial sector, doubling the per capita income and current industrial output. The policy will aim at increasing the export share of Tamil Nadu from current 15% to 20%. Special emphasis on development of thrust areas like Bio-Technology, Information Technology, Telecommunication, Pharmaceuticals, Food processing, etc. will be one of the key features of the policy.

Tenth Plan Proposals

For the Tenth plan, it is expected that investments will come from the private sector and the State Government will provide infrastructural support. The direct assistance will be

(1) by providing State Capital Subsidy (2)Generator Subsidy and (3) Mega Project subsidy. The programme wiseallocation of the outlay of Rs. 200 crores will be as follows:

1. State Capital Subsidy - The Government provides capital subsidy to set up new industries and also for expansion, diversification, modernisation, renovation, etc. TIIC is functioning as a nodal agency for disbursement of this subsidy. Based on the subsidy disbursement made during the Ninth Plan it is estimated that on an average Rs. 26 crores of capital subsidy is claimed per year. There was a backlog of previous years amounting to Rs. 80 crores. Therefore, an outlay of Rs. 120 crores is provided to TIIC in the Tenth Plan towards disbursement of State Capital Subsidy.
2. Generator Subsidy - The Government is providing subsidy for providing generators to Medium and Large Industries in order to avoid production loss due to power interruptions. During the last five years an amount of Rs. 4 crores at the rate of Rs. 0.80 crores per year has been granted as Generator subsidy. This subsidy is retained at the same level of Rs. 0.80 crores per year and an outlay of Rs. 4 crores is provided for the Tenth Plan.
3. Mega Projects subsidy - Consequent to the withdrawal of sales tax based incentives since January 2000, there is no major incentive for mega projects. Many States have, therefore, introduced subsidies to compensate part of infrastructure development costs of mega projects. In this setting, to improve attractiveness of Tamil Nadu, it becomes imperative to introduce a mega project subsidy for projects with investments exceeding Rs. 100 crores.

An amount of Rs. 4.82 crores has been provided towards subsidy for reimbursement to Ford Motors Ltd., Rs. 5.38 crores for Hyundai and Rs. 0.7 crore for TIDCO in the Budget Estimate for the year 2002-03. In the coming years, the claims from new entrepreneurs are likely to increase. Therefore, a total outlay of Rs. 50 crores at the rate of Rs. 10 crores per year is provided for sanction and disbursement of Mega projects subsidy in the Tenth Five Year Plan.

4. Share capital assistance to Public Sector Undertakings for implementing special infrastructure development - The Government is providing share capital assistance to the State Public Sector Undertakings for implementing special infrastructure development. The Government have provided a sum of Rs. 5 crores in the Budget estimate for the year 2002-03 for forming the Roads in Sugar factory areas and Rs. 9.62 crores for sugar cane cess fund. Government of India is also providing funds for share capital assistance for implementing special infrastructure development being implemented through SIPCOT. A total share capital assistance of Rs. 26 crores is provided towards Share Capital Assistance to be extended to the Public Sector Enterprises for promotion of Infrastructure facilities during Tenth Five Year Plan period.

2

Recent Trends in Indian Industries

ITES - BPO MARKET

Over the past decade, the Indian BPO segment has witnessed significant transformation. Starting with basic data entry tasks, the industry graduated to a high proportion of voice-based services and a range of back-offi ce processing activities. The last 3-4 years have seen the scope of services expanding to include increasingly complex processes involving rule-based decision making and even research services requiring informed individual judgment.

The rapid expansion in scope of BPO has been accompanied by an equally rapid adoption across a range of vertical industries. This wide range of services may be summarised into four broad categories comprising Finance and Accounting (F&A), Customer Interaction Services (CIS) and Human Resource Administration (HRA), and a wide range of other vertical-specifi c and niche services.

F&A services manage or support aspects of the fi nance and accounting functions of businesses. This includes activities such as general accounting, transaction management (accounts receivables and payables management), corporate fi nance (e.g. treasury and risk management, and tax management); compliance management and statutory reporting, etc. This segment accounts for approximately 40-45 percent of Indian BPO.

CIS includes all forms of IT-enabled customer contact; inbound or outbound, voice or non-voice based support used to provide customer services, sales and marketing, technical support and help desk services.

The HR administration services include payroll and benefi ts administration, travel and expense processing, talent acquisition and talent management services, employee and manager self-service delivery services, employee communication design and administration. This segment accounts for about two percent of Indian BPO.

BPO is witnessing an increasing emphasis on the cost-plus, additional strategic levers that it can deliver include innovation of the underlying business process being outsourced, improved competitive positioning, managing customer expectations, elevation of the strategic role of the retained organisation, optimal resource allocation, support for globalisation of their businesses, and technology support and access. This has also resulted in heightened C-level attention resulting in enterprise-wide evaluation of BPO opportunities – which is in turn opening new avenues to explore. This steady expansion in scope coupled with low penetration levels is supporting high growth for BPO.

INDIAN IT - BPO SECTOR

India's IT-BPO Performance in 2006

The Indian IT-BPO sector (including the domestic and exports segments) is growing at an estimated 28 percent in FY2007.[1] Total revenue aggregate for the sector is expected to exceed USD 47.8 billion, nearly a ten-fold increase over the aggregate revenue of USD 4.8 billion, reported in FY1998, and direct employment is likely to cross 1.6 million.[2] As a proportion of national GDP, the revenue aggregate of the Indian technology sector has grown from 1.2 percent in FY1998 to an estimated 5.4 percent in FY2007. Net value-added by this sector, to the economy, is estimated at 3-3.5 percent for FY2007.[3]

Service and software exports remain the mainstay of the sector; FY07 export growth likely to beat forecasts and exceed 32 percent.5 While the US and the UK remain the dominant markets, contributing to 67 percent and 15 percent of total exports respectively, fi rms are also keenly exploring new geographies for business development, and to strengthen their global delivery footprint. Banking, Financial Services and Insurance, and Technology (Hi-tech/ telecom) are the main verticals, accounting for nearly 60 percent of the total; Manufacturing, Retail, Media, Utilities, Healthcare and

Transportation follow – also growing rapidly. IT services exports, accounting for 55-57 percent of total exports, are growing at an estimated 36 percent and are expected to reach USD 18.1 billion in FY2007. Newer areas of application and infrastructure management, testing, etc. are gaining traction, with their share in the business-mix growing steadily. BPO continues to grow in scale and scope, with fi rms increasingly adopting a vertical focused approach. Total exports for this segment are expected to exceed USD 8.3 billion in FY 2006-07, growing by 32 percent over the previous year. Lastly, increasing traction in offshore product development and engineering services is supplementing India's efforts in own IP creation. This group is growing at 22-23 percent and is expected to report USD 4.9 billion in exports, in FY 2006-07.

Service-line expansion is aiding service providers to take on larger and more complex deals, and is driving up the average ticket size of contracts awarded to Indian fi rms. High offshore component of delivery and superior execution in multi-location delivery continue to be key differentiators. Broad-based industry structure; IT led by large Indian fi rms, BPO by a mix of Indian and MNC third-party providers and captives, refl ects the depth of the supply-base. While the larger players continue to lead growth, gradually increasing their share in the industry aggregate; several high-performing SMEs also stand out.

The domestic market is also picking-up, showing defi nite signs of breaking-out of the trend of hardware linked growth with the contribution of software and services exceeding that of hardware for the fi rst time in FY 2005-06. The total size of the domestic market is expected to cross USD 15.9 billion in FY 2006-07, a growth of 21 percent over FY 2005-06. Although this segment has been led by MNCs in the past few years, Indian fi rms are gradually gaining ground. Overtime this segment could become a larger SME play, as the mid-sized fi rms increase their levels of IT adoption.

INDIAN HARDWARE INDUSTRY

Hardware accounted for about 49 percent of the total domestic IT-BPO spends in FY2006, its share falling below the 50 percent mark for the fi rst time ever. While pricing continued to slide across key categories, domestic hardware revenues grew by 20 per cent in FY2006 and are expected to exceed USD 7.5 billion, growing at about 17 percent in the current fiscal.

PCs, notebooks and servers continued to lead hardware spending across vertical markets in FY2006. Networking equipment, peripherals and storage witnessed strong demand in select sectors including Discrete Manufacturing, Telecom, Oil and Petrochemicals, and IT-BPO.

Interestingly, desktop shipments outside the top four metros grew 3-5 times faster than in the top four metros – an indication of the growing penetration of IT adoption in the country.

IT SOFTWARE & SERVICES MARKET

The Indian IT Services Exports Scenario

Services exports, accounting for nearly two thirds of the total, are estimated to be growing at 32.6 percent in FY2007. This beats the industry forecast of 27-30 percent, estimated earlier – at the beginning of the year (June 2006).

Strong fundamentals including a large base of skilled talent, demonstrated quality and service delivery expertise at a signifi cant cost advantage and an enabling environment have ensured that India attracts a disproportionately larger share of the global demand for offshore IT-ITES – and continues to drive India's export led growth.

The top 40 publicly listed Indian fi rms have reported a top line year-on-year growth of nearly 35 percent, over the fi rst half of the current fi scal. MNC owned captive units have been scaling up their operations steadily with the headcount estimated to be growing by about 25-30 percent this year.

DOMESTIC MARKET

The domestic IT market is beginning to come out of the shadows of the export segment. The overall size of the domestic market, comprising hardware, software and services (IT-BPO), grew by an impressive 29 percent in FY2006, and is forecast reach USD 15.9 billion in the current fi scal (FY2007). With an increase in the spend on software and services, and the outsourced model gaining noticeable traction, the domestic market is beginning to refl ect the service line depth that characterises maturing markets. In fact, spends on software and services (IT-BPO) outweighed the total spending on hardware, for the fi rst time ever in FY2006 and are expected to continue to gain share in FY2007.

BFSI, Manufacturing, Telecom, and the Government are the key vertical markets driving growth in domestic IT spending across categories including hardware systems, networking, storage, security, enterprise application products and related services. Education, Retail and Healthcare are a few emerging areas expected to drive additional growth. BFSI, Telecom and Consumer Durables are the early adopters of BPO in the domestic market and currently account for about three-fourths of the business in this space.

BPO demand in the domestic market has witnessed noticeable growth over the past few years. As the Indian economy becomes more globally integrated, businesses in India are beginning to face increasing levels of global competition and being push to deliver world class levels of product and service quality. BPO has emerged as an effective means of entrusting specialists with the task of consistently delivering the desired high-levels of quality – leaving the client organisations to focus on their core businesses.

Increasing competition and growing emphasis on customer satisfaction is also driving the public sector organisations towards BPO. Last year, Air India outsourced its domestic customer service operations to third-party providers. This year, the Indian Railways announced its plans to establish Railway Enquiry Franchisees across the country. The success of these early initiatives by the public sector is of critical importance to the domestic BPO sector as they will add signifi cant scale and serve as proof-of-concept for an even larger market opportunity.

SECURITY ENVIRONMENT

IT definitely has raised India's bar globally because of its unmatched value proposition - in terms of the skill sets, higher productivity coupled with quality and scalability. The Information Technology sector has indeed played a significant role in transforming India's image globally. A "secure and reliable" environment—defined by strong copyright, IT and cyber laws—is an imperative for the growth and future success of the ITS/BPO industries. NASSCOM has been proactive in pushing this cause and ensuring that the Indian Information Security environment benchmarks with the best across the globe. ITS/BPO companies in India are taking as many precautions as possible to ensure that data and personal information of their customers is protected. That means following international best practices, getting procedures audited by independent parties and making sure that these procedures are up to date and are being closely followed.

Security Environment in India

- Indian companies have robust security practices comparable to those followed by western companies. Indian companies primarily comply with BS 7799 – a global standard that covers all domains of security

Security Environment: Country Comparison

Law	**India**	China	Philippines
IPR			
Copyright	√	√	√
Patent	Product patents-2005	*	*
DATA PROTECTION			
Data Protection Laws	Comprehensive framework-2004	x	x
Vertical Specific Laws	x	x	x
CYBER			
Digital signatures	√	√	√
Hacking	√	√	√
Privacy	√	√	√

- Companies sign Service Level Agreements (SLA), which have very strict confidentiality and security clauses built into them at the network and data level. Such SLAs also cover all relevant laws that the companies want its offshore providers to comply with and actions that can be taken in case of breaches
- Spending on security ranges from 5% to 15% of the IT budget
- Laws such as the IT Act 2000, Indian Copyright Act, Indian Penal Code Act and the Indian Contract Act, 1972 provide adequate safeguards to companies offshoring work to US and UK
- Most of the BPO companies providing services to UK clients ensure compliance with UK Data Protection Act 1998 (DPA) through contractual agreements
- Companies dealing with US clients require compliance depending upon the industry served. E.g. Healthcare requires compliance with HIPAA, Financial services require compliance with GLBA. To ensure compliance with such laws, Indian vendors follow security practices as specified by clients such as security awareness, protection of information, non-disclosure agreements, screening of employees, etc. Further, clients conduct periodic audits to ensure compliance
- Many companies in India are undergoing/have undergone SAS 70 Audit. SAS-70 assignments helps service companies operating from India to implement and improve internal controls, ensure minimal disruptions to business from clients' auditors, and is potent marketing tool in the face of increasing competition.
- Insurance premiums paid by Indian BPO companies for insuring themselves for security breaches have been declining since the past two years-a telling indicator of the robust security practices being followed by Indian companies

KNOWLEDGE PROFESSIONALS

India has successfully leveraged its fundamental advantages of abundant talent, a keen focus on quality and security, lower cost-structure coupled with an enabling business environment to achieve a marked lead in the global outsourcing arena. This is refl ected in India's dominant and growing share of the global pie. Over FY2001-2006, India's share in global sourcing has grown from 62 percent to 65 percent for IT and 39 percent to 45 percent for BPO. The visibly higher preference for India is driven by its unmatched superiority when measured across a range of parameters that determine the attractiveness of a sourcing location.

- Abundant talent: India's young demographic profi le is an inherent advantage.
- Sustained cost competitiveness: The signifi cant and sustained cost advantage, attributed to the wide differential in wage-costs and productivity gains achieved by fi rms in sourcing from India, continues to be a compelling driver of decisions to source services from India.
- Quality orientation, superior process delivery and a keen emphasis on information-security
- Quality business infrastructure: Rapid growth in the quality and scale of Grade A real estate (around 25 million sq ft of real estate space is being added per annum) and telecommunications infrastructure – the key elements of business infrastructure required for running an IT-BPO operation, have been instrumental in supporting the growth of the sector.
- Enabling business policy and regulatory environment: The Indian government has encouraged this sector by providing incentives and non-fi nancial assistance, and by creating enabling regulations.

KEY HIGHLIGHTS OF THE NASSCOM-IDC STUDY ON THE DOMESTIC SERVICES (IT-ITES) MARKET OPPORTUNITY

The Indian Information Technology (IT) and IT Enabled Services (ITES) success story and its paradigm changing impact on global service delivery is now a well acknowledged fact. However, much of the success achieved by the sector has been attributed to the meteoric growth in exports – that has overshadowed the latent opportunities unlocked and growth observed in the domestic market over the past few years.

SPOTLIGHT ON THE DOMESTIC IT SERVICES MARKET OPPORTUNITY

Domestic demand for IT in India is witnessing a gradual transformation from being predominantly hardware driven towards a solutions oriented approach – resulting in a growing emphasis on services. In fact, revenue growth in the services segment alone has reported faster growth than that for the overall domestic IT market (including hardware, software and services) over the past few years. As depicted in the following chart, this trend is expected to continue over the forecast period.

The liberalization of Indian economic policy, de-regulation of key sectors and progressive moves towards further integrating India with the global economy has been a key driver of increased IT adoption in the country. This is best reflected in the fact that most indigenous players in telecom and banking, two key sectors with significant multinational corporation (MNC) participation, have significantly upgraded their levels of IT adoption to offer best-in-class services comparable to those offered by the global competition and these two sectors together account for approximately 35-40 percent of the domestic spend on IT services. Similar competitive pressures in other more recently deregulated service sectors such as airlines and insurance, and the uptake in the manufacturing and industrial sectors; and the several large e-governance initiatives launched by the government under the National E-Governance Plan (NEGP) are expected to provide sustained growth in domestic demand for IT services over the next few years. Over the next five years, domestic spending on outsourced IT services is projected to more than double, from INR 103 billion in 2004 to over INR 238 billion in 2009.

Five Year Revenue Forecasts for Key Service Lines in the Domestic Market (INR Million)

Breakups	2004	2005	2006	2007	2008	2009	CAGR
IT Consulting	4,784	5,669	6,775	7,774	9,109	10,674	17.4%
System Integration	34,011	42,979	51,900	62,065	72,960	85,399	20.2%
Application Development	13,997	17,115	19,852	22,586	25,113	27,924	14.8%
End-to-end Outsourcing	6,328	8,221	10,247	12,343	14,344	16,850	21.6%
Discrete Outsourcing	16,731	21,055	25,819	31,401	36,262	41,509	19.9%
Deploy and Support	23,631	28,321	32,907	37,651	42,510	48,,186	15.3%
IT Education and Training	4,126	4,879	5,609	6,534	7,260	8,067	14.3%
Grand Total	103,606	128,239	153,109	180,354	207,559	238,607	18.2%

Source: IDC, 2005

Systems integration and network integration make up a high growth-large size category within the IT services engagements. These services will continue to be prime drivers of the domestic IT services market in the enterprise segment due to the increasing growth in the enterprise application implementation and increased demand for network integration from telecom & banking verticals.

Domestic IT Services Revenues by Key Vertical Markets (2004)

The financial services, communications and media, and manufacturing verticals accounted for over 3/4th of the revenues earned by service providers in the domestic IT services market in 2004.

The growth projections for IT service revenues in the domestic market may be further accentuated by addressing some basic issues highlighted by the findings of the surveys conducted as a part of this study.

A significant portion of the domestic corporate IT spends still lies in-house, predominantly driven by a perceived lack of focus by service providers on the domestic market and a perceived absence of value generated by outsourcing.

It is estimated that in-house spending on IT services (including training costs, salaries of in-house IT staff and associated overheads) still accounts for more than half of the corporate IT spend in India, while the outsourced / vendor addressed spends account for just 45 percent of the total.

Comparison of the Vendor Addressed Market and the In-house Spend by Key Services (INR During the research study, IDC undertook in-depth interviews with CIOs. There was a strong perception among a majority of the CIOs that domestic customers were not a focus area for IT service providers and that the IT service providers rarely offer Indian customers the kind of commitment and expertise that they provide their large (and necessarily more lucrative) global customers. The CIOs also strongly believe that the potential of the domestic market is still not appreciated by many of the IT services players.

Further, there continues to be a relative poor awareness of the potential of using IT as an enabler of competitive advantage. As cost arbitrage is not a strong enough justification for outsourcing in India, the IT service providers need to clearly articulate their value proposition and relate it to business benefits.

IT services vendors should be able to assist the CIOs to focus on generating business value from IT investments, by offering total solutions and end-to-end services.

As the level of IT investment increases, there is a change in the perceived role of IT from a support function to an enabler of competitive advantage. There is increasing pressure on the CIO(s) to justify the IT investment by demonstrating the value delivered from IT investments. The increased expectations from IT requires them to move from routine IT operations to strategic IT management. The challenges they face in making this transformation has to do with the existing complexities in their IT environments, which make the IT departments and the CIOs spend most of their time and effort in day-to-day operations.

The IT services vendors have a key role to play in helping the CIOs make this transformation. New offerings and service delivery models need to be developed that can assist the CIOs in streamlining their IT operations to such a level that they can then devote their IT investments and efforts to transformational initiatives.

Verticalised solutions are becoming increasingly important, and IT service vendors need to develop domain skills and offerings.

Verticalisation of IT services is a definitive emerging trend and users are demanding services tailored to their needs. Mature IT customers are today looking for total solutions that can solve their business challenges rather than at IT hardware, software, and services as discrete elements.

IT vendors today, need to develop new or customize existing offerings to address the specific needs of each vertical/market segment. Such an approach, based on solution-orientation, is enabling IT service providers to offer sustainable value to customers.

While the larger services vendors have specific vertical practices and teams, the medium- and small-sized IT services vendors need to focus on select verticals and develop their skills in these. Service providers need to extend strong end-to-end service capabilities to domestic customers, as the IT services market moves to high-value, annuity engagements.

The evolution of the IT services landscape is defined by the market graduating from low-value long-term services (such as basic maintenance and support) to high-value one-time services (such as system integration) and then on to high-value long-term services (such as discrete and end-to-end IT outsourcing).

The vendors who will gain from this shift are those who will have the capability to offer end-to-end services.

The transformation that is needed.

Larger and mature IT users are increasingly looking for end-to-end IT services and this will be a major growth engine for the market. This market segment will be dominated by a few large IT services vendors who have the size and the capabilities to address this demand. The development of the domestic IT services market will need to become more broad-based. To achieve sustained development, new verticals will need to be penetrated as it is not sufficient to increase business from only the currently addressed verticals.

A large proportion of the current IT services market is predicated on the banking, financial services and telecom verticals. While IT services for these verticals will continue to show strong growth, new verticals will need to be developed to increase the rate of growth of the IT services market in India.

As the Indian economy opens further opens up, other verticals including manufacturing, travel and tourism, healthcare, entertainment will increasingly look towards IT to increase competitiveness. For both new and existing verticals, the small and medium business (SMB) segment will represent an important source of growth for the domestic IT services market.

Spotlight on the Domestic ITES-BPO Market Opportunity

ITES-BPO is a very nascent segment of the domestic market, driven by voice based services with customer care and sales and marketing activity accounting for approximately 70 percent of the total.

Domestic ITES-BPO Revenues (INR Million)

	2004	2005	2006
HR	2428.9	4412.5	8019.5
F&A	2563.9	2975.4	3454.1
Customer Care	7696.1	16161.8	33939.7
Sales & marketing	8465.2	12019.6	17756.4
Other	2059.2	2449.4	2914.6
Total	23213.3	38018.6	66084.4

Source: IDC, 2005

Currently, the BFSI and Telecom verticals account for over 70 percent of the demand for ITES-BPO services in the domestic market.

Domestic ITES-BPO Revenues by Vertical Market (2004)

Verticals	% Share (2004)	Typical Processes Outsourced
Banking and Financial Services	47.4	Customer support, marketing and sales, collections, billing, transaction processing, market analytics, HR
Telecom	24.1	Customer support, cross-selling, loan processing, claim processing, market analytics, data validation, HR
Manufacturing (Consumer Durables/Automobile)	12.2	Customer support, sales and marketing, transportation, supply chain management, accounts payable/receivable
Others (IT-ITES, Aviation, Hospitality, Retail)	16.4	HR, Customer support, marketing and sales, billing, transaction processing, analytics, etc.

Source: IDC, 2005

While cost savings have been the primary driver of offshore outsourcing, vendors do not have comparable differences in labour costs to leverage while serving the domestic market. As a result, the primary motivation for the domestic market, in its early years of evolution are not cost savings but access to specialist skills and freeing client resources to focus on the core business. Scalability and process efficiency is expected to return some degree of cost savings in the domestic market as well. However this may not compare with the levels achieved by overseas (e.g. US/UK) clients.

Notwithstanding its relatively smaller contribution to the industry revenues, this segment has over the past twelve-eighteen months witnessed a noticeable increase in interest and activity on the part of customer organisations as well as service providers.

While the market activity (contracts announced and deals known to be in the negotiation stages) signal growth in the segment, like in IT services, future growth may be accentuated if a few lingering issues are addressed.

Some of the key findings from the ITES-BPO leg of the user-organization survey conducted by IDC as a part of this study include:

- While BPO/ITES penetration (to external/independent entities) is still very low, a sizeable proportion of end user organisations have an internal division to focus on these specific business processes indicating growing adoption of process based work-flow. This is a critical stage in the maturity of user organisations for them to consider / be able to outsource.
- Willingness to move from an in-house captive sourcing model to outsourcing is very low. Satisfaction with existing systems, lack of trust in outsourced service providers, high cost of services, unavailability of suitable vendors and lack of skilled personnel (with vendors) being the most commonly cited reasons for not looking at outsourcing.
- Demonstrated focus on serving the domestic market and showcased examples of successful engagements with domestic customers are key factors that would make outsourcing a more attractive alternative for end users.

About the Document

This document contains the key highlights of a study conducted by NASSCOM in association with IDC India to better understand the domestic services (IT-ITES) market opportunity.

This study comprised primary interactions with over 390 user organisations and over 40 service providers, and also leveraged IDC India's existing knowledge of trends in the domestic market context.

Key Highlights of the IT-BPO sector performance in FY 2007-08

IT Industry-Sector-wise break-up

USD billion	FY2004	FY2005	FY2006	FY2007	FY2008 E
IT Services	**10.4**	**13.5**	**17.8**	**23.5**	**31.0**
-Exports	7.3	10.0	13.3	18.0	23.1
-Domestic	3.1	3.5	4.5	5.5	7.9
BPO	**3.4**	**5.2**	**7.2**	**9.5**	**12.5**
-Exports	3.1	4.6	6.3	8.4	10.9
-Domestic	0.3	0.6	0.9	1.1	1.6
Engineering Services and R&D, Software Products	**2.9**	**3.8**	**5.3**	**6.5**	**8.5**
-Exports	2.5	3.1	4.0	4.9	6.3
-Domestic	0.4	0.7	1.3	1.6	2.2
Total Software and Services Revenues	**16.7**	**22.5**	**30.3**	**39.5**	**52.0**
Of which, exports are	**12.9**	**17.7**	**23.6**	**31.3**	**40.3**
Hardware	**5.0**	**5.6**	**7.1**	**8.5**	**12.0**
-Exports	n.a.	0.5	0.6	0.5	0.5
-Domestic	n.a.	5.1	6.5	8.0	11.5
Total IT Industry (including Hardware)	**21.6**	**28.2**	**37.4**	**48.0**	**64.0**

N.A.: Not available

Note: Figures may not add up due to rounding off.

Source: NASSCOM

GLOBAL SOURCING TRENDS IN 2007

- Worldwide technology products and related services sector spends are estimated to have grown at 7.3 per cent to nearly reach USD 1.7 trillion in 2007
- IT-BPO services, growing at an above-sector-average rate of nearly 8 per cent, remain the largest category, accounting for an increasing share of the worldwide technology sector revenue aggregate.
- Outsourcing continues to be the primary growth driver, sustained by gradual shifts in regional spending patterns– with increasing traction in Europe and Asia Pacific offsetting a marginal decline in share of the Americas.

- Underlying this steady growth in services spends is the increasing adoption and continued evolution of the global sourcing supply-chain. Global sourcing of technology related services is estimated to have grown by about 30 per cent to reach USD 70-76 billion in 2007.
- Increasing emphasis on innovation-led growth added to the secular trend in technology related spending, with IT-enablement.
- Global delivery now being recognized as complementary means of effectively increasing productivity, reducing time-to-market and thereby increasing the returns on innovation investment.

INDIAN IT-BPO PERFORMANCE IN FY2008

- The Indian IT-BPO revenue aggregate is expected to grow by over 33 per cent and reach USD 64 billion by the end of FY2008.
  - o IT exports (including hardware exports) are expected to cross USD 40.8 billion in FY2008 as against USD 31.9 billion in FY2007, a growth of 28 per cent.
  - o Domestic IT market (including hardware) is estimated to reach 23.2 billion in FY2008 as against USD 16.2 billion in FY2007, a growth of 43 per cent
- The direct employment in the sector is expected to reach nearly 2 million, an increase of about 375,000 professionals over FY2007.
  - o IT services exports, BPO exports and Domestic IT industry provides direct employment to 865,000, 704,000 and 427,000 professionals respectively.
- As a proportion of national GDP, the Indian technology sector revenue has grown from 1.2 per cent in FY1998 to an estimated 5.5 per cent in FY2008.

SOFTWARE AND SERVICES EXPORTS FY 2008:

Exports remain the mainstay of the sector and are estimated to reach USD 40.3 billion in FY2008, contributing nearly 64 per cent to the overall revenue aggregate.

IT services (excluding BPO, product development and engineering services), contributing to 57 per cent of the total software and services exports, remains the dominant segment and is expected to cross USD 23 billion, a growth of 28 per cent in FY2008.

Split by service offerings in IT Services

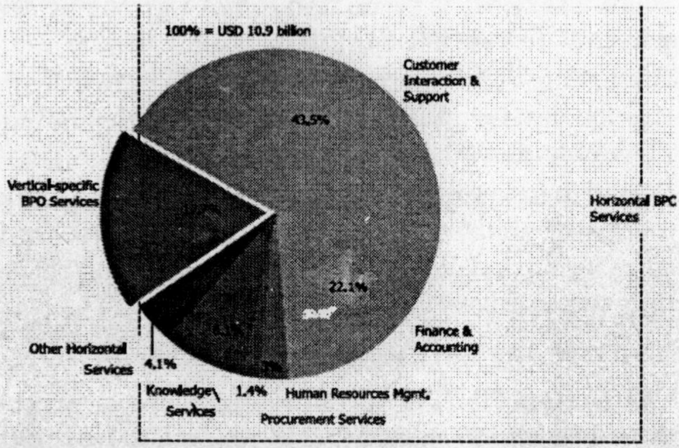

Split by service offerings in BPO services.

BPO services, accounting for over 27 per cent of the export aggregate, is the fastest growing segment across software and services exports driven by scale as well as scope. Export revenues for this segment are expected to cross

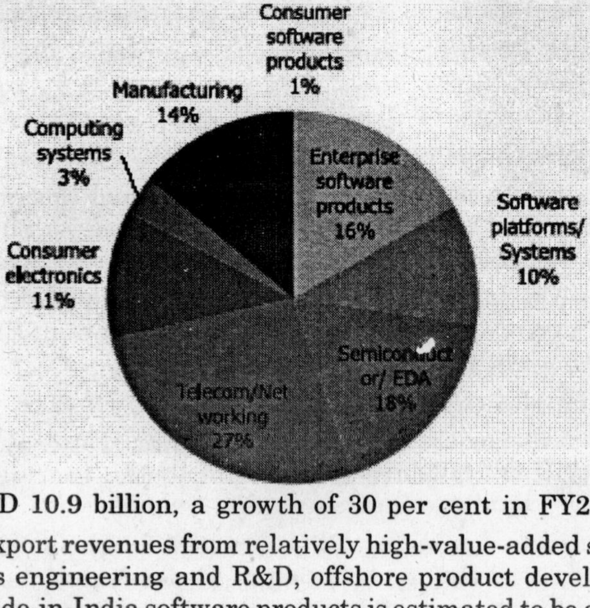

USD 10.9 billion, a growth of 30 per cent in FY2008.

§Export revenues from relatively high-value-added services such as engineering and R&D, offshore product development and made-in-India software products is estimated to be growing at over 27 per cent, and are forecast to reach USD 6.3 billion in FY2008.

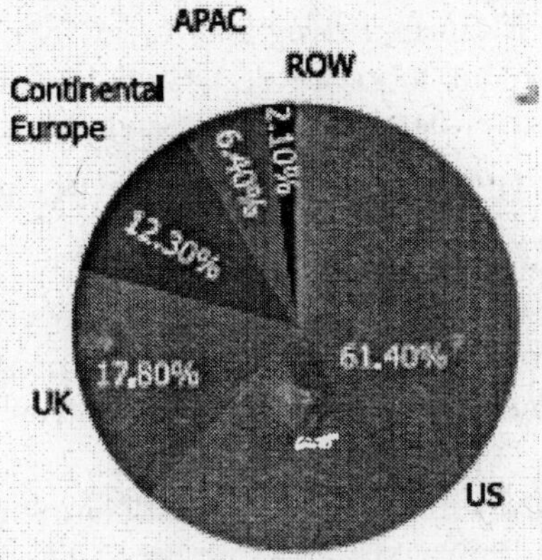

Split by service offerings in S/w products & Eng. Services.

Geographic market exposure of IT-BPO Exports.

While US & UK remained the largest export markets (accounting for about 61 per cent and 18 per cent respectively, in FY2007), the industry is steadily increasing its exposure to other geographies. Exports to Continental Europe in particular have witnessed notable gains, growing at a CAGR of more than 55 per cent over FY2004-2007

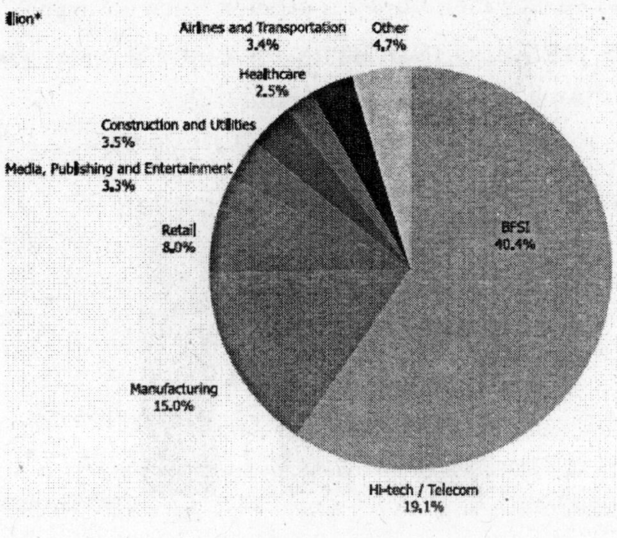

Banking, Financial Services and Insurance (BFSI) remains the largest vertical market for Indian IT-BPO exports, followed by High-technology and Telecom accounting for nearly 60 per cent in FY2007. Manufacturing and Retail followed, contributing 23 per cent to the aggregate. Other key segments include Media, Healthcare, Airlines and Transportation, and Utilities.

VERTICAL SPLIT FOR INDIAN IT-BPO EXPORTS

DOMESTIC IT MARKET IN FY2008

Technology adoption in the domestic market also reported steady gains in 2007. This segment is expected to cross USD 23 billion in FY2008, reporting healthv growth across all key segments.

- o Hardware remains the largest segment of the domestic market, and is expected to grow at 44 per cent in FY2008.
- o Domestic IT services spends are estimated to be growing at about 43 per cent in FY2008.

Software and services and BPO spending growth in the domestic market is being supported by increasing adoption, and is expected to grow by over 42 per cent and 45 per cent, respectively. Growing levels of technology adoption are now accompanied by a steady appreciation of the rupee, is also making India more attractive as a market – even for players that had earlier maintained a stricter focus on exports.

INDIAN ITES-BPO INDUSTRY : NASSCOM ANALYSIS

The Indian ITES-BPO Scenario

Employees ITES-BPO (in '000)

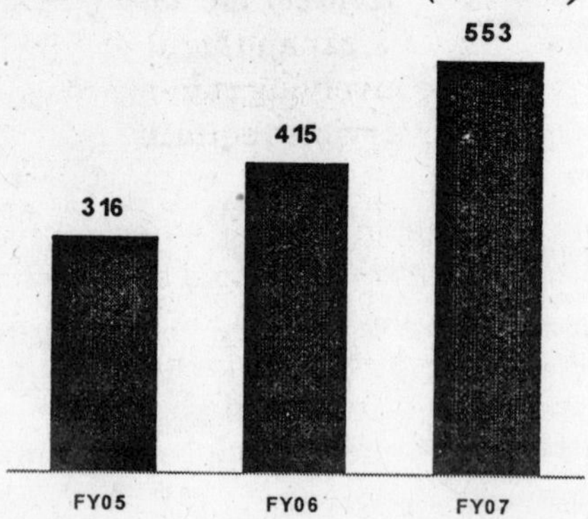

The Indian ITES-BPO segment has witnessed a steady growth. BPO exports are growing at about 33.5% percent and have exceeded FY06 expectation at USD 8.4 billion in FY2007.

***Exports ITES-BPO* (USD million)**

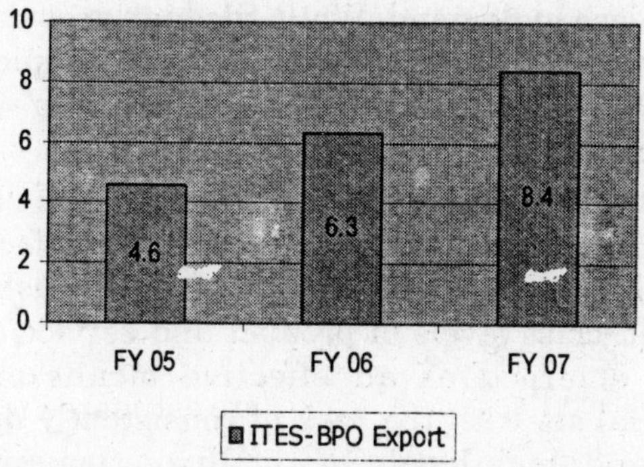

Key Highlights of Indian ITES-BPO Sector Performance

- Indian ITES-BPO exports grew from USD 6.3 billion in FY 2005-06 to USD 8.4 billion in FY 2006-07 expected to grow to USD 10.5-11bn in FY08.
- ITES-BPO employee base has grown to 553,000 in FY 07 from 415,000 in FY 06
- Over the past decade, the Indian BPO segment has witnessed significant transformation. Starting with basic data entry tasks, the industry graduated to a high proportion of voice-based services and a range of back-office processing activities. The last 3-4 years have seen the scope of services expanding to include increasingly complex processes involving rule-based decision making and even research services requiring informed individual judgment.
- The rapid expansion in the scope of BPO has been accompanied by an equally rapid adoption across a range of vertical industries. This wide range of services may be summarised into four broad categories comprising Finance and Accounting (F&A), Customer Interaction Services (CIS), Human Resource Administration and niche business services

Key Highlights of Domestic BPO Industry

- BPO demand in the domestic market has witnessed noticeable growth over the past few years. The annual revenue aggregate of the domestic market for ITES-BPO grew to USD 1.2 billion in FY 2006-07 from USD 0.9 billion in FY 2005-06, illustrating a significant increase in demand. While the high growth rate may be attributed to a small-base effect, the rapid adoption of BPO in the domestic market is receiving well-deserved attention.
- As the Indian economy becomes more globally integrated, businesses in India are beginning to face increasing levels of global competition and being pushed to deliver world class levels of product and service quality. BPO has emerged as an effective means of entrusting specialists with the task of consistently delivering the desired high-levels of quality – leaving the client organisations to focus on their core businesses.

Contrary to concerns of India's eroding cost competitiveness, best-in-class players have sustained profitability – while maintaining above-average growth. With significant bandwidth capacity lying unutilized and the steady advancement in technology making access faster and less expensive than before, it is likely that the share of telecommunications in the cost structure of an IT-BPO firm may further decline. Firms are also managing to lower their facilities costs by expanding into other tier-II locations.

Finally, there is scope for further leveraging operational levers to drive efficiencies in the organisation. A detailed industry benchmarking exercise, underway since 2005, has revealed that there is wide variation in the internal practices adopted across the industry, and suggests that the adoption of industry best-practices can further enhance operational excellence in Indian IT-BPO firms. This is also being evidenced in the performance of some of the best-in-class players. Contrary to concerns of rising wage inflation eroding the sustainability of India's cost-advantage, especially over the past two years, leading players have managed to grow at an above average rate– while sustaining their high levels of profitability.

Key Growth Drivers of Indian ITES-BPO Exports

- Abundant Talent- India's young demographic profile is an inherent advantage complemented by an academic infrastructure that generates a large pool of English speaking talent. Talent suitability concerns are being addressed through a combination of government, academia and industry led initiatives. These initiatives include national rollout of skill certification through NAC (NASSCOM Assessment of Competence), setting up finishing schools in association MHRD to supplement graduate education with training in specific technology areas and soft skills and MoU's with education agencies like UGC and AICTE to facilitate industry inputs on curriculum and teaching and develop faculty development programme.
- Sustained cost competitiveness- India has a strong track record of delivering a significant cost advantage, with clients regularly reporting savings of 25-50 percent over the original cost base. The ability to achieve such high levels of cost advantage by sourcing services from India is driven primarily by the ability to access highly skilled talent at significantly lower wage costs and the resultant productivity gains derived from having a very competent employee base. This is further complemented by relative advantages in other elements of the cost structure (e.g. telecom) that contribute to India's cost competitiveness – even when compared to other low-cost destinations.
- Continued focus on quality- Demonstrated process quality and expertise in service delivery has been a key factor driving India's sustained leadership in global service delivery. Since the inception of the industry in India, players within the country have been focusing on quality initiatives, to align themselves with international standards. Over the years, the industry has built robust processes and procedures to offer world class IT software and technology related services.
- World class information security environment- Stakeholders of Indian BPO recognise fool proof security as an indispensable element of global service delivery. Individual firm level efforts are complemented by a

comprehensive policy framework established by Indian authorities, which has built a strong foundation for an 'info-secure' environment in the country. These include strengthening the regulatory framework through proposed amendments to further strengthen the IT Act 2000, scaling up the cyber lab initiative, scaling up the National Skills Registry (NSR) and establishing a self regulatory organisation.

- Rapid growth in key business infrastructure- Rapid growth in key business infrastructure has ensured unhindered growth and expansion of this sector. The BPO sector has been a key beneficiary with the cost of international connectivity declining rapidly and service level improving significantly. The growth is taking place not only in existing urban centres but increasingly in satellite towns and smaller cities. Critical business infrastructure such as telecom and commercial real estate is well in place; improving other supporting infrastructure a key priority for the government. STPI infrastructure available across the country and magnitude of investments shows government support to the industry.
- Enabling Business policy and Regulatory environment- The enabling policy environment in India was instrumental in catalyzing the early phases of growth in this sector. Policy makers in India have laid special emphasis on encouraging foreign participation in most sectors of the economy, recognising its importance not only as a source of financial capital but also as a facilitator of knowledge and technology transfer. The Indian ITES-BPO sector has benefited from this approach, with participating firms enjoying minimal regulatory and policy restrictions along with a broad range of fiscal and procedural incentives.

3

Information Security Environment in India Nasscom Analysis

Most Indian companies that are aiming to go global will require certifying their ability to maintain proper security levels when scouting for international clients. Information security is no more a mere legal requirement but it is fast becoming a factor for companies to compete on and grow businesses. A "secure and reliable" environment—defined by strong copyright, IT and cyber laws—is an imperative for the growth and future success of the ITES BPO industries.

NASSCOM has been proactive in pushing this cause and ensuring that the Indian Information Security environment benchmarks with the best across the globe. Indian ITeS-BPO companies today adhere to international best practices – they are regularly audited by independent certified auditors, comply with international standards at the highest levels, update procedures and practices regularly and meet - if not exceed - the worldwide information security standards to ensure that data and personal information of international customers is adequately protected.

SECURITY ENVIRONMENT IN INDIA

Indian companies are known for their quality deliverables. International certifications like ISO 9000 and CMM went a long way in establishing this reputation. Likewise following international standards in information security is also helping Indian companies build credibility among customers. While most Indian BPO firms are recognized for high quality processes and services, information security practices need to be constantly reviewed and updated according to the rapidly changing environment. Customer data demands special focus. Currently, the information security environment in India is:

- Indian companies have robust security practices comparable to those followed by western companies. Indian companies primarily comply with ISO 27001 – a global standard that covers all domains of security.
- Companies sign Service Level Agreements (SLA), which have very strict confidentiality and security clauses built into them at the network and data level. Such SLAs also cover all relevant laws that the companies want its offshore providers to comply with and actions that can be taken in case of breaches.
- Laws such as the IT Act 2000, Indian Copyright Act, Indian Penal Code Act and the Indian Contract Act, 1972 provide adequate safeguards to companies offshoring work to US and UK
- Most of the BPO companies providing services to UK clients ensure compliance with UK Data Protection Act 1998 (DPA) through contractual agreements.
- Companies dealing with US clients require compliance depending upon the industry served. E.g. Healthcare requires compliance with HIPAA, Financial services require compliance with GLBA. To ensure compliance with such laws, Indian vendors follow security practices as specified by clients such as security awareness trainings, access control, data encryption and obfuscation, non-disclosure agreements, screening of employees, penetration testing etc. Further, clients conduct periodic audits to ensure compliance.
- Many companies in India are undergoing/have undergone SAS 70 Audit. SAS-70 assignments helps service companies operating from India to implement and improve internal controls, ensure minimal disruptions to business from clients' auditors, and is potent marketing tool in the face of increasing competition.

NASSCOM'S SECURITY INITIATIVES

NASSCOM has taken a holistic view of Information Security through its 'Trusted Sourcing'[1] Initiative to strengthen the regulatory framework and further improve India's attractiveness as an outsourcing destination. This multi-pronged initiative is targeted at employees, organizations, enforcement agencies and policy amendment, through a '4E Framework' Engagement, Education, Enactment and Enforcement.

NASSCOM has been working closely with the ITeS - BPO industry in India, to create a robust and secure Information Security culture, and in association with other stakeholders like the Indian Government on the issue of creating a relevant regulatory environment. All these initiatives aim to further strengthen information security environment, together with initiatives being rolled out by NASSCOM and the ITeS - BPO industry. NASSCOM, with the Indian government has also laid the foundation for the required legal framework through the proposed Amendments to the Indian IT Act of 2000[2] which includes laws and policies concerning data security and cyber crimes and the Indian Copyright Act of 1972 which deals with copyright issues in computer programs.

Trusted Sourcing Initiative

This initiative seeks to reinforce India as a secure and reliable technology partner. NASSCOM has also instituted the 4E framework to establish India as a trusted sourcing destination. This framework ensures highest standard of information security in the outsourcing industry in India.

NASSCOM'S FLAGSHIP INITIATIVES

Data Security Council of India (DSCI) - Self-Regulatory Organisation (SRO)*

The DSCI is an independent, self-regulatory body which has been set up to establish, popularize, monitor and enforce privacy and data protection standards for India's IT and ITeS-BPO industry. It has also set up a 21 member Steering Committee to guide DSCI in the technical aspects.

- DSCI is headed by a Board of Directors with Mr Shyamal Ghosh as the Chairman
- The DSCI steering committee is headed by Jerry Rao, Chairman, MphasiS. The first meeting of the committee took place on 14 September 2007 and sub-groups were set up to look into current security status and the

interests of organisations and develop a business model for DSCI.

- The new office of DSCI was inaugurated on Oct 15 2007 at Niryat Bhawan, New Delhi.

National Skills Registry (NSR)

Launched in January 2006, NSR is a centralized database of all employees of the IT services and BPO companies in India and contains third party verified personal, qualification and career information of IT professionals. The objective of NSR is to improve recruitment practices in IT and BPO industry, which will in turn help in maintaining India's global competitive advantage.

- As of November 2007, over 160,000 employees across 54 companies are registered with NSR
- The target is to take this number to touch 500,000 by March 2008.

NSR Milestones

1.	MOU signed between NASSCOM & NDML	18-A
2.	NASSCOM & NDML conducts road-shows in Bangalore, Chennai, Delhi , Hyderabad & Mumbai to showcase National Skills Registry	Nov/l
3.	Soft Launch of National Skills Registry	28-D
4.	Satyam Computers, Mphasis, TCS, CMC, ICICI Onesource, GENPACT become first few subscribers to join NSR	Dec/
5.	Point of Service(POS) facilities started in Delhi, Bangalore and Mumbai	Jai
6.	7. National Skills Registry was inaugurated by Hon'ble Minister for Communications and Information Technology Mr. Dayanidhi Maran	18-J.

NSR SYSTEM IS ISO27001 CERTIFIED

Amendments to the Indian IT ACT

The Union Cabinet (on October 16 2006) has approved the amendment to the IT Act 2000. NASSCOM worked with the government to evolve recommendations for amendments to further strengthen the Indian IT Act 2000. The recommendations are focused around protecting overseas customer data and tightening the punishment for defaulters. We understand that these amendments have incorporated most of the recommendations, and are hopeful that this will lead to better handling of cyber crime by enforcement authorities. We expect this to be discussed in the forthcoming session of the parliament.

Additionally, most Indian IT BPO companies conform to global standards such as ISO 27001 and also specific standards depending on the country/sector they cater to. For example in the US, Healthcare requires compliance with HIPAA, Financial services require compliance with GLBA.

NASSCOM's Education Initiatives

Sustaining India's talent edge to fuel the next wave of IT-BPO industry growth.

India offers a unique combination of attributes that have established it as the preferred offshore destination for IT-BPO, abundant talent pool being the key one. From India's young demographic profile (an inherent advantage), to its vast network of academic infrastructure that churns out 3.1 million graduates annually, to its English-speaking workforce, the country offers an unmatched mix of human-power benefits to organizations.

Various studies including NASSCOM-McKinsey Study 2005 throws up some interesting insights to validate India's positive human-power status:

- *The number of IT-BPO professionals employed in India grew from less than 200,000 people in 1998 to over 1.6 million in 2007, largely because of the country's demographic profile and network of high-quality academic institutions.*
- *India currently has around 347 institutes of higher education and 16,885 colleges with a total enrollment of over 9.9 million. These produce around 495,000 technical graduates, nearly 2.3 million other graduates and over 300,000 post-graduates every year.*
- *Even at current levels of employability, India has the largest pool of suitable offshore talent, accounting for 28*

percent of the total suitable pool available across all offshore destinations.

- *India's emergence as a preferred outsourcing destination has created the need for about 2.3 million professionals by 2010. Based on current estimates, a shortage of 0.5 million skilled knowledge workers may arise if remedial action is not taken.*

Despite the strong fundamentals (of a disproportionately large talent pool), already there are growing concerns about parts of the existing available talent pool being unsuitable for employment due to a skill gap.

It's become imperative to enhance the Indian talent pool to maximize the industry's potential and enable the sector to further catalyze the country's galloping economic growth rate.

To address this challenge, NASSCOM and the Indian IT-BPO sector have taken the lead in ensuring that requisite remedial actions are undertaken – well in time – to avoid any form of a talent crisis.

NASSCOM has over the last few years created a major workforce development platform and launched several initiatives, in partnership with the Government and academia that aim to bring positive changes to the Indian education system and its orientation towards building employable students.

THE PYRAMID APPROACH

NASSCOM has taken the employment pyramid approach to better understand the industry's skills requirement and create specific education and development initiatives basis that approach; most recent being working with Ministry of HRD to set up new IIITs and Finishing schools and extending NASSCOM Assessment of Competence (NAC) to IT services sector.

The base of the pyramid represents simple technical skills (including entry level jobs in the BPO industry and vocational jobs like networking, hardware maintenance, etc.). The middle stands for skills which are mainstream and account for the majority of the existing shortage in the industry, while the top of the pyramid, represents high-end technology skills (in areas such as bio-informatics, embedded software, product architecture, DSP, VLSI, program management and multimedia convergence), which are niche today, but will become mainstream in the near future.

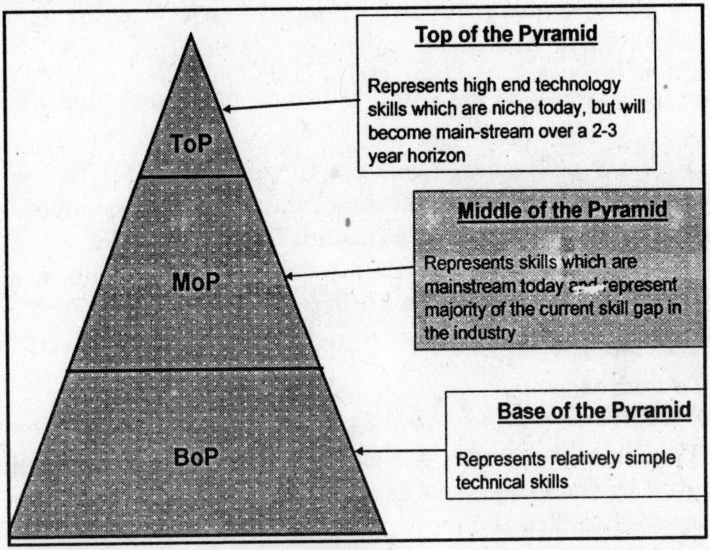

NASSCOM'S EDUCATIONAL AND WORKFORCE ENHANCEMENT INITIATIVES

The Top end of the Pyramid

One of the biggest human-power challenges being faced at the level of higher-end education is the paucity of Ph.Ds and research scientists. Currently, post-graduate education is lagging behind undergraduate learning, with barely a handful of takers for the top-of-the-line Ph.D programs.

1.

Set-up new IIITs - NASSCOM has been working with Ministry of Human Resource Development on a proposal to create "top of the pyramid," highly specialized professionals with skill sets in emerging, "on-the-horizon" technologies that are not yet mainstream. These will typically include research in areas such as banking, insurance, analytics, remote sensing, water, agriculture, energy, transportation, environment, geosphere, natural sciences, nanotechnology, healthcare, networks and mobile computing, image processing, and cyber security, among others.

The aim of these institutions will be to:

- generate cutting-edge research and technology
- enhance and produce competent professionals and engineers
- incubate new companies and clusters
- nurture existing clusters of knowledge-based companies

Ministry of Human Resource Development (MHRD) with support from NASSCOM and the IT industry has recommended the launch of five new IIITs (Indian Institutes of Information Technology). based on the Public-Private Partnership model, by the year 2008. In all, the Ministry of Human Research and Development aims to set up around 20 IIITs over the next few years.

The Middle Level of the Pyramid

This area represents the skills which are most commonly required by the IT services segment. It is also the market that is expected to face the largest skill shortage and a number of NASSCOM initiatives have been focused at this level.

1. NAC-Tech- Encouraged by the success of its Assessment and Certification program (NAC) for the BPO sector, NASSCOM is looking at offering a similar testing and accreditation offering, NAC-Tech, for the IT services sector starting this academic year. The aim is to make NAC-Tech an industry standard for evaluating students aspiring to find jobs in the technology/engineering industries. NAC-Tech will also help the industry, academic institutions and individual colleges to understand the potential of their students and determine their caliber, in terms of industry relevance and employability.
2. IT/Engineering Finishing School – Another pioneering initiative by NASSCOM in partnership with the Ministry of Human Resource Development is the "Finishing Schools for Engineering Students" program, which is expected to enable young technical graduates to become industry-ready.

The "Finishing School" for engineering graduates who are still seeking employment has been launched in a pilot mode in May 2007. The pilot has been conducted during the summer months of May-June, 2007, for a period of eight weeks in eight institutions, including IIT Roorkee and seven NITs—Calicut, Durgapur, Kurushetra, Jaipur, Surathkal, Trichy and Warangal.

The "Finishing School" is covering the curriculum provided on technical and soft skills development. The students will get an opportunity to reinforce some basic engineering skills and in addition, acquire industry-specific knowledge and skills, soft skills, and management and employment skills, which are being delivered by trained faculty and practicing IT and ITES industry consultants.

As part of the program, the students will also receive periodical feedback on their performance and undertake a final exam that highlights their ability in the area of rational, analytical thinking processes identified in a problem solving environment. The students will have the opportunity to take the NAC-Tech (NASSCOM Assessment of Competence–Tech), an employment benchmarking test and participate in a Job Fair.

3. The IT Workforce Development (ITWD) program- The initiative was created keeping the issues and concerns of the industry at one end and challenges of the academia at the other end.

- As part of this initiative, NASSCOM has been nurturing the IT industry-academia interface through workshops and conferences, faculty sabbaticals, training programs and mentorship initiatives to ensure better synchronization between IT education and the industry requirements. The one-day industry-academia workshops for instance, have already been held in Kolhapur, Madurai, Tirupati, NCR, Dharwad, Coimbatore, Jaipur, Vizag, Lucknow, Hyderabad, Kolkata, Pune and Chennai. These have helped improve industry-academia interactions within different regions, enable a flow of information and discussion on the IT industry and create a plank for experience sharing. The faculty training workshops (or sabbaticals) are enabling faculty to realize the gaps in the present style of teaching and the approach to take in the core areas.

- As part of the mentorship program, IT companies are providing consistent and continuous guidance for over 12-24 months to a particular college(s)/institute(s) and enabling it to transform into a center where quality education is imparted.
- Closely working with academic bodies such MHRD, AICTE and UGC to standardize the curriculum and pedagogy
- Encouraging research and survey-oriented projects to showcase the best practices in the area of industry academia alliances and developing White Papers on certain fundamental and critical requirements such as curriculum, information on engineering institutions and skills sets desired/available pan India.

The Bottom of the Pyramid

In order to develop entry-level human-power, especially for the BPO industry, and equip them with relevant hard and soft skills that ensure employability, NASSCOM has launched a key endeavor, the NAC.

NASSCOM's Assessment of Competence (NAC) - NAC was launched as an industry standard assessment and certification program to ensure the transformation of a "trainable" workforce into an "employable workforce" hence creating a robust and continuous pipeline of talent for the BPO sector.

NAC successfully completed its pilot phase in 2006 and was rolled out in Rajasthan where 2500 people took the NAC test. A job fair was held in association with the Department of Information Technology & Communication (DoIT&C) and Government of Rajasthan after the scores were released in Jaipur in March 2007.

Now NAC is being taken to the next level, by proliferating it across Tier II and Tier III cities and towns that can be strengthened into BPO hubs and used as playgrounds for nurturing job-ready professionals. By the end of the year, NAC will be rolled out in various states of India, including Tamil Nadu, Gujarat, Chandigarh, Andhra Pradesh, North-Eastern

States and West Bengal amongst others. In order to build a mindshare for NAC, awareness campaigns are being organized at colleges/universities in these regions, before the test is conducted. Students are being briefed about the BPO industry and the opportunities it offers in terms of jobs

In the future, NAC will help align educational curriculum offered by universities and colleges in the country with the needs of the ITES-BPO sector. The initiative is also expected to help ITES-BPO players reduce their hiring costs, improve efficiencies, enlarge the candidate pool and perhaps more importantly reduce; if not remove the current escalation the market is seeing in entry level wages.

NATIONAL SKILLS REGISTRY

The IT software and services industry is one of India's outstanding successes. It is now India's top exporter, and provides direct employment to over 1.6 million people directly and over 6.4 million indirectly (For 1 job created in IT-ITES, 4 jobs are created in rest of the economy) in sectors such as commercial real estate, physical security, transport, catering, hospitality and mortgage banking industries. It is contributing to better governance and efficiency, even as it has transformed the image of India abroad. The industry is making a significant positive impact on the Indian economy and the people of this country.

According to NASSCOM-McKinsey report 2005 the IT-BPO exports are expected to reach US$ 60 billion in 2010, from approximately USD 4 billion in FY 2000. (The industry clocked US$ 31.3 billion from IT-BPO exports in 2007).

Today, issues such as governance, physical security, business continuity, logical security, safeguarding IP, software change management and personnel security are becoming key for both customers and outsourcing service suppliers. These issues, if not properly handled, could derail the growth and hopes of the IT industry.

The Indian IT-BPO companies need to continuously raise the standards for the safety of the employees and the clients. These issues are being taken extremely seriously, not only by NASSCOM, but also the government, the legal authorities and the police.

In recognition of these, NASSCOM - working closely with industry has taken a number of pro-active steps.

NASSCOM has undertaken an initiative to create, operate and maintain a national database of employees working in the IT/BPO sector in India, known as the National Skills Registry (NSR): A centralized database of all employees of the IT services and BPO companies in India. Launched in January 2006, NSR is a pan-India online database containing third party verified personal, qualification and career-related information of IT–BPO professionals. As of July 2007, over 125,000 employees across 43 companies are registered with NSR. With the positive response received by the industry, the target is to take this number 4 times over to touch 500, 000 by December 2007.

NASSCOM will also be rolling out a series road shows to generate awareness in the next six months across 8 cities.

Objective

The objective of NSR is to improve recruitment practices in IT and BPO industry, which will in turn help in maintaining India's global competitive advantage. It is an employee-friendly measure to minimize any misuse of employee identity. The ownership of the data resides with the IT professionals and prospective employers will be able to view the verified resume only if authorised by the professional.

Implementation of NSR

The NSR implementation agency is National Securities Depository Limited (NSDL), a decade old depository offering services to over seven million investors. NSDL Database Management Limited (NDML) - a subsidiary of NSDL is responsible for creating, operating and maintaining this database of IT professionals. The database is voluntary in nature.

Validation & Registration

The database for BPO employees will require authorisation by the candidate himself. IT/BPO aspirants and existing industry employees can go and register themselves either online (www.nationalskillsregistry.in) or through empanelled points of sales (PoS), and provide details like their name, educational qualification, professional qualification, previous employment information, photograph and fingerprint, on NSDL database. There is a validation history associated with each section that will reflect who was validated what when. This would be charged at Rs. 300-500 per person. NSDL will also have an empanelled group of background checking agencies.

IT or BPO employees can approach any of these agencies and ask them to run verification checks for which the charges would be Rs 1,500-2,000, or the same can be done by their existing or prospective employers after an authorisation by the employee. Firms that use information from the registry are expected to contribute the results of their validation efforts back to the registry.

BENEFITS TO STAKEHOLDERS

Employees

- Increasingly, the foreign clients, especially, government or public bodies, are insisting on background check of an individual before recruitment. The employee resume will be ready for showcasing to such clients and thus ensure better employment opportunity for them
- There are several undeserving candidates who fake their resume to grab employment opportunities. IT professionals can prevent such people from taking away an opportunity they deserve, by being a part of this database
- The employer will save time on background check since the employee background information is only a click away. This will result in faster completion of HR processes (formalities).
- As more and more IT professionals join the database, Industry may decide to recruit only such candidates that have registered in the database. If someone is already registered, he/she will be in a better position to avail of the new opportunities.

Employers

- Menace of bloated resume will be eliminated as pre-verified facts are available for cross-checking
- Risk of engaging any employee on the basis of fake/forged documents is minimized

- Benefit of back ground check done by any of the NASSCOM member companies will be available to all other members of the industry. This will save cost and time involved in having background check done
- Indian IT/BPO industry can confidently claim higher standards of recruitment practices in front of international customers, through NSR

Customers

- The customers can view employee information-his background, qualifications, etc. directly, depending on employee's consent
- Pro-active step by Indian IT/BPO industry to ensure customer information is in safe and secure hands

NSR Milestones

1. MOU signed between NASSCOM & NDML 18-Aug-05
2. NASSCOM & NDML conducts road-shows in Bangalore, Chennai, Delhi , Hyderabad & Mumbai to showcase National Skills Registry Nov/Dec 05
3. Soft Launch of National Skills Registry 28-Dec-05
4. Satyam Computers, Mphasis, TCS, CMC, ICICI Onesource, GENPACT become first few subscribers to join NSR Dec/Jan 06
5. Point of Service(POS) facilities started in Delhi, Bangalore and Mumbai Jan 06
6. National Skills Registry was inaugurated by Hon'ble Minister for Communications and Information Technology Mr. Dayanidhi Maran 18-Jan-06

NSR System is ISO27001 certified

List of companies who have joined NSR – as of July 2007

1. 24/7 Customer

2. Accenture
3. Aviva
4. AXA
5. Citigroup
6. CMC
7. Cognizant
8. Customer Op.Serv
9. DELL
10. Deutsche
11. FirstSource
12. Franklin Templ
13. Fusion
14. GENPACT
15. HCL - BPO
16. HP
17. i - flex
18. IBM Daksh
19. Inautix
20. Infosys
21. iSoftTech
22. Intelenet
23. JP Morgan
24. KPIT Cummins
25. MindTree
26. Mphasis
27. NeST
28. NIIT
29. Perot
30. PHILIPS
31. Quatrro BPO
32. Sasken
33. Satyam
34. Scope
35. Syntel

36. TCS
37. Tech Mahindra
38. Wipro
39. Wipro BPO
40. WNS
41. Xchanging
42. Zensar
43. Zenta

National Skills Registry is another milestone for the Indian IT/BPO industry. Together, we will leave no stone unturned and we aim to make India the "Fort Knox" of security, positioning ourselves as the gold standard for security as we are today for quality.

4

Data Security Council of India

A SELF REGULATORY INITIATIVE IN DATA SECURITY AND PRIVACY PROTECTION

Background

The phenomenon of globalization has led to creation of innovative business models and provided unprecedented benefits for the global economy. The Indian IT and ITeS/BPO sector had played a pivotal role in this irreversible trend and contributed to the national economy in no small measure. However, the unbundling of business processes has also brought in its wake some unforeseen challenges in the area of data security and privacy.

The Indian ITeS and BPO industry, which started with the advantage of low-cost human resources, has now moved on to add quality and diversity as it differentiators. With companies maturing and successfully coping with the issue of scaling up and expanding, will now need to tackle the problem of offering consistent data security to the customers at an affordable cost. The security landscape is constantly evolving, as the threats, consumer perceptions and legislative and regulatory strategies keep changing. These are the challenges that will need to be met with effective responses.

The Indian ITES/BPO companies are striving hard to ensure the security of data and privacy protection. They are following the stringent security controls specified by their customers through contracts. However, many a times, the problem can not be contained by an individual company, irrespective of the cost incurred, and requires industry-level solutions. Successful security solutions require a convergence of the three components, viz. technology, people and processes. Further, a single instance of information security breach can tarnish the entire industry's image and the country's reputation as a safe destination for data. Smaller companies lack dedicated resources for handling security and need cost-effective approaches for demonstrative security levels. There is an urgent need to provide a protected environment for data and privacy for IT and ITeS sector in India, through the establishment of rules and standards that promote ethics, quality and best practices.

NASSCOM has been proactive in pushing this cause for ensuring that the Indian Information Security environment benchmarks with the best across the globe. As a part of its Trusted Sourcing initiative, NASSCOM is in the process of setting up the Data Security Council of India (DSCI) as a Self Regulatory Organization (SRO) to establish, popularize, monitor and enforce privacy and data protection standards for India's ITeS-BPO industry.

GUIDING PRINCIPLES

DSCI is envisaged as a credible and committed body to uphold a high level of data privacy and security standards. DSCI shall be based on the following five guiding principles:

1. Self-Regulation: The structure and operating procedures of DSCI rely primarily upon self-regulation. Industry, rather than a governmental body, is best positioned to develop appropriate data privacy and security standards based upon its greater knowledge and understanding with the practical commercial issues involved. A self regulatory approach will allow DSCI to evolve and respond more effectively to developments in overseas and domestic markets.
2. Adoption of best global practices: DSCI shall adopt the best global practices, drawing upon U.S. laws, the European Union Directive and Safe Harbor Framework, OECD guidelines, and Asia Pacific Economic Cooperation (APEC) Framework in designing the Code of conduct, which in turn, will continue to evolve with time and experience.
3. Independent Oversight: The composition of governing body of DSCI shall be balanced with adequate

representation of independent directors and industry specialists.

4. Focused Mission: Initial focus of DSCI shall be its core mission of establishing itself with significant membership with focus on evolving the Code of Conduct and promoting a culture of privacy and security through education and outreach.
5. Enforcement Mechanism: DSCI shall promote and encourage voluntary compliance of the code, but, in due course, will seek to create a mechanism for enforcement of the code to enhance its credibility among a variety of stakeholders

Structure

DSCI shall be a not-for-profit organization, registered under section 25 of the Companies Act. It would have a diversified membership associated with Data Security and Privacy Protection. This could include: companies in information technology (IT) and IT enabled services (ITeS) sector, companies other than in IT/ITeS sector, Academic or research Institutions and universities. DSCI will thus seek to develop a diverse membership, unified in its pursuit of its objectives. Activities of DSCI members could be in the fields of provision of IT/ITES services, consultancy, research and development and manufacturing. Irrespective of the field of specialization, all DSCI members will be expected to share and support the objectives of DSCI and to operate in a manner consistent therewith.

DSCI shall be headed by a Board of Directors with balanced representation from industry and independent individuals. In the technical aspects, it will be guided by a Steering Committee, which will have experts from the various domains of security.

Mission

The key objectives of DSCI will be:

- To enable Indian IT/ITeS organizations to provide high standard of security and data protection by adopting the best practices.
- To develop, monitor and enforce an appropriate security and data protection standard for the Indian IT/ITES

industry that would be adequate, cost effective, adaptable and comparable with the global standards

- To build capacity to provide security certification for organizations.
- To create a common platform for promoting sharing of knowledge about information security and foster a community of security professionals and firms.
- To create awareness among industry professionals and other stakeholders about security and privacy issues.

ACTIVITIES

DSCI shall function as an enabler to the IT and ITeS industry to grow at a rapid pace by facilitating the adoption and enforcement of the prescribed security standards and best practices. It plans to undertake the following activities.

1. Awareness through Security Forums: Creation and functioning of Security Forums throughout the country for creating awareness among the involved entities and individuals about the importance and measures for data protection.
2. GAP analysis: Analyzing the existing standards and best practices adopted by the industry in India and industry at the international level.
3. Devising standards and best practices: Consolidating, devising and enforcing ethical standards and best practices in line with international standards for creating a secured environment for data in India that would be cost effective and easily adoptable.
4. Research: Carrying out research in the field of data privacy and protection in the context of Indian situation.
5. Conferences: Organizing national and regional conferences on data security issues.
6. Certification: Certifying the companies who adopt the standard proposed by DSCI.

Keeping in view the broad objectives, DSCI, as a Self Regulatory Organization, would be a credible and committed body for upholding an effective data privacy and security standard in India, thereby enabling member companies with competitive edge to sustain their rate of rapid growth.

SECTORAL TRENDS OF INDIAN ECONOMY

The different sectoral trends of Indian economy has been encouraging for the investors. The astronomical rise of the Indian industry across all verticals have facilitated the growth of Indian economy. The main contributors for the overall rise of the different sectoral trends of Indian economy has been the manufacturing and service industry. Today, India along with china is regarded as the manufacturing hub of the world. In the service sector India still holds dominating position in the world market.

Some key facts of the sectoral trends of Indian economy are discussed as below -

- India's economy grew at 9.3% in quarter April-June and it was driven by manufacturing, construction and services sector and agriculture sector
- GDP factor for the first quarter of 2007-08 was at Rs 7,23,132 crore, registering a growth rate of 9.3% over the corresponding quarter of previous year
- Manufacturing registered 11.9% growth
- The passenger vehicles sector grew by 11.61% during April-May 2007
- Electricity, gas & water supply performed well and recorded an impressive growth rate of 8.3%
- Construction growth rate rose to 10.7%
- Trade, hotels, transport and communication registered a growth rate of 12%
- Financing, insurance, real estate and business services recorded an impressive growth rate of at 11% during the 1st quarter of this fiscal
- Community, social and personal services maintained a decent growth rate of 7.6%
- The growth rate of agriculture, forestry & fishing' and 'mining & quarrying' are estimated at 3.8 per cent, and 3.2 per cent, respectively during the 1st quarter of 2007-2008
- Exports grew by 18.11% during the 1st quarter of 2007-2008 and the imports shoot up by 34.30% during the same period

- India's FOREX reserves (excluding Gold and SDRs) stood at $219.75 billion at the end of July ' 07
- The food sector is estimated to be of US$ 200 billion and it is expected to grow to $310 billion by 2015
- Stocks of food-grains grew by 13.1% to 17.73 million tonnes
- The annual inflation rate was 4.45% for the week ended July 28, 2007
- India's Balance of Payments is expected to remain comfortable
- Merchandise Exports recorded strong growth

According to reports, the productivity trends of different sectors of Indian economy and its subsequent growth is estimated to be around 8% and above until 2020. Further, at this rate, the Indian economy will become the second largest economy in the world after China.

Further, the World Bank has ranked India as one of the top economic reformers worldwide. It simplified business registration, cross-border trade, and payment of taxes, eased access to credit and strengthen investor's interest. The sectoral trends of Indian economy indicates robust growth of Indian industries especially manufacturing, construction, and service industry.

Can Indian Software Firms hold their own Against MNCs?

While MNCs position India on the global map by their continued investment in the country, they also pose competition to the local firms in segments like consulting and software services. Pankaj Mishra pits Indian software firms against the MNCs and tries to find out if it's a 'win-win' or a 'win-lose' situation for the Indian software industry Jack Welch, former CEO of General Electric, the world's most respected company, in his autobiography describes how he met Wipro's Azim Premji for the first time in India. That was the time when GE was looking for strategic partners in India and Welch was perhaps one of the first to identify India as the outsourcing hub. "The quiet one, Azim Premji came in and gave a thoughtful presentation as to why his company, Wipro, was the right partner for GE."

Later Welch forged a JV with Wipro for medical systems and also became one of the largest outsourcers to the Indian software industry. GE accounts for more than two percent of the software outsourced to India. Wipro benchmarked GE's 'six sigma' process and became what Welch describes as "the poster child of the Indian hi-tech industry". Since then, Indian software firms -essentially services firms-have not only benchmarked the best practises, but have also started competing with the IBMs of the world.

But there is a school of thought which believes that with the MNC software house presence increasing in India, the outsourcing pie shared by the domestic firms is in danger. The traditional outsourcers like Cisco, Ford and GE are moving more work to their own development centres in the country.

What are the strengths, weaknesses, opportunities and threats that Indian software firms face in light of the MNC presence? Is it a win-win situation for both sides or will the local outfits be badly affected in the long run?

Strengths

It all started with the great 'Y2K' boom when 'India' brand became popular in the global software services arena. While the Indian firms went through a kind of 'identity crisis', firms like Infosys, TCS, Wipro and HCL Technologies helped the Indian software industry graduate to a mature and reliable option for the outsourcers.

"In the software services arena, Indian brand equity is very high. Not only because of the cost effectiveness, but also because the Indian firms are now looked upon as quality-driven organisations," says S Gopalakrishnan, co-founder and member of the Board, Infosys.

It would not be fair to expect Indian firms to undertake marketing investments anywhere near to what firms like Microsoft do. Microsoft invests nearly $1 billion annually in promoting and enhancing Windows. Similarly, it could take a few more years to build 'high value' equity in the consulting segment but in the services arena, Indian firms enjoy an enviable reputation. Today, India is perceived as the hub for offshore development and firms like Wipro have already started branding their Offshore Development Centres (ODC).

"ODCs in India today are commoditised, branding is the only logical option. Wipro is trying to define brand attributes by branding its ODCs," says Sangita Singh, vice president of marketing at Wipro Technologies. Everything boils down to the kind of positioning Indian firms have been striving to achieve. Till now, the positioning has been the 35 percent cost advantage and around 10-15 percent production improvement. It is high time the likes of Wipro, TCS and Infosys change gears and position their services at a better overall value proposition.

Weaknesses

The Indian software industry has traditionally been software services oriented, which ironically has become one of the weaknesses for Indian firms who want to move up the value chain by developing products. We have players like HCL Technologies, TCS, Infosys, Wipro and NIIT who have now started to move up the value chain of the software development cycle and enhance focus on R&D services. The flip side however, is that most of these Indian players are also aggressively tapping the IT enabled services arena, which according to many analysts is not 'high value' work.

But there is a fundamental difference in the type of software development done by the likes of Oracle and Microsoft as compared to, say, Wipro or Infosys. "At Oracle, we are not involved in any kind of custom development or software services. We only undertake product development and designing," says Ranjan Chak, executive director of the Oracle India Development Centre.

Microsoft, Oracle, Adobe and SAP are all doing product-oriented development. "We have to understand that these MNCs are exploiting Indian talent to use it as their R&D base. The type of development undertaken is very different," admits Gopalakrishnan.

The services tag is like a double-edged sword. While on one hand it has become a 'cash cow' for the Indian firms, on the other hand it acts as a stumbling block for companies like Talisma and ITTIAM when they go to sell products. But when it comes to high-end consulting and productised solutions, Indian firms have a daunting task ahead in terms of shedding the 'cost-effective services' image.

"Indian firms don't have sufficient brand equity in high-end consulting, but then if we look at the MNC subsidiaries in the country, they are all employing Indian professionals," says Gopalakrishnan. He adds that it is not realistic to expect products like operating systems and databases to come from the Indian firms at present, because the Indian IT industry is not mature enough. But Gopalakrishnan feels that developing products is not a 'capability issue' for Indian firms. "Let's not forget that even the Indian subsidiaries of these MNCs are employing Indian talent only," he says.

However, this argument seems weak when one considers that firms like TCS and HCL Technologies have been around for almost two decades and yet no significant product offering has emerged.

Opportunities

Developing world-class products or offering high-end consulting services like the Big Five consulting firms are the two routes available for the Indian software industry in its efforts to move up the value chain. The opportunity for the Indian IT industry lies in the success of firms like Sasken, ITTIAM, Talisma, Trivium and i-flex, who are capable of establishing the 'India brand' in the global product arena. The 'big five" who are services oriented should now be looking at growing fast in the consulting space either by acquiring companies, or by developing those competencies in-house.

Threats

According to Sunil Mehta, vice-president, Nasscom, the MNC firms account for a mere 15 percent of the total software exports done from India. "Indian firms will continue to get outsourcing deals and the multinational vendors are no threat," he says. The only MNC development house posing a direct threat to the Indian firms is IBM Global Services. Other vendors like Oracle, Microsoft, SAP and Cisco are oriented towards their in-house product development efforts. Competition is very intense in the A-PAC region, which has emerged as a new geographic market for the Indian firms.

IBM Global Services has an established brand equity, which helps it command premium rates. "With IBM Global Services India (IGSI) business growing in the A-PAC region and diversification into new business segments like AMS, we see IGSI becoming the cornerstone of service delivery for IBM worldwide-specifically the A-PAC region," says IBM Global Services India director Uday Shukla.

However, an important point to note is that IGSI also has the same Indian talent pool. "The market for software services is competitive and globally IBM Global Services operates in the same sphere as other Indian companies. Every organisation that competes for business brings to the table a certain value proposition. Our value proposition is proven IBM technology and expertise coupled with the best from the Indian talent pool," says Shukla.

Undoubtedly, as the Indian firms try to move up the value chain and pitch for consulting projects, competition from IBM Global Services will get more intense. "We are now competing more and more with IGSI and there are instances wherein we have lost contracts to them," says Gopalakrishnan of Infosys.

MNC's Presence Conducive

A close look at the first generation of Indian IT entrepreneurs reveals that most of them, at some point in their career, worked for an MNC. "There is no doubt that the Indian software industry owes a lot to MNC vendors, who not only gave them international exposure, but also cultivated the entrepreneurial spirit in them," says Chak of Oracle. He further adds that the presence of players like Microsoft and Oracle has helped local players.

Most of the MNCs have a 'leadership' program in place, which enhances the entrepreneurial skills of their Indian executives. Microsoft's India Development Centre is also developing managers who can take on responsibilities at the company's headquarters in Redmond.

When the MNCs like Microsoft and Oracle started telling the world that their Indian subsidiaries were rolling out new products aimed at the global market, an awareness was created that India was a good place to do business in the field of software, and the 'India brand' gained further equity.

As Srini Koppolu, director of Microsoft's India Development Centre proudly puts it, "Today, the IDC is a self-contained unit with program managers, testing professionals and developers. We usually wait for the charter to come from Redmond for working on any new product or solution. With the kind of expertise we have garnered, we are now even in a position to suggest our own products. Everyone from Bill (Gates) to Steve (Ballmer) is excited about the group."

Achieving Synergy

Although the MNCs account for a mere 15 percent of total software exports from India, the kind of work done by them endorses the fact that high-end research and development can be done right here in India. But it is very unlikely that the likes of Oracle and Microsoft will ever outsource product development to Indian firms.

If we take a close look, the Indian software industry has two options-it can either take the product route aggressively or the likes of Wipro and Infosys should move up the value chain by offering end-to-end consulting like, for instance, PriceWaterhouse Coopers. It's high time the 'big five' of the Indian software industry steer away from low-billing-rate maintenance projects that are detrimental to the objective of establishing the Indian IT industry at the higher end of the value chain. Software India has to shift to high-value strategic outsourcing or Business Intelligence projects which could result in huge, sustainable revenue streams that could see the industry through to its ambitious revenue projection estimates.

And for a 'win-win' relationship to emerge between the MNCs and Indian firms, the latter would have to achieve more strategic proximity with the former. JVs on the lines of Wipro-GE Medical Systems should be pursued more intently, while at the same time continuing with the usual work being outsourced by the MNCs.

GROWTH OF THE INDIAN IT INDUSTRY

If the Indian IT industry continues to grow, a few large players, especially those that are merely banking on past performances and goodwill, are bound to falter, believes *MOHAN BABU*

Indian IT majors are beginning to project a uniformly optimistic view of the forthcoming fiscal year. Case in point,

Infosys, during its first quarterly announcement (Y 2005) painted an extremely rosy picture of its growth, setting the expectation for about a 40 percent growth during the coming fiscal year. Two major factors contributing to this buyout outlook include subsiding ruckus over outsourcing and the strengthening of US dollar (against the Rupee). The resilience shown by the American economy, which incidentally accounts for a large percentage of Indian IT exports, is also helping. The signs of optimism are everywhere in the Indian IT landscape, ranging from statements emerging out of executive interviews to optimistic reports from industry bodies like Nasscom. Behind all the signs of optimism, however, there are a few voices of concern over the trends shaping up.

A leading Indian business in a recent article set a cautious tone with the following remark "Finally, in the very success of the Indian IT companies lies the seeds of a future tragedy. The stocks have appreciated significantly in the past 12 months, so much so Infosys, Wipro and Cognizant all trade for more than 35 times the calendar 2004 earnings estimates. This means investors need to pay even closer attention to the risks." The article went on to analyse various issues, including attrition at top Indian companies and added, "IT biggies like Wipro and Infosys are not only losing people at the entry level, but also experienced professionals at the middle and senior management level. The top Indian IT companies starting to lose key software developers, project managers and high level executives to leading US tech companies such as IBM, Oracle and Accenture."

I began to think of some of the issues raised by the article and exchanged notes with some of my knowledgeable peers who had an insight into the trends in the Indian IT industry. One friend responded saying that he believed that the churn at the middle/top levels in Indian companies might in fact turn out to be a blessing in disguise since it would lead to more opportunities for juniors to move up. He also felt that for the kind of work being done by a majority of software services companies, most people weren't indispensable.

The vacuum created by the exit of a few senior project managers or a delivery head are routinely being filled by eager second-line managers. More than a conscious risk mitigation strategy, the existence of a 'pyramid structure', coupled with aggressive hiring during the past few years has ensured an abundant supply of talent in many of the large organisations.

Another factor propelling Indian IT is the fact that the business is "highly commoditised" and the business models of most large software service organisations have been built around economies-of-scale. It also helps that the sheer momentum created by stratospheric growth during the late nineties has lead to sufficient inertia to sustain the current pace of growth. The fact of the matter is that the growth has definitely "slowed" from ninety or hundred percent during the late nineties to thirty and forty percent growth the industry is currently experiencing. This relative slowing of growth has by no means deterred investors for whom a forty percent growth is still hugely appealing; the Indian IT industry still promises higher returns and growth than most other sectors.

Issues like high rates of attrition are also moot since attrition in one or two companies leads to a widening depth of the overall talent pool available in the industry. Added to this is the 'reverse brain drain' of Indian NRIs and technologists overseas who are not just observing the trends but are also beginning to return back to partake in growth. At a macro level, Indian IT is bound to see a sustained rate of growth, regardless of the issues faced by individual players.

And, this is where I would like to end my discussion of this topic by wondering aloud: "If the Indian industry continues to grow, a few large players—especially those that are merely banking on past performances and goodwill—are bound to falter. What would it take to trip the 800 pound gorillas that are merely moving because of sheer inertia?" Any thoughts and comments on this are more than welcome.

RECENT TRENDS IN RECRUITMENT

The following trends are being seen in recruitment:

Outsourcing

In India, the HR processes are being outsourced from more than a decade now. A company may draw required personnel from outsourcing firms. The outsourcing firms help the organisation by the initial screening of the candidates according to the needs of the organisation and creating a suitable pool of talent for the final selection by the organisation. Outsourcing firms develop their human resource pool by employing people for them and make available personnel to various companies as per their needs. In turn, the outsourcing firms or the intermediaries charge the organisations for their services.

Advantages of outsourcing are:

1. Company need not plan for human resources much in advance.
2. Value creation, operational flexibility and competitive advantage
3. turning the management's focus to strategic level processes of HRM
4. Company is free from salary negotiations, weeding the unsuitable resumes/candidates.
5. Company can save a lot of its resources and time

Poaching/Raiding

"Buying talent" (rather than developing it) is the latest mantra being followed by the organisations today. Poaching means employing a competent and experienced person already working with another reputed company in the same or different industry; the organisation might be a competitor in the industry. A company can attract talent from another firm by offering attractive pay packages and other terms and conditions, better than the current employer of the candidate. But it is seen as an unethical practice and not openly talked about. Indian software and the retail sector are the sectors facing the most severe brunt of poaching today. It has become a challenge for human resource managers to face and tackle poaching, as it weakens the competitive strength of the firm.

E-recruitment

Many big organizations use Internet as a source of recruitment. E- recruitment is the use of technology to assist the recruitment process. They advertise job vacancies through worldwide web. The job seekers send their applications or curriculum vitae i.e. CV through e mail using the Internet. Alternatively job seekers place their CV's in worldwide web, which can be drawn by prospective employees depending upon their requirements.

Advantages of recruitment are:

- o Low cost.
- o No intermediaries
- o Reduction in time for recruitment.
- o Recruitment of right type of people.
- o Efficiency of recruitment process.

STEEL AND CONSTRUCTION INDUSTRY - RECENT TRENDS

Steel as a basic ingredient in construction has come a long way in the evolution chain. While the Eiffel Tower made in steel stands tall as the landmark for Paris, the Howrah bridge and Vidyasagar Setu across River Hooghly in Calcutta sing laurels to the amazing capabilities of this ingenious building material. The tallest building in the world, viz. Petronas Twin Towers of Kuala Lumpur, Malaysia have high-strength steel-reinforced concrete frame, with the exterior sheathed in stainless steel. The record-breaking height of 451.9 m has been attributed to the steel spires, forming the integral pinnacle of the Petronas towers.

An international survey conducted recently has indicated a relationship between the proportional share of steel in construction and the national Gross Domestic Product (GDP). The study has indicated that the consumption of steel in construction induces a faster pace in the growing economy. In 1996-97 the total production of finished steel in India stood at 22.72 million ton and in the fiscal year 97-98 production was at a level of 23.37 million ton. The total consumption of finished steel in 1997-98 by all sectors was indicated as 22.6 million tonnes.

The Housing construction sector besides being an opportunity for catering to the housing need is a major kick starter for the economy. For every one crore rupees of investment in housing, nearly 290 industries in the building material sector get activated besides the core manufacturing sector constituting cement, steel and bricks. The consequent employment opportunities generated amount to an order of nearly 750 man-years. Thus we achieve a three-in-one solution of employment generation, economic development and human development through investments in housing. The application of steel in construction is catching on at a fast pace in the developing world. Starting from the reinforcement as a basic ingredient of RCC, steel is being used for every conceivable application replacing timber in the provision of joinery and household furniture.

Despite construction segment being the backbone of infrastructure development, the proportionate share of domestic consumption of steel has shown a gradual but distinct decline over the past a few years. From the high of 51 per cent market share in 1982-83, it came down to 46 per cent in 1987-88. During 1997-98 it further got lowered to 41 per cent. In 1997-98, total consumption of steel by this sector was 9 million tons which was only 41 per cent of the total steel consumption in India. The per capita consumption of steel in India is one of the lowest, being around 15 Kg. compared to 700 Kg. in Japan and 500 Kg. in USA. Presently, the usage of steel in the construction segment is dominated by traditional mild steel long products. Of late, some specialised products such as corrosion resistant structural bars have come into use but the overall share of flat and special products in the pool of construction materials remains much below the international level. The alarming trend of decline in steel usage in Indian construction industry, in favour of reinforced and pre-stressed concrete in buildings, bridges and railway sleepers is contrary to the scenario in the international arena.

In India, growth of urban population during the past decade indicates higher growth for metro cities. There are 6 mega cities (4 million plus) and 23 metropolitan cities in the country, which are expected to increase to 40 by 2001 AD. There are also, 300 large towns (0.1 million) and 3,396 small and medium towns (less than 0.1 million population). With economic liberalisation and expected higher economic growth, rate of urbanisation in India in coming decades is likely to increase. This will put an unprecedented demand for growth of urban areas with adequate housing and associated infrastructure.

The National Buildings Organisation (NBO) had estimated the urban housing shortage in 1991 at 8.23 million dwelling units. Keeping in view trends from 1961-1991 in the nature of additionality in housing stock, the overall urban housing shortage of 7.57 million DUs was projected for 1997. As per 1991 census of India projections, out of 22.9 million housing shortage, 8.23 million DUs was in urban areas while 14.67 million DUs in rural areas. With the additionality of 16.5 million in housing stock in five years, the net shortage has been estimated to be 6.64 million DUs by 2001. The new housing demand during the period 1997-2002 has been gauged as 8.8 million dwelling units.

It is estimated that the urban housing sector alone would require a total investment of Rs.1,21,371 crores during the next five years to meet the requirement of housing shortage of 75.7 lakhs DUs, upgradation of 3.2 lakh semi-pucca EWS units and the additional construction requirement of 86.7 lakh units. The total fund requirement including rural housing need would be 1,50,000 crores whereas the total availability is Rs.52,000 crores only from the formal sector (Rs.34,000 crores for urban and Rs.18,000 crores for rural housing).

The average percentage investment of steel in normal construction is estimated as 9 per cent of the total cost of the project. This means that every crore of investment in construction requires 9 lakhs of investment in steel. This means that every crore worth of construction utilises nearly 54 tonnes of steel at prevailing market rates. Accordingly in order to meet the requirements in construction, an investment of Rs.33,423.4 crores in steel will be required to meet the infrastructural investments till year 2006.

The National Sample Statistics Organisation has estimated that the materials component accounts for more than 75 per cent to 78 per cent of the construction cost in residential housing. The break-up of the total construction cost indicates that I ron and Steel accounts for 10.35 per cent of the total construction cost in urban areas and 7.87 per cent in the rural areas. Building materials and Technology Promotion Council (BMTPC) has estimated the cumulative expenditure by households on iron and steel in the period 2001-2011 at Rs. 945,174 million in urban areas and Rs. 359,349 million in rural areas.

The aggregate demand for Steel in construction sector identified for the period 1996-2001 is 63.63 million tonnes while the projections for the period 2001-2006 is 100.57 million tonnes and for period 2006-2011 is 158.72 million tonnes. Assuming that construction sector accounts for consumption of 45 per cent of the steel produced, the projections for availability indicate 64.67 million tonnes during the period 1996-2001, 104.15 tonnes during 2001-2006 and 167.74 tonnes during 2006-2011, indicating a trend of surplus availability in the housing sector against projected demand.

According to BMTPC estimates, the requirement of finished steel during the period 1996-2001 will be 8.65 million tonnes in urban housing and 3.31 million tonnes in rural housing. The requirement for the entire construction sector would be 63.63 million tonnes. The declining uses of steel in construction sector is certainly a matter of concern for the steel industry and overall growth of economy. And therefore, there is urgent need to provide a stimulus to the uses of steel in the sector. For this, perhaps, we may have to introduce a sensitisation programme for those engaged in the construction sector to enable them to better comprehend the advantages of usage of steel in construction.

INDIAN SILK EXPORTS

Export of Indian silk during the first quarter of the current financial year rose by 30% in value terms. Union minister of state for textiles G N Ramachandra said exports were placed at $74.8m ($60m for the same period in '99-00). Decline in Chinese exports of silk products and rising demand for Indian products were attributed to be the main reasons for this encouraging performance of the domestic silk industry. "We are confident that silk exports would rise by 20% this financial year (compared to last financial year), he added.

The textile ministry would be convening a meeting during the first week of August of weavers, reelers and traders to discuss the issues relating to silk waste exports from India. The ministry is also planning to raise the production of raw silk from 14,000 tonnes to 20,000 tonnes during this financial year.

TRENDS IN SPICES EXPORTS

The Spices Board may not achieve the export target of Rs. 2,000 crore for the current year. Spices exports have dropped both in terms of quantity and value in the first two months of the current financial year. Exports during April-May '00 have dropped to 30,820 tonnes, valued at Rs.235.07 crore, from 52,254 tonnes, valued at Rs. 399.38 crore in the corresponding period of last year. Overall exports during '99-00 touched about 2.08 lakh tonnes, valued at Rs. 1,861.02 crore against the target of 2.17 lakh tonnes, valued at Rs.1,748 crore. In '98-99 exports touched 2.31 lakh tonnes, valued at Rs.1,758.02 crore. This year the Spices Board has fixed the export target at 2,27,750 tonnes, valued at Rs.2,000 crore.

Countries such as Vietnam, Indonesia and Malaysia are dominating the market as far as pepper is concerned. Similarly, China and Nigeria have grabbed a sizeable market for ginger this year. Export of chillies has also come under serious pressure as Pakistan is out with its stock. This is for the first time in the last 4-5 years that Indian exporters are playing second fiddle. Currently Indian exporters are exporting purely on the basis of quality and long standing business relations. Exports of pepper have dropped from 10,897 tonnes, valued at Rs. 204 crore to 4,000 tonnes, valued at Rs.85.60 crore. Similarly, exports of chilli have dropped from 13,667 tonnes, valued at Rs. 55.73 crore to 9,000 tonnes, valued at Rs.30.60 crore.

Exports of turmeric have dropped from 7,968 tonnes, valued at Rs. 24.63 crore to 4,500 tonnes, valued at Rs. 13 crore. Also, ginger exports have dropped from 1,433 tonnes, valued at Rs.4.06 crore to 230 tonnes, valued at Rs 1.71 crore. Exports of seed spices, such as coriander, has dropped from 3,404 tonnes, valued at Rs. 7.95 crore, to 2,500 tonnes, valued at Rs. 6.25 crore. Exports of cuminseed have dropped from 1,691 tonnes, valued at Rs.10.88 crore, to 500 tonnes, valued at Rs.3.06 crore. Similarly celery exports have dropped from 521 tonnes, valued at Rs.1.40 crore to 200 tonnes, valued at Rs. 51 lakh. Fennelseed exports have dropped from 644 tonnes, valued at Rs.2.96 crore, to 250 tonnes, valued at Rs. 1.12 crore and exports of fenugreek dropped from 2,204 tonnes valued at Rs 3.96 crirem to 1,100 tonnes, valued at Rs.2.75 crore.

EXPORT TRENDS OF MUSHROOM

World Production

The major varieties of mushrooms produced in the world are European or white-button mushroom (*Agaricus bisporus*),

Oyster mushroom or Dhingri (*Pleurotus* spp), Chinese or paddy-straw mushroom (*Volvariella volvacea*), shitake mushroom (*Lentinus edodes*) and *Auricularia* spp. Among these the most widely cultivated species is the *Agaricus bisporus*, which accounts for almost 38% of the total mushroom production. About 2,000 varieties of mushrooms grown in the world are edible. These varieties are grown in diverse regions of the world. The white-button mushroom is grown in the U.S.A, France and China.

The Oyster mushroom is concentrated in China, which accounts for over 80% of the production. It is also grown in South Korea and Italy. India is not a major producer of any of the mushroom varieties, but it does cultivate mushrooms. The variety gaining maximum importance in India has been the white-button mushroom, which registered the highest growth rate in production.

World Trade

Only about 45% of mushrooms produced are consumed in the fresh form. The rest of the 55% is processed with 5% in the dehydrated form and 50% in the canned form. This is because their shelf life in the fresh form is very short. Hence mushrooms are traded in the world market mostly in the processed form.

Netherlands is the largest exporter of canned button mushrooms with a market share of about 38.5%. China is another significant exporter of the processed form of this variety, accounting for almost 30% of world trade. France is another important exporter, contributing to about 13.5% of the world exports.

As far as the import market is concerned, the most significant buyer of canned white button mushroom is Germany. This country alone accounts for almost 40% of the world imports. USA also imports canned mushroom, accounting for about 19% of the world imports.

Importers of button mushrooms

Germany

U.S.A.

France

Belgium

Sweden

Norway

U.K.

India's Exports

Out of about 2,000 edible mushrooms known, about 280 species are produced in India. The most important mushroom collected in India is the Guchhi (Morchella species), which is dried and exported to Western countries, rather than being consumed domestically.

Domestic consumption of canned mushrooms is quite low in India, it has managed to foster exports due to the huge marketable surpluses. It was only after 1990 that the export level of mushrooms began to pick up substantially. Currently, although there are only two major exporters of canned mushroom, namely Flex Foods and Ponds Ltd. and five new companies have entered the market recently. Countries like the Switzerland and the USA have ranked as comparatively consistent importers of canned mushrooms from India in the recent years.

5

Imperialism and the Indian Economy: Recent Trends

After the end of the Second World War the international economic decision making process was handed over to the Transnational Corporations (TNCs) by the developed world so that the sovereign states of the third world countries became insignificant economically and politically. In the year 2000 out of the world's top 100 economies, 54 were TNCs and 46 were countries, while just 3 years ago (1998) the TNCs were only 51. Globally out of the top 500 corporations listed by *Fortune*, the US dominates with 185 followed by Japan with 104 corporations. Together they account for 58 per cent of the total. They dominate 70 per cent of the world's trade and 80 per cent of the world's foreign investment. (*Global Corporate Power, 2001,* Public Interest Research Centre, Delhi). To help the TNCs to attain this objective the G-7 countries especially promoted three organisations viz. the International Monetary Fund (IMF), the World Bank (WB) and the World Trade Organisation (WTO). To promote the interests of the Transnational Corporations this *Trimurti* (trinity) ordered the developing countries to dismantle and destroy all public sector enterprises as in India, which had been promoted and funded by governments.

In the developing economies the growth of the local private sector was entirely dependent on investment policies made by the government in the public sector. This was the advice given in the forties by the then champions of the private sector known as the Bombay Club to Pandit Nehru. Even today the capitalists of the world are demanding that the governments of the developing countries develop infrastructure as capital investments in these projects are relatively high and profits from infrastructure start pouring in quite late. The recent experience in India with TNCs like Enron in the power infrastructure sector is relevant to show that these organisations are not in the least interested in 'proper' business dealings. They merely wish to exploit the hungry people of the third world. They bribe the politicians of the mainstream political parties to get sovereign guarantee (in the case of India this was given by a government which resigned before the ink of its signature on the guarantee paper dried) and by selling the product at an astronomically high price after jacking up costs artificially. Let us see how many skeletons the Justice Department of the US will bring out from the cupboards of Enron!

The main theme propagated by the G-7 countries in the 21st century is 'globalisation' as is exposed nakedly in the 'war on terrorism'. The destructive activities of the US were globally challenged from the very beginning, though in an unorganised form. In Seattle the WTO meeting had to be cancelled and subsequently protesters in larger numbers followed these capitalist gangsters wherever they went – Washington, Bangkok and in Genoa. In the last city one Italian student was shot dead by the police and several hundred protesters were wounded, but none of these seven gangsters (G-7) who are paid fabulous commissions by the TNCs, condemned the brutal use of force by the Italian government on unarmed civilian protesters. Rather they resolved to continue to support the policies of the TNCs and so promote and strengthen the destructive agenda of world capitalism. They selected Doha, an island in the Gulf ruled by an oil rich autocrat as the safe venue of the latest WTO ministerial meeting in November 2001. They sent a clear signal that in future such important meetings, whose decisions affect the world's population would take place either on the high seas under the supervision of the US Marines or in spaceships piloted by the Pentagon. Nobody knows how Mexico can be a safe haven for the next meeting of WTO in 2003!

They refuse to see the writing on the wall. It clearly reads that the day is not far off when militant mass protests both north and south of the equator will compel these shortsighted world exploiters to wind up their destructive economic policies.

What is unfolding in the backyard of the US in Argentina cannot be ignored. A country moulded, structured and run by the TNCs under the direct supervision of the US and its *Trimurti* (WB, IMF and WTO) with an average per capita income of around $ 8000 per annum is declared bankrupt at the end of 2001. The US president is not in the least bothered about the 36 million people of the devastated economy of Argentina. It is the US which ordered the privatisation programme in Argentina over the last decade. Now more than 50 per cent of its population is economically devastated and those who were rich yesterday are now on the streets beating pots and pans because their *peso* and US dollar accounts have vanished overnignt. The consecutive four years of recession has sent around twenty per cent of the workers home. A forty per cent devaluation of the *peso* in one stroke after maintaining an artificial parity of one *peso* equal to one US $ over a decade has created nervousness among the TNCs and affluent people of Argentina.

In India one US $ was equivalent to Rs 25 in 1990-91 and after the successful implementation of the Structural Adjustment Programme supervised by the IMF the rupee has depreciated by around 100 per cent to more than Rs 48 per $ today and our rulers have advised people to accept this devastation as a simple *fait accompli*. In the sixties the then Finance Minister was asked to quit for devaluing the Indian currency. Our present Finance Minister refuses to give up his chair though he is at the centre of many financial scams. This is the democratic accountability of the BJP brand! Our honourable prime minister being a faithful supporter of the *hindutva* of the RSS brand first visited Pasupati Mandir, a hindu siva temple at Kathmandu, before attending the SAARC meeting and after its conclusion he expressed his government's complete faith in the autocratic monarchy.

Supporters of 'globalisation' understand clearly that today only finance capital is fully 'globalised'. In a fraction of a second the 'capital' of International Financial Institutions (IFI) can fly from one continent to another and has the power to make or destroy any region or any single country. It happened in Latin America a number of times and in 1997-98 it was repeated in South East Asia and this may happen any moment in South

Asia too. But what about the millions of unskilled rural labour? Can they move an inch freely beyond their respective territorial boundaries? Rather they are tortured if they try to enter any country without permission. Surplus labour is bottled up in respective underdeveloped economies. Wealth too is not globalised; rather it is more and more concentrated in the hands of the few. Three men – Bill Gates, Paul Allen and Warren Buffet – own assets equivalent to those owned by 600 million people in the world's 48 least developed countries. The ratio between the income of the top fifth and bottom fifth of humanity is 74 to 1 compared to 30 to 1 in 1960.

90 per cent of the world's patent rights are held in the richest countries and poor countries are heavily charged for their use. Described as 'patent king' by *Fortune*, Jerome Lemelson, a US citizen, owns a staggering portfolio of 558 patents, with companies paying him nearly $1.5 billion in licensing fees (*Fortune* May 14, 2001). Pharma TNCs have already expressed their strong resentment of the recent WTO decision to discuss whether patent rights on medicines can be waived for diseases like HIV/AIDS, TB and malaria if individual countries need it in national emergency and for public health. Recent nervousness on the anthrax epidemic in the US and the high prices charged for Cipro by Bayer of Germany created lot of protest in Canada and the US. Canada was forced by public opinion to ignore this patent right in the interests of her own people.

Elementary seeds traditionally used in the developing countries from previous years' crops are banned now under the Intellectual Property Rights (IPRs) rules of WTO. The farmers' right to use old seed can't be denied by any order of WTO or any other organisations, they are accustomed to it since the days of their forefathers. The US government permission to TNCs to produce and sell 'terminator' and other genetically modified seeds (GMS) will cause disaster to the third world's agricultural economy Two thirds of our population till today depends alone on cultivation as the main source of livelihood. The United Nation's Development Programme reports that the richest 20 per cent of the world's people account for 86 per cent of global consumption, the poorest 20 per cent receive only one per cent. Naturally the children of the poor have to die due to acute malnutrition. The G-7's armoured tank of global capitalism is marching ahead ruthlessly. The number of protesters at Seattle was much smaller than those at Genoa and the day is not far away that a new united and well organised powerful resistant group will emerge throughout the world as history is the witness that militant working class trade unions emerged and flourished with the increasing exploitation of labour as the destructive face of capitalism kept on unfolding.

GRAVEYARD OF CAPITALISM – INDIA'S LEAD ROLE

The approach paper to the Tenth Five-Year Plan (2002-07) prepared by the Hindu fundamentalist party – the BJP admits that 'the economy is currently in a decelerating phase and urgent steps are needed to arrest the deceleration and restore momentum. This reversal is all the more difficult because it has to take place in an environment where the world economy (led by USA) is slowing down.' (p. 2). The USA Labour Department reports that unemployment in the US in December 2001 reached 5.8 per cent against 5.4 per cent in the previous month. The rough estimate is that since 11th September 2001 more than one million people have lost jobs in the US. Ford recently declared the retrenchment of 35,000 of its workers in different factories of the world. Daily reports in the media of retrenchment and layoffs in the US are no longer news. The US President's plan to reduce tax rates and increase government spending are opposed vehemently by the opposition Democrats but they fully endorsed the war on Afghanistan. It is known that during the last 11 years Japan has failed to revive the 'market' after using all types of both conventional and non-conventional tools to revive it.

The Indian brokers of international capitalism use the words 'growth', and 'development' to prove that the Indian economy is moving in the right direction and that foreign investors should bring in more US dollars as purchase consideration of our economy plus the agreed commissions due to politicians and bureaucrats. From the early fifties we are having a conventional 'Hindu' rate of growth of 3.5 to 4 per cent per annum, since the 1980s when India started contracting more foreign loans it crossed 5 per cent growth rate with the help of an artificial invisible sector called the tertiary sector or services. The GDP growth rate during the pre-reform period (1980-81 to 1990-91) was 5.6 per cent and in the post-reform period (1990-91 to 2000-01) it went down to 5.1 per cent. In 1950-51 services contributed only 27.5 per cent of the GDP, in 1990-91 its share was increased to 40.6 per cent and by 2000 it was virtually half (49 per cent) of the GDP. The democratically elected government's only concern is to satisfy the demands of the elite section of the population by providing them with the latest technology in communication systems, digital stock exchanges, modern five-star hospitals, five-star hotels, cable T.V., credit and debit cards, telebanking facilities and other services. The same government has no time to attend to the problems of the majority of the population without whose vote these people cannot capture the seats in either states' capitals or at the centre. Starvation deaths take place despite 60 million tons of food rotting in the government warehouses. The governments at the centre and in the states take their own time to fix the selling price of this grain. The governments know that the people will never purchase this grain at 'below the poverty line' (BPL) price because it is higher than the local market price.

At the same time the well-to-do cultivators in increasing numbers are committing suicide year after year in different states due to the failure of crops and the heavy outstanding loans taken from moneylenders at huge interest rates, though the financial institutions are flooded with idle funds. In such a situation it is a cruel joke that the same corrupt, inefficient and insensitive government tries to show to the world India's military power, of course, subject to approval of world's 'peace keeper' – US, to take revenge on Pakistan for attacking India's legislatures and parliament buildings. The mainstream political parties have no political will to provide services for compulsory education for children, pure drinking water and modern hospital facilities for the vast millions without whose vote they can't enter into the legislatures.

In the pre-reform period 1980-1991 growth in commodity production was around 5 per cent per annum and in the post-reform period 1991-2001 it went down to 4.3 per cent per annum. It is peculiar that the share of service sector in the GDP is increasing but widespread retrenchment is also carried out mercilessly in this area. Retrenchment in the banking sector is very successful without any protests; rather people went to court complaining why they were not considered for retrenchment (State Bank of India employees and now Corporation Bank employees are also demanding retrenchment). The trade unions run by the revisionist political parties can't explain why they failed to politicise their workers, rather they taught them all these years only to extract an extra penny from the employers. Real growth of commodities both in agriculture and in industry instead of increasing during this period of reform declined and this downhill journey is still continuing. In real terms this is called 'structural adjustment programme' and is dictated by the World Bank and the IMF and was introduced by Narasimha Rao and now has been taken up by Atal Behari Vajpayee. The G-7 masters are more than confident that Mr. Vajpayee's 'nationalist' government will fulfil its obligation to hand over the economy to foreigners.

DESTRUCTION OF INDIAN AGRICULTURE

The Food Corporation of India warehouses are overflowing with around 60 million tons of foodgrains against the economic holding requirement of 16-17 million tons. This huge stock does not mean that everything is rosy on the agricultural front. The growth rate in agricultural production during 1980 to 1991 was 3.84 per cent but it declined to 1.24 percent during 1990-91 to 2000-01. Do we require the existing elaborate Agricultural Ministry to continue without any responsibility and accountability to the nation? Not only 'food security' is absolutely uncertain but also the supply of raw materials for the various industries cannot be assured when the government is bent upon destroying it. Its performance in the last decade is shameful in the entire country. The rainfall in 2001 was better and uniform throughout the country and kharif production was better than previous years. The same better performance is anticipated for the rabi crops too.

According to the Central Statistical Organisation (CSO) the growth rate in agriculture, forestry and fishing in the first and second quarters of 2000-01 was 0.6 and 0.5 per cent respectively but it increased to 2.3 and 3.4 per cent respectively in 2001-2002. The higher growth in the second quarter of this year is due to an increase of production of 2.7 per cent and 12.2 per cent in rice and pulses respectively. However, the poor man's food, coarse cereals' production declined by 0.4 per cent during the kharif season of 2001-02. Production of oilseeds and cotton has also gone up in comparison to last year. Without providing basic structural land reform and institutional financing arrangements for *lakhs* of small and marginal farmers, long-term agricultural production growth cannot be sustained.

The government is bent upon introducing corporations into the agricultural sector. Already TNCs like Cargill, HLL, ITC and so on are in agricultural business and the days are not far off when even big landowners in the villages will work as paid labour under the TNCs. Today the small and marginal farmers have small assets in the form of land, a thatched house and may be one or two animals in the villages, but gradually this will be history unless people stop the corporatisation of farming as suggested in the agricultural policy of the government. Foodgrain production growth in the pre-reform period was 3.46 per cent per annum and in the post-reform period it went down to 1.22 per cent. With the population growing at slightly less than 2 per cent per annum, what will happen with such an insignificant rate of growth of foodgrain?

In this scenario in agriculture and allied activities, how long it will take us to assure the hungry millions of not one but two square meals a day? The government says that 26 per cent of the Indian population or 260 million people (equivalent to the total population of the USA) are below the poverty line and they don't have the purchasing power to purchase grain from the Public Distribution System. Why should they not be mobilised to take control of the Food Corporation of India warehouses in scarcity areas? The World Bank's 'structural reform' has virtually destroyed our rural economy. WTO's insistence on removing restrictions on imports has resulted in unemployment for millions of cultivating families. The TNCs are dumping the Indian market with cheap edible oil, green coconut, milk, tea, fruit etc. Even the imported genetically-modified wheat and soya bean are cheaper than that of our own country. There is huge direct and indirect financial aid given to these TNCs engaged in agriculture by the developed countries which WTO tactfully ignores but it raises objections to our paltry subsidies. It is high time the 'riyot coolie sangathans' (peasants' and agricultural workers' unions) should organise the peasants and landless workers of the country to take over control in different parts of our rural economy.

INDUSTRY IN INDIA IS IN A DEEP COMA

FMCG (Fast moving consumer goods) companies like Hindustan Lever, Proctor and Gamble, Nestle India etc. belonging to the TNCs are eagerly waiting for increased purchasing power in the rural economy. Their sales are below normal for months. In the same manner consumer durable producers who happen to be mainly from foreign countries are waiting for demand to grow and tractor and other agricultural equipment producers are all keeping their fingers crossed (A list of foreign companies in the consumer goods sector is given in the appendix). Indian and foreign industrialists are virtually going bankrupt due to the loss of India's vast rural market. Share prices in the Bombay Stock Exchange refused to rise even after the 'dream budget' of February 2001. The big bull Ketan Parekh is in jail after looting public money from banks and mutual funds. Three big co-operative banks in Gujarat have gone bankrupt recently because the banks' directors decamped with huge public funds.

The largest government mutual fund chairman was sent to jail in 2001 and the 1992-share scam hero, Harshad Mehta, died when investigations restarted against him last year. Let us see whether the new Joint Parliament Committee (JPC) which is inquiring into the share scam finds fault with any of our respected politicians, businessmen and bureaucrats. It is already agreed that the fake Mauritius route is kept open for Foreign Institutional Investors to allow fraudulent transactions involving billions of US dollars. Many of our politicians are party to this organised fraud on the country. Our own long-term lending institutions like IDBI, IFCI, ICICI and so on are already in the sick list because of their shortsighted lending policies ordered on political and non-business considerations. After the collapse of the Dhabol project of Enron, no one speaks of the quantum of loss suffered by these lending institutions. In the same manner UTI, LIC, GIC and almost all the public sector banks have sunk more than Rs 60000 *crores* of public deposits in bad debts which were given to many top business houses and most of them are in the habit of committing such criminal activities as part of their business philosophy. Why not issue an ordinance to scrap the 'secrecy' clause in the Negotiable Instrument Act and let the people know the true face of these honourable members of the Bombay Club who are championing the cause of privatisation and development. If TADA can be brought back as the Prevention of Terrorism Ordinance, don't these looters of public funds deserve to be in jail as terrorists instead of functioning as the advisers to the government to frame policies for the next budget?

Growth in industrial production in the pre-reform period (1980-81 to 1991-92) was not bad, it was around 7.8 per cent but it declined to 6.0 per cent in the post-reform period (1992-93 to 1999-2000). The slowdown in the production of capital goods was particularly sharp, from 9.4 per cent to 5.9 per cent, which showed the unwillingness of industrialists to invest in the capital goods sector; rather they found imported capital goods more economical. This is the main strategy of the World Bank-dictated New Economic Policy – destroy all types of indigenous production capacity, specially the capital goods sector which is the backbone of any developing economy and make the developing countries permanently dependent on the developed ones. This is the road map of neo-imperialism. A new trend is visible among Indian manufacturers – not to make any fresh investment in plant and machinery in India; rather they are entering into joint ventures in China for its lower cost. They will produce their branded products in China and import them to India as their manufactured items. That is why they desire that Indian tariff rates should be reduced to nil to destroy our own industrial capacity for the sake of higher profit for the industrialists. In this way India's industrial production capacity may go down in the near future and the country will be reconverted into a colony of the west.

In the economic advisory council of the present prime minister there are eminent industrialists and representatives of all of the three Apex Chambers of Commerce – FICCI, CII and ASSOCHAM. Despite their presence Indian industry is getting weaker; there is no plan to strengthen our industrial base to fight against foreign aggression. The government thinks that the economy is of less importance, communal politics and the appeasement of the TNCs are of more immediate interest. The following Table explains how industrial production failed in two consecutive years.

Growth in Industrial Production (in per cent)

Industry	2000-01		2001-02	
	Q1	Q2	Q1	Q2
Mining and Quarrying	5.0	3.8	0.0	0.6
Manufacturing	7.0	6.0	2.3	2.3
Electricity, Gas and Water supply	5.7	3.0	3.3	4.8
Construction	8.4	8.4	2.5	4.1
Trade, Transport etc	9.7	7.3	5.2	6.2
Finance, Insurance etc	9.5	9.8	9.9	11.0
Community, Social and Personal Services	6.0	9.3	6.2	6.1
GDP at factor cost	6.1	6.2	4.4	5.3

(Business Standard 1.1.2002)

The above figures are from the estimate of the Central Statistical Organisation. Various organisations like the National Council of Applied Economic Research and the Institute of Economic Growth are confident that the growth of GDP for 2001-02 will be less than 5 per cent. GDP growth for the first half was 4.85 percent. The manufacturing sector has maintained a *status quo* over the first two quarters at 2.3 per cent with no visible signs of a pick-up against a high 6 per cent in the corresponding periods last year. Similarly construction, which grew at 8.4 per cent last year, reported growth of only 4.1 per cent this time. The mining sector also showed a sharp fall from 3.8 per cent last year to 0.6 per cent this year. However, electricity grew from 3 per cent last year to 4.8 per cent this year. The financial sector grew from 9.8 per cent last year to 11.0 per cent this year.

The vocal Bombay Club of our industrialists, which demanded liberalisation and privatisation in the early 1990s and had doubts about globalisation, is finding it difficult to survive in the market. All attempts are made by it to retain control over their individual empires and save themselves from foreign acquisition. Buy back of their own company's shares is going on at full speed. At the same time foreign companies are buying back the shares of their subsidiaries from the public and converting them to 100 per cent subsidiaries and withdrawing from listing in Indian stock exchanges. Our companies are going to foreign countries to collect capital by selling shares called by various names like American Depository Receipts (ADRs) and /or Global Depository Receipts (GDRs). Joint ventures with foreign companies are being terminated and Indian partners are being asked to leave with some compensation. Mergers and acquisitions among TNCs are going on at full speed in the international market and new companies are coming up with more financial power and monopolistic controls.

To give an example, Time Warner and America Online Inc. have merged and their the deal value is around $105 billion. Likewise two British giant pharmaceutical companies, Smith Kline Beecham plc. and Glaxo Welcome plc., have merged, the deal value is over $77 billion. In the automobile industry in 1998, the car manufacturing company, Daimler Benz AG of Germany merged with the Chrysler Corp of US resulting in the formation of a $40 billion corporation. It is rumoured that the Citibank group will acquire Standard Chartered Grindley Bank's India's business. Microsoft of US was charged with unfair trade practices and punished. The Justice Department of the US has taken up the Enron issue and many politicians who accepted bribes including the auditor's firm Anderson are in the hit list. In this country we do not have any law against unfair trade practices, the sick Monopolies and Restrictive Trade Practices Commission is dying a natural death. Politicians and bureaucrats who accepted bribes in India from TNCs including Enron must also be exposed in this investigation.

On the demand of Indian industry for a 'level playing field' the government is reducing the interest rate at a faster speed than expected but nevertheless unsold stocks continue to pile up in the warehouses as demand has dried up. In the US, whom we are imitating, the Federal Reserve Authority during the last one year reduced the bank rate eleven times from 6 per cent to 1.75 per cent. Even then they required a full-fledged war to try to revive their decaying capitalist economy. Companies are offering various allurements to sell their products. Costly advertisements say: one extra shirt or one extra soap if one purchases two shirts or two soaps. The selling and advertisement cost is rising higher but the wages bill is being reduced every day by retrenchment and layoffs. The loss of employment is reducing further the demand for goods and services. Business liquidation is going on at a fast speed. The government is directed to amend labour laws and give up all the protection now assured to organised industrial labour, which accounts for less than 10 per cent of total labour, and to make closures an easy task. Senior citizens, widows and the poor who kept money in post offices and whose only source of income is from interest on past savings find it very difficult to meet minimum requirements when the interest rate is going down every day to help the rich.

Some of them have already started starving and many of them may be compelled to commit suicide in future. Labour is threatened with reduced interest income on their long-term saving in their Provident Funds lying with the Government. Before the economies of the G-7 countries caught cold, the Indian economy was already flat with severe pneumonia. This is the infection injected by the WTO and we have already destroyed the inbuilt immunity system by demolishing the public sector at the insistence of our foreign lenders now ruling as masters to whom we owe more than US $100 billion. In this crisis hour our public sector could save us from the onslaught of world depression.

A similar economic situation happened with Argentina, which was forced to privatise its public sector, allowing the TNCs to rule the country. The Vajpayee government faced great criticism when it sold public sector units like Modern Foods and BALCO, but it hardly respects public protest because it is a fascist regime. It is moving very fast to sell both the airlines of the Indian public sector. Rs 12000 *crores* have to be realised by the sale of the public sector units to meet the budget deficit. This is more important to this government than the security of the nation's economy.

WORKERS ARE THE WORST SUFFERERS

Our worry is that in such a devastating situation with declining production and loss of job opportunities, where will the millions of unskilled and semi-skilled workers go and earn for their family members one square meal a day?

According to the Economic Surveys the annual growth rate of jobs in the organised sector, which never employed more than 10 per cent of the total workers, during 1990 to 1999 was only 0.77 per cent. In terms of absolute increase in the number of employment during the above period, it was around 1.96 *lakhs* per year against 70 to 80 *lakh* new job seekers every year assuming a 2 per cent growth in the labour force per annum.

During 1998 and 1999 there was no increase in employment in the organised sector, rather through various schemes there was competition to hand over pink retrenchment slips to the workers. During the last three years four public sector units have retrenched, through the Voluntary Retirement Scheme, more than 12,00,00 employees.

The break up was as follows: Bharat Heavy Electricals 10,712, Coal India Ltd. 90,000, Hindustan Zinc Ltd, 1,443, Steel Authority of India Ltd 20,000 (*Business Standard* 25.8.01). Every day these figures become stale as fresh batches are given marching orders.

The railways are asked to retrench 30,000 employees every year. The Fifth Pay Commission was ordered by the government to recommend a 10 per cent reduction in the central work force. Since the early nineties all vacancies created due to retirement and resignation in central government offices were not filled up and from the current year, the Finance Minister announced in his Budget speech, out of 3 per cent vacancies in government departments each year due to retirement, only one per cent will be filled up and thus in the next five years a 10 per cent reduction in government employment will take place.

At the same time every day Cabinets both at the centre and in the states are expanding to provide berths to new political criminals, shamelessly unmindful of the fact that each minister is provided with a large team of officials just to serve and wait.

CONCLUSION

The above analysis of the Indian economy after 10 years of experience of the New Economic Policy tries to focus on how a constitutionally formed central government can treat with contempt the thrust area of the Indian Constitution: to keep India as a sovereign democratic republic. The mainstream political parties have colluded with the G-7 countries to follow steadfastly a single point agenda – to expand the horizon of capitalism and make the one billion people's market in India an exclusive protected area for their selfish exploitation. Our freedom fighters are feeling restless in their graves. This is probably the price one has to pay for an independence bargained by negotiations by politicians at the back of the people and not gained by a fierce fight and sacrifices like that of China and Vietnam.

TO USE OR TO MISUSE

That is the Question Industries Need to Think Over

Water use in industry is a double-edged sword. On one hand it puts immense pressure on local water resources. On the other, wastewater discharged from the industry pollutes the local environment. Water is required, often in large volumes, by industries as process inputs in most industries. In other cases, like food and beverage and chlor-alkali industry, water is used as a raw material: turned into a manufactured product and exported out of the local water system.

However, in most industries it is essentially used as input and mass and heat transfer media. In these industries a very small fraction of water is actually consumed and lost. Most of the water is actually meant for non-consumptive process uses and is ultimately discharged as effluent.

Quantity and Quality

The amount of water available matters but so also does its quality. Industry requires water of good quality for its use, and for this it uses cleaner upstream water. However, the water it discharges is always of lower quality than the feed water and this wastewater is discharged downstream. At best the wastewater discharged represents a quality that can be recycled for lower grade of industrial use and at worst represents water quality which is unsuitable for every use other than navigational puposes. In other words, this water is unfit for usage, is seldom used by the industries and usually used for certain agricultural purposes or by villagers to meet their daily needs.

Of wastes and wants: Water use in India

Of wastes and wants: Water use in India			
Industrial Sector	Annual wastewater water discharge (million cubic meters) (%)	Annual consumption (million cubic meters)	Proportion of water consumed in industry
Thermal power plants	27000.9	35157.4	87.87
Engineering	1551.3	2019.9	5.05
Pulp and paper	695.7	905.8	2.26
Textiles	637.3	829.8	2.07
Steel	396.8	516.6	1.29
Sugar	149.7	194.9	0.49
Fertiliser	56.4	73.5	0.18
Others	241.3	314.2	0.78
Total	30729.2	40012.0	100.0

Note: For methodology see www.downtoearth.org.in
Source: Estimated by CSE based on the wastewater discharged data published by CPCB in "Water quality in India (Status and trends) 1990 - 2001".

Major Consumers

Water consumption depends on the type of industry. Whereas thermal power, textiles, pulp and paper and iron and steel are highly water intensive sectors, industrial sectors like chlor-alkali, cement, copper and zinc and plastics require little water. Data on actual water consumption in India is absent. However, the data on wastewater discharge by various industrial sectors in the country is available. The data on wastewater discharge has been complied by CPCB. According to CPCB, the total wastewater discharged by all major industrial sources is 83,048 million litres per day (mld). This includes 66,700 mld of cooling water discharged by thermal power plants (TPPs). Out of the remaining 16,348 mld of wastewater, TPPs generates another 7,275 mld as boiler blowdown water and overflow from ash pond.

Is it possible...

In the absence of data on actual water consumption is it possible to chalk out a water consumption pattern for Indian industry? The Centre for Science and Environment (CSE) has attempted to arrive at an estimate based on the wastewater data of CPCB.

According to CPCB the annual water consumption in Indian industry is 40 billion cubic meters and the annual wastewater discharge is about 30.7 billion cubic meter. Therefore, the overall ratio of wastewater discharged to freshwater consumption in Indian industry works out to be about 0.77. That is, for every cubic meter of water consumed by

Indian industry, 0.77 cubic meters of wastewater is discharged. Considering this, CSE has estimated the possible water consumption in various industrial sectors in India (See table: Of wastes...).

Guzzlers

Inefficent water use by industry

The ratio of water consumption and economic value creation in Indian industry is poor. For every cubic metre of water that Indian industry uses, it generates merely US $7.5 economic productivity

Country	Industrial water use (billion cubic metres)	Industrial productivity (million US $)	Industrial water productivity (US $ / cubic metre)
Argentina	2.6	77171.0	30.0
Brazil	9.9	231442.0	23.4
India	15.0	113041.0	7.5
Korea, Rep.	2.6	249268.0	95.6
Norway	1.4	47599.0	35.0
Sweden	0.8	74703.0	92.2
Thailand	1.3	64800.0	48.9
United Kingdom	0.7	330097.0	443.7

Source: *World Bank, 2001*

Thermal Power Plants (TPPs): Most TPPs in India are owned by the government. Indian TPPs are one of the highest consumers of water as compared to their global counterparts. On an average, for every 1000 Kwh power, Indian TPPs consume as much as 80 cubic meters of water. The water consumption in the modern TPPs in developed countries is less than 10 cubic meters for every 1000 Kwh. The major reason for this atrocious figure is the widespread prevalence of 'once-through cooling systems'.

Pulp and paper: Water consumption in Indian pulp and paper industry is significantly higher than in developed countries:

Complete discharge of paper machine wastewater, which can be recycled easily.

Use of chlorine-based bleaching technology in wood and non-wood based mills. Due to the presence of chlorine compounds in the bleach wastewater, it cannot be used as 'black liquor' for energy generation and hence is discharged.

Textiles: The textile industry in India guzzles double the accepted amount for consumption.Why is this so? A major factor is obsolete technology which permits minimum recycling and reuse of process water. For instance, most textile mills in India do not use counter-current washing systems; instead they use clean water at every stage of the wash cycle. Similarly the reuse of final rinse water from dyeing for dye bath make-up or reuse of soaper wastewater, is absent in most mills.

Iron & Steel: The Iron & Steel sector is also water intensive industry. In India, approximately 80-85 per cent freshwater consumed in this sector is discharged as effluent. In contrast, in USA over 95 per cent of the water used for steel production and processing is recycled.

Consequently, while the Indian steel companies consume about 10-80 cubic meters water to produce a single tonne of steel, in the US only 5-10 cubic meters of water is needed. Global best practice for wastewater discharge in integrated iron and steel plant is less than 0.1 cubic meter per tonne steel (See tables: Inefficient water use...;

Comparatively very poor). Indian industry will have to reduce its voracious appetite for water. Water, the once inexhaustible natural resource, is going to be one of the most important factors to decide the growth and development of Indian industry in the future.

Comparatively very poor: Indian industry vs Global best		
Sector	**Average water consumption in Indian industry**	**Globally best**
Thermal power plant	On an average 80 m^3/ mwh(1)	Less than 10 m3/mwh(2)
Textiles	200-250 m3/ tonne cotton cloth(3)	Less than 100 m3/ tonne cotton cloth(2)
Pulp & Paper	• Wood based mills: 150 - 200 m3 / tonne(3) • Waste paper based mills: 75 -100 m3/ tonne(3)	• Wood based mills: 50 - 75 m3 / tonne(4) • Waste paper based mills: 10 25 m3/tonne(4)
Integrated Iron & steel plant	10-80 m3 per tonne of finished product (average	5 -10 m3 per tonne of finished product. Best is around 25 m3)(practice - less than 0.1 m3 wastewater per tonne finished product(5)
Distilleries	75-200 m3/ tonne alcohol produced(6)	Data not available
Fertiliser industry	• Nitrogenous fertiliser plant - 5.0 - 20.0 m3/ tonne(3) • Straight phosphatic plant - 1.4 - 2.0 m3/ tonne(3) • Complex fertiliser - 0.2 - 5.4 m3/ tonne(3)	An effluent discharge of less than 1.5 m3/ tonne product as P2O5(2)

Source: 1. No credible data available. Estimates done by CSE from wastewater discharge data from "Water Quality in India, Status and trends (1990-2001), CPCB, MoEF" and annual electricity generation data from "Annual Report (2001-2002) on the working of state electricity boards and electricity department, Planning Commission." 2. Pollution prevention and abatement handbook, World Bank. 3. Environmental management in selected industrial sectors - status and need, CPCB

& MoEF, February, 2003. 4. Green Rating of Pulp and Paper Sector, CSE. 5. Integrated Pollution Prevention and Control (IPPC), Best available techniques reference document on the production of iron. 6. Environmental performance of Alcohol industry in UP, UPPCB, 2000-2001.

This study, produced by Accenture in collaboration with the Confederation of Indian Industry (CII), examines the future opportunities that Information and Communications Technology (ICT) will deliver for India. It is based on a unique and wide-ranging survey of over 200 Indian business leaders across all major industries and identifies the important trends that will shape and advance the efforts of business, government and civil society to achieve wider ICT access and usage across the economy. The survey reveals widespread recognition that ICT will play a crucial role in delivering social advances and economic growth to India.

Our research suggests that 87 percent of Indian businesses believe that socio-economic disparities between rich and poor communities represent the most significant obstacle to the sustainable growth of the Indian economy. And 88 percent believe that the increased usage of ICT will be a major determinant in overcoming these disparities and thereby advancing growth in the next five years. Many businesses are already running ICT-driven operations in low-income markets in India; the central government and several states have instigated a number of ICT programmes; and non-governmental organisations are conducting numerous ICT-based initiatives. This activity is driven by the belief that ICT can have a disproportionately positive impact on society, the economy and business.

Global ICT supply bases are shifting towards emerging economies and growing consumer markets in these economies are demanding more ICT products and services. India is pivotal in this relocation. Our research indicates that 94 percent of businesses believe the usage of ICT has been a major reason for India's recent economic growth. The country has built a reputation as a fast-learning, ICT-savvy trailblazer among emerging economies. Companies continue to move operations to India to benefit from the country's low-cost, skilled ICT workforce. More of the country is becoming "connected" and rapid innovation and fierce competition are driving down technology prices. Yet paradoxically India's story continues to be marred by poverty and inequality.

Access to quality education, health and employment are still far out of reach for many millions in India. Moreover, the country's increasing population, especially in deprived regions, creates ever greater pressure for rapid improvements in basic living standards and employment opportunities. ICT is one of the few tools that will allow India to address these critical issues across its vast and diverse population and geography. The country clearly has much to offer and much to gain from the ICT revolution.

Indian business people believe that the next phase of ICT-led growth will come from three main sources:

Supply-side Opportunities

As access to ICT in low-income markets improves, emphasis is likely to shift from well-known demand side benefits towards supply-side benefits such as more efficient supply chains, better communication, improved productivity and lower input costs.

Catalytic Impact of ICT

ICT delivers spill-over and multiplier effects which will bring new growth opportunities across all industries. The telecommunications, agribusiness, education and financial services sectors are expected to be significant beneficiaries.

Improving Access to Education

ICT is expected to play a central role in the provision of, and access to, quality education across India.

A statistical annex to the study sets out some of the wider survey findings beyond this specific scope.

Both Accenture and the CII believe that building a strong understanding of the role of ICT will improve India's prospects for greater and more equitable growth. The creation of digital opportunities has been an important strategic focus for Accenture over the past decade and is embedded in its thinking and approach towards Corporate Citizenship. CII's theme of "Competitiveness for Sustainable and Inclusive Growth" reflects the Confederation's commitment to balanced development that encompasses all sectors of the economy and all sections of society. Both organisations believe that there are real opportunities for business to collaborate with government and civil society and for all sides to make great progress. This study is our contribution to that debate.

The study concludes with four imperatives to help the Indian economy to capitalise on ICT-enabled growth:

1. Invest in Human Capital: both by building a wider ICT-enabled workforce and by improving basic education across India.
2. Create Coherent Infrastructure: The ICT industry itself needs to build a strong view of the appropriate infrastructures, standards and systems of interoperability that are critical in the delivery of ubiquitous access to ICT.
3. Build Partnerships Between the ICT Industry and Government: cooperation at all levels is essential to ensure that the development of India's ICT environment is responsive to local requirements and is implemented efficiently.
4. Ensure Affordability and Relevance of Content: devices, their ongoing usage and access to content and applications must all be affordable. Content must be relevant and delivered appropriately for each community.

6

Pharmaceuticals in India: A Business and Regulatory Outlook

INTRODUCTION

After decades of slow growth, India's economy is now advancing rapidly. From 1996 to 2006 its GDP grew at an average rate of 7% yearly, and this growth figure increased to 10% in 2006. It is expected to keep growing at 7% or higher over the next five years. With the fourth-largest economy in the world (as measured by purchasing power parity), India is finally coming into its own as a major world economy.

Total medical spending in India is growing quickly, driven by better-off Indians willing to pay privately for modern care from private hospitals. This increased spending creates many opportunities for foreign pharmaceutical companies. India's $9 billion pharmaceutical market saw 10% growth in 2006, and double-digit growth is predicted to continue through 2012. In addition, the country's low labor costs, large existing pharmaceutical manufacturing base, and sizable patient population make it an excellent location for Western companies to do contract manufacturing, clinical research, and R&D.

DEMAND

India's population, the second largest in the world, should not be described as one big pharmaceutical market. Most of its 1.1 billion citizens are rural or low-income and lack even basic access to Western medicines. The market, rather, is to be found in India's growing middle and upper classes in urban areas such as Mumbai, Kolkata, New Delhi, and Bangalore. If being in the middle class is measured by earning at least $1,000 per year, there may be as many as 100 million potential customers in India's major cities.

India is now going through a public health transition typical of rapidly developing countries. Once, ailments such infectious diseases, malnutrition, and gastrointestinal disorders were the predominant diseases requiring treatment. Today, though, with rising incomes, more and more Indians are able to drink, smoke, and lead more sedentary lives. As a result, "lifestyle" diseases such as cancer and cardiovascular disease are receiving more attention. Cases of cardiovascular disease, for example, are predicted to increase from 29 million in 2000 to 64 million in 2015, rising to 34% of all deaths.

Currently, the dominant drug types on the Indian market are still anti-infective and gastrointestinal. However, greatest growth is predicted in coming years for cardiovascular, oncological, diabetes, and psychiatric drugs. Since Western companies have many new and innovative drugs in these types, which may not be available generically in India, they are prime areas of opportunity.

HEALTHCARE PROVIDERS

In theory, much healthcare is available for free in India. There is a large network of over 160,000 public hospitals, clinics, and health centers at the national, state, and local level. However, in practice, these providers are barely acceptable. Public facilities are overcrowded and poorly staffed and funded. Although services are supposed to be free, patients must often pay for supplies like bedsheets, bandages, and drugs. Bribes can also be necessary to get faster treatment. Almost always, when patients have the freedom to choose, they will opt for private hospitals over public.

For-profit private hospital chains, such as Apollo, Max, and Fortis, have flourished in India over the past two decades. Serving both well-off Indians and medical tourists from the West, they tend to offer much higher standards of treatment with better staff, training, and equipment. Their fees, while low by Western standards, are significant to Indian incomes. In total, the majority of medical costs in India are paid for privately and out-of-pocket. It is private spending, not public, which is the basis of future growth.

INDUSTRY

The Indian pharmaceutical industry has historically been characterized by a large number of small factories. There are over 10,000 pharmaceutical plants, and only about 300 are large or medium-sized. However, parts of the pharmaceutical manufacturing sector have developed to become more competitive in foreign markets. The Indian API industry had sales of about $2 billion in 2005, making it the third largest producer in the world. Over 90 Indian factories now have FDA approval. Global pharmaceutical companies such as GlaxoSmithKline, Sanofi-Aventis, Pfizer, and Abbott also have their own manufacturing facilities in India, making use of low local labor costs.

Despite the traditional focus on generics, original R&D is becoming a more practical option in India. This is partly due to the abundance of trained scientists in the country. For example, the Indian company Torrent Pharmaceuticals drew attention in 2004 when it licensed a new cardiovascular compound to Novartis. Large Indian firms are also players in R&D: GlaxoSmithKline has a wide-ranging drug discovery and development alliance with Ranbaxy.

Finally, India's low costs, availability of talent, and large population have made it a major site for international clinical trials. In 2002, the total clinical trial market in India was about $20 million; by 2005, this figure had risen to nearly $100 million. India is home to over 100 CROs, as well as many clinical testing sites of foreign pharmaceutical companies.

Regulatory Structure

India has a federal form of government, and the medical regulatory structure is divided between national and state authorities. The principal national drug authority in New Delhi is the Central Drug Standards Control Organization (CDSCO). CDSCO is often referred to as the DCGI, which stands for Drug Controller General India, the title of its head official. There are also 35 state-level Food and Drug Administrations, one for each of India's states and territories.

The DCGI registers all imported drugs, new drugs, and drugs in selected categories. It also has responsibility for clinical trials and quality standards. The state FDAs register all other products, accredit manufacturing plants, and conduct the bulk of quality monitoring and inspections. The Indian cabinet has approved a plan that would bring all drugs under a new Central Drugs Authority, modeled on the US FDA. This may be approved by Parliament in a legislative session during the summer of 2007, but if so it will be phased in over time.

The DCGI has a shortage of reviewers, often relying on outside experts to provide opinions. To pursue regulatory approvals effectively, a company must use a regulatory professional with significant experience in applications for foreign companies. This professional must also be in a position to spend a significant amount of time in New Delhi (where the DCGI is located) following up on applications.

Most of India's pharmaceutical product policy is governed by the Drugs and Cosmetics Act (DCA). The DCA was first enacted in 1940 and has been amended many times since then.

New Drug Registration

Drugs count as "new drugs" in India if they fall into one of the following categories: (1) drugs never marketed in India; (2) drugs with new therapeutic purposes or dosages that have not been marketed in India; (3) new fixed-dose combinations of two or more drugs; and (4) any drug which was first approved in India less than 4 years ago, unless it is included in the Indian Pharmacopoeia. Also, all vaccines are treated as new drugs, unless notified otherwise by the DCGI.

New drug registration is applied for officially in Form 44. The required attachments to the form vary depending on the type of new drug. All submissions require basic dosage and indication information, test specifications of active and inactive ingredients, listing of any applicable patents, and the raw material manufacturer.

Finished drugs with new active ingredients that have never been marketed in India require full pre-clinical and clinical testing information. These fall into the following categories: chemical and pharmaceutical information; animal pharmacology; animal toxicology; human clinical data from phases I, II, and III; bioavailability and bioequivalence; and other special studies as appropriate. Besides information on safety and efficacy, the DCA also requires comprehensive information on the marketing status of the drug in other countries. Information must be provided for any countries where the drug has marketing approval, investigational new drug approval, or has been withdrawn or rejected. Prescription information, samples and testing protocols, and the proposed product monograph, labels, and cartons, must also be submitted.

It is possible to relax some of the requirements on a case-by-case basis, especially in the category of animal toxicology. This relaxation can be requested if a drug has been marketed for several years in other countries and its safety has been well-demonstrated. However, tests for animal pharmacology and animal toxicology are defined very closely in Schedule Y of the DCA, all the way down to the species and exact numbers of animals to be used in each test.

New fixed-dose combinations, new dosages and indications, new bulk drugs, and anything which was first approved less than 4 years previously, have significantly fewer requirements in the new drug process.

They all require chemical and pharmaceutical information, including stability studies and testing specifications, as well as package inserts and labels. Anything taken orally requires bioavailability, bioequivalence, and comparative dissolution data. Anything taken by intravenous infusion or injection requires sub-acute animal toxicity data. New indications, dosages, or fixed-dose combinations require therapeutic justification that satisfies the DCGI of their safety, which can vary case by case and requires consultation and coordination.

New drug registration has a fee of 50,000 rupees, or about $1,200. There is no fixed time frame in which the application has to be reviewed, but a typical range is about 12-18 months.

Clinical Trial Approval

Clinical trials are also applied for in Form 44, the same form used for new drug approval. Much of the same information as for new drug approval must be included, with the exception of reports on clinical trials that are still in the future. The Investigator's Brochure, study objectives and rationale, case record forms, informed consent documents, list of study locations, sponsor authorization letter, etc. must also be attached.

However, in late 2006, the government clarified additional information that should be submitted in the case of simultaneous global trials. Besides normal Form 44 information, this includes a list of all worldwide trial sites and numbers of subjects at each site, all serious adverse events reported from other sites, and the status of the trials at other sites.Phase III clinical testing generally must be conducted in India to receive new drug approval. This can only be waived in occasional cases, typically when the government is interested in a product for public health reasons and there is ample foreign data.

A previous rule was that for drugs discovered in foreign countries, Phase I trials could not be conducted in India unless they were supplementary to Phase I trials which had been completed elsewhere. However, the new rules in late 2006 also allowed first-time Phase I trials in India as long as they are conducted simultaneously to other foreign Phase I trials.

Import Drug Registration

All drugs to be imported in India require their own import registration. This is independent from new drug registration. New drugs to be imported into India must first be registered as new drugs under Form 44 and then as imported drugs under Form 40. The contents of Form 40 are fairly routine, but are still substantial. There is some overlap with the new drug application contents. Since clinical testing results are fully provided in new drug applications, they need only be summarized for form 40. However, information on regulatory status in other countries, GMP certification of the manufacturer, and items such as stability data, manufacturing methods, toxicity tests, bioavailability and bioequivalence, batch testing certificates, and inserts and labels must be included in full.

The process of receiving import registration can take up to a year, and it must be done after new drug registration. Once you have import registration for a drug, you can apply for a simple import license, which is needed to actually let the drug in through customs.

MANUFACTURING

Most manufacturing is licensed by state FDAs, but new drugs, blood products, sera, and vaccines require approval from the DCGI. Manufacturing permission is fairly simple compared to new drug approval. Besides basic information on the site, information must be furnished that the drug is being made to therapeutically justified specifications, and has new drug approval if appropriate. A GMP standard has also been recently implemented, under the name of "Schedule M." This may drive out many smaller drug manufacturers as it is enforced more strictly.

Intellectual Property Issues

Since 1970, in an effort to develop the local pharmaceutical industry, India's patent laws were changed to allow pharmaceutical processes to be patented, but not pharmaceutical substances. This made it completely legal to copy patented drugs, as long as they were made by a slightly different method. This led to the rapid development of small-scale bulk drug and formulation manufacturers in India. As a result, it became extremely difficult for Western pharmaceutical drug companies to succeed there.

However, when India joined the World Trade Organization in 1995, it committed itself to remedying its patent system to comply with international norms within ten years. In 1999, a provisional system allowing marketing exclusivity was created, and finally, in 2005, the patent laws were amended to allow product patents also.

Intellectual property rights are still comparatively weak in India, making it difficult to enforce patent protections. However, it is widely believed that a corner has been turned. India's large domestic companies such as Nicholas Paramal, Ranbaxy, and Dr Reddy's Laboratories are increasing their research and development budgets in order to compete under the new patent regime. Global pharmaceutical firms have also been using the judicial system to prosecute infringers. The patent change has helped build confidence among Western companies that India is now worth the effort. For example, Bristol-Myers Squibb and Merck, which had terminated some of their Indian presence in the 1990's, returned in 2004 and 2005 respectively, citing the improved business and IP environment.

However, the new patent regime does not apply retroactively. Drugs discovered before 1995, even if patented elsewhere, are still copyable. Also, the new system only allows for the patenting of drugs discovered after 2005, when the system was implemented. New indications for drugs are not patentable, and neither are new chemical forms of existing substances unless they increase efficacy. This is why, if foreign pharmaceutical companies want to enter the Indian market with proprietary drugs, they should focus on bringing new drugs into India. These are the drugs that can be patented locally, brought first to market, and hopefully protected in court.

CONCLUSION

With a nontransparent regulatory system, fragmented geographic markets, and much local competition, India is not a place where easy success can be expected. However, its burgeoning economy, greater market openness, and the improved patent regime have altered the playing field. The potential of India for R&D, manufacturing, and sales now outweighs its drawbacks in many cases.

Although India's business environment has improved greatly over the past decade, it is still a very complex country to operate in, and many obstacles can appear along the way. Due diligence and careful selection of regulatory professionals and business partners is essential to succeed there.

Country	Market Size (US$)
Japan	$55 billion
China	$20 billion
India	$8.8 billion
Korea	$6.3 billion
Taiwan	$2.5 billion
Hong Kong	$1.5 billion
Thailan	$1.5 billion
Singapore	$400 million
Indonesia	$350 million
Philippines	$300 milllion
Malaysia	$210 million

7

Medical Device Market Opportunities in India

INTRODUCTION

For a long time, India was closed to many foreign markets through government protectionism and a nationalistic tariff system. Today, however, India is ripe for market entry for many industries, including medical devices. Entering soon (or expanding one's business there) will help keep Western enterprises from being left out of India's exponential growth.

India is a country of 1.1 billion people, with its $4 trillion GDP (adjusted for purchasing-power parity) making it the fourth-biggest economy in the world. After being stuck at a low rate of growth for many years, it has been booming since the 1990's. From 1996 to 2006 GDP grew at an average rate of 7%, and is still not slowing down. Within that picture, the $1.75 billion medical device market is a strong sector, with 8% growth in 2005 and double-digit growth foreseen for coming years.

MARKET CHARACTERISTICS

To understand the medical markets in India the first thing to remember is that, for foreign market entrants, the consumer base is *not* one billion people. Even today, a majority of Indians are too poor to afford more than the most rudimentary health care. Rather, the market is the middle and upper classes in the teeming cities, numbering around 150 million and counting. With no comprehensive national health insurance, and an inadequate public health network, it is mostly the private sector fulfilling their new demands for quality health care. About 75% of medical expenditures in India are paid privately.

India is home to a number of large, modern private hospital chains (Apollo, Wockhardt, Fortis, and many others). These groups purchase high-end medical equipment to serve both their demanding local customers and India's more than 100,000 annual "medical tourists" from other countries.

The device categories poised for the highest growth in India are those connected to its changing disease profile. As Indians increasingly lead sedentary lifestyles, smoke, and eat more, lifestyle diseases such as cardiovascular disease and cancer are on the rise. Imaging, diagnostic, and surgical devices to treat these diseases are well-situated. Cardiological equipment currently makes up about 20% of India's total device market, while imaging equipment is about 15%. Other growth sectors include ophthalmological equipment, general surgical devices, orthopedics, and plastic surgery equipment. Imports make up over 60% of all devices by value and dominate the high-end market, with foreign devices seen as more effective and reliable.

OBSTACLES

Though India's business environment has improved markedly over the last 15 years, in some ways it is still a difficult country to work in. Assistance on the ground by experts with medical device experience is indispensable.

India's regulatory system is complex and can be difficult to navigate. Up until very recently, there were no regulations for medical devices as a class. Today, though, various devices (i.e., hypodermic syringes, cardiac stents, and orthopedic implants, among others) are designated as needing registration as drugs under the Drugs and Cosmetics Act. A few specific devices, such as diagnostic X-ray equipment, have individual registration requirements instead. The government has drafted a medical device law, which may streamline the process but include many more medical devices (requiring registration) within a year or two.

For devices that need it, registration may take up to a year, and will require a regulatory professional prepared to spend a significant amount of time in New Delhi following up. The manufacturer may authorize the importer to apply for registration, or may designate an independent third party (in-country) to make the application and hold the license, which helps keep distribution options flexible. Obviously, if your company has its own office there, direct registration is possible.

As noted above, India has no comprehensive national reimbursement system. However, a patchwork of different government programs sometimes reimburses for devices, but more to public hospitals than to private ones. However, private health insurance will soon become a part of the landscape. In 2004, only 1% of Indians had private healthcare coverage, but with high demand and aggressive marketing, this figure is expected to rise to 10% by 2010.

Finally, while tariffs have been eliminated altogether for some types of medical devices, many still have tariffs ranging from 5-36%. These are expected to go down further in the future.

MARKET ENTRY STRATEGY

Distribution networks in India are extremely dense, layered, and difficult to penetrate without connections and experience. Therefore, it is recommended to find distribution partners or set up a joint venture, not jump in and set up your own operation at first.

Large Western medical companies often choose to create a joint venture with similarly large local companies. One of the best-known examples is the long association of GE with Wipro, which put in a great deal of expertise and capital to make and market diagnostic equipment in India.

Smaller companies, on the other hand, usually work through distributors. They may also set up a small representative office to do advertising and market research, as well as keep tabs on the distributor. Finding the right partner is essential, and lack of due diligence can doom the whole process. Both parties should also try to align their mutual expectations as much as possible, since cultural differences make strategic disconnect hard to fix.

In crafting a marketing strategy for India, it is vital to think regionally. Is it really "all one country"? India's billion citizens speak 24 major languages, practice 6 major religions, and are divided into thousands of ethnic groups. To market to multiple regions of India, you may need multiple distributors.

Any pressure to sign an exclusive distribution agreement should be resisted, since very few distributors have the capacity to market to the whole country satisfactorily.

You should not assume that just because India has a large middle class (per capita income $3,000-20,000), they will snap up your high-end products quickly. Brand recognition in the US will not necessarily carry over in India. Market research is a must, and you may find you need to adjust a device's features or pricing. Some hospitals may be after advanced equipment, but their budgets are still smaller than hospitals in the West. A key way to stand out in the Indian market is through offering excellent after-sale service, which domestic competitors are often poor at.

Some companies combine market entry with starting up manufacturing operations in India, since it should enhance sales due to significant cost-cutting. Clinical trial and R&D outsourcing are also becoming more popular, helped by India's huge patient base and relatively cheap scientists.

India is not a place to get rich quick. Preparations take time and money, and there will be bumps on the road. But with a good product, the right partners, and a locally-adapted strategy, capturing part of its market will pay off for decades to come. Finally, when doing business in India, it is extremely important to remember their business culture is more aligned with the Middle East and East Africa as opposed to East Asia.

MARKET, REGULATORY, IMPORT AND INVESTMENT REGIME

The purpose of this discussion is to provide an overview of the major aspects of the market, law and policy related to pharmaceuticals in India, as well as law and policy on patents, trademarks, investment and company law. It is not meant to provide legal or commercial advice on which any business or investment commitments may be based.

The data and other statistics presented in this report have been collected from published sources generally felt to be reliable (newspapers, published research, company data, business magazines) but are not intended to be a substitute for detailed market studies and sales analyses. They are only given to provide "order of magnitude" data.

Pharmaceutical Industry

Country Background

Major demographic statistics on India are as follows:

- Population : 1 billion (48% female / 52% male)
- Population growth rate: 1.6%
- 58% of population is aged less than 25 years of age, 83% below 45 years
- Over 70% of the population lives in rural areas
- 302 towns account for 65% of the urban population
- The per capita income is estimated at US$400
- The population earning income over US$1000 per annum (the "middle class") is approximately 150 million people.

Economic Policy Drivers

The major features of the country's economic policy are as below.

- The country has a democratically elected Government, which is very involved in setting economic policy
- Traditionally (until 1991), the system was heavily socialist oriented, but with a substantially large private sector (including several joint venture foreign companies), operating subject to Government licensing and other controls.
- Liberalization since 1991 has resulted in fewer controls and licenses and encouragement of foreign investment in priority areas
- Foreign trade was restricted, and imports of consumer goods were effectively banned. However, India is now a WTO member, and quantitative restrictions on consumer goods imports have been considerably reduced, with free imports of most goods to be permitted by 2002.

Business Environment

The market is being opened to foreign investment and products, but with a preference for local manufacture as opposed to imports. There are also tariff barriers for consumer goods and pharmaceuticals, with high excise and sales taxes. In addition, there are certain non-tariff barriers in terms of product standards and cumbersome factory and other licensing procedures, and reservation of some products for a strictly defined "small scale sector."

Health Care System Profile

A few particulars of the prevailing health care system are provided below:

- Pharmacies : 150,000 (urban), 150,000 (rural)
- Number of doctors: 500,000
- Number of nurses: 600,000
- Hospitals: 15,000 (55%, Government owned, 45% other)
- Dispensaries and health centers: 180,000 (130,000 are sub-centers with basic services)
- Hospital beds: 1000,000 (60% Government, 40% other)
- Medical insurance: very limited. Re-imbursement is mainly from companies/institutions to employees.
- Medical colleges: 126
- Medical graduates: 15,000 per annum

Note: These statistics pertain only to the Western (allopathic) system of medicine. Only 25% of the population has access to or uses such medicine. The rest depend on traditional indigenous medicine, mainly ayurvedic, and unani, as well as homeopathy.

Pharmaceutical Industry Profile

A current profile of the Indian allopathic pharmaceutical industry, is provided below:

- Size of domestic market (value): US$3 billion
- Per capita annual consumption: US$3
- Number of units in manufacturing: 23,000 (1.2% in formulations, the rest in bulk drugs)
- Number of brands: > 6,500 in 77 therapeutic segments
- Market growth rate (value): 14%
- Imports: 4% of total
- Market share of multinationals (incorporated in India): 40%
- Market share of Indian companies: 60%
- Indian drug prices are among the lowest in the world

Pharmaceutical and other Related Regulation

The major source for pharmaceutical regulation is the Drugs and Cosmetics Act 1940 (DCA), and the Drugs and Cosmetics Rules (DCR) made there under. This legislation applies to the whole of India and all products, whether imported or made in India. The legislation is enforced by the Central Government (Department of Chemicals and Fertilizers, Ministry of Chemicals and Petrochemicals) in New Delhi, which is responsible for overall supervision. The office of the Drug Controller of India (DCI) has prime responsibility. However, at the field level, enforcement is done by the individual State governments through their Food and Drug Administrations. Matters of product approval and standards, clinical trials, introduction of new drugs, and import licenses for new drugs are handled by the DCI. However, the approvals for setting up manufacturing facilities, and obtaining licenses to sell and stock drugs are provided by the State Governments. Price controls are in effect on certain drugs, by virtue of the Drug Prices Control Order 1995 (DPCO) (as amended from time to time), under the Essential Commodities Act. (ECA). Other relevant, but general legislation is administered by Government Ministries in charge of Civil Supplies, Law, Industry, etc.

PRODUCT APPROVAL

Definition of "Drug"

The DCA provides the definition of a "drug." It is a definition which includes:

"all medicines for internal or external use of human beings or animals, and all substances intended to be used for or in the diagnosis, treatment, mitigation or prevention of any disease or disorder in human beings or animals, including preparations applied on the human body for the purpose of repelling insects like mosquitoes. such substances (other than food) intended to affect the structure or any function of the human body or intended to be used for the destruction of vermin or insects which cause disease in human beings or animals as may be specified from time to time by the Central Government in the Official Gazette"

The definition of a drug also includes substances intended for use as components of a drug (including empty gelatin capsules) and such medical devices for treatment, mitigation, and diagnosis of disease or disorder in human beings or animals as may be specified from time to time.

Approval Procedures for New Drug

There is no requirement for any registration of a drug in India. However, there is need for approval from the DCI to import, market, or manufacture a "new drug." All new drugs (drugs not previously used in India or in use for less than four years) proposed to be introduced must be approved for import or manufacture in India by the DCI. The application for permission to import or manufacture must be accompanied by the appropriate dossier as follows.

Data requirements

The full set of data to be submitted consists of:

- Introduction: description of drug and therapeutic class
- Clinical and pharmaceutical information
- Animal pharmacology
- Animal toxicology
- Human/ clinical pharmacology (Phase I)
- Exploratory clinical trials (Phase II)
- Confirmatory clinical trials (Phase III)
- Special studies
- Regulatory status in other countries
- Marketing information

All items above may not be required for all drugs. In case the drug is already approved and marketed abroad, then only Phase III trials may be required in India. Further, such trials would need to be conducted on at least 100 persons spread over 3-4 locations in the country. However, the DCI may agree to dispense with the need for local clinical trials, if it is in the public interest and if it can use the data of trials carried out in other countries. Similarly, the submission of data related to animal toxicology, reproduction studies, teratogenic studies, perinatal studies, mutagenicity and carcinogenicity may be relaxed or modified in case the drugs are in use overseas for several years and there is adequate published evidence regarding the safety of the drug. Permission from the DCI has to be obtained to import samples for clinical trials and to carry out the clinical trials in India.

In case the new drug is a fixed dose combination (FDC) of existing approved active ingredients, and these are merely being combined for convenience and provision of a stable acceptable dosage form and the ingredients are unlikely to have significant interaction of a pharmacodynamic or pharmacokinetic nature, then no additional animal or human data are generally required and marketing permission may be granted if the FDC has an acceptable rationale. However, if the combination is being done for the first time, and a claim is being made, and/or the combination is likely to result in a significant interaction of a pharmacodynamic or pharmacokinetic nature, then it is treated in the same way as any other new drug.

The period taken to give approval to a new drug largely depends on whether clinical trials will be required by the Drug Controller. It is not possible to estimate the time, and the law lays down no time limit. However, it can be assumed that after the submission of the full (final) dossier, it may take around three months, though this is only an estimate. The actual time taken depends on the amount and effectiveness of follow-up that is done by the local agent with the concerned authorities.

Product Standards

No drug can be imported, manufactured, stocked, sold or distributed unless it meets the quality and other standards laid down in the DCA. For instance, for patent or proprietary medicines (medicines not listed in the Indian or other pharmacopoeia), the product should comply with the ingredients displayed in the prescribed manner on the label or container and such other standards as may be prescribed. The DCR contains these standards.

There are general standards for all patent or proprietary medicines, tablets, capsules, liquid orals, injections and ointments. In patent medicines that contain vitamins, the content of active ingredients shall not be less than 90% of the labeled contents (however more than 100% of the labeled contents is allowed). In other cases excluding antibiotics and enzymes, the lower limit is 90%, but the active ingredient cannot exceed 110% of the labeled contents. In case of drugs included in the Indian pharmacopoeia (IP), the drug must comply with the standards of identity, purity and strength specified in the current edition of the IP (or if not specified in the current IP, then in the previous IP), as well as such other standards as may be prescribed. Similar standards apply to drugs not in the IP, but included in the official pharmacopoeia of another country. Standards are also prescribed for other types of drugs such as sera, antigens and other biological products.

Drugs should not be misbranded, adulterated, or spurious. Misbranded drugs are those that are not properly labeled, or the label makes false or misleading claims, or if damage to a drug is concealed, or if a drug is made to appear of greater therapeutic value than it really is. Adulterated drugs are those that contain any filthy, putrid or decomposed substance, or which has been prepared or packed under unsanitary conditions or contaminated with filth, or it contains any toxic or poisonous substance or contains colors other than those permitted, or if it has been mixed with any substance so as to reduce its quality or strength. Permitted colors for drugs are prescribed by the DCR, and these include certain natural colors, artificial colors, coal tar colors, and aluminum or calcium salts (lakes) of the permitted water soluble colors.

The Central Government has the power to prohibit the import, manufacture or sale of any drug, including those that are deemed as "irrational drug combinations." For instance, the import and manufacture of Fenfluramine and dexfenfluramine is prohibited. Similarly, other banned drugs include fixed dose combinations of vitamins with anti-inflammatory agents, tranquilizers or analgesics or tetracycline and vitamin C.

Labeling

No drug can be sold in India without being appropriately labeled. The label must be printed in indelible ink and must contain the trade name as well as the proper name of the medicine, the net contents in terms of weight, measure, volume, etc. The contents of active ingredients must also be provided in the prescribed manner. The name and address of the manufacturer and the address of the premises where the drug has been manufactured, the batch number, and date of manufacture must be provided, as well as the drug license number under which it is manufactured (if manufactured in India).

In the case of certain products (including vitamin products even if in combination with other drugs), the label should bear the date of manufacture, and the date of expiry of potency fixed by the manufacturer and the import license number if the product is imported. As per the Standards of Weights and Measures Act, 1976 (SWM) and the Packaged Commodities Rules, 1977 (PCR) made there under, an imported package (whether of drugs or any other item) also has to bear the name and address of the importer, and the retail price thereof. The SWM also prescribes the size and contents of the principal display panel to be on each container. Under the SWM, there are requirements as to standard contents of packages in certain cases.

For certain drugs, the period between the date of manufacture and the date of expiry of potency is laid down. In addition, for certain drugs the pack sizes have also been specified.

Certain drugs have to be sold under medical prescription only, and these have to be labeled accordingly along with the schedule of the DCA under which they are classified. Certain other drugs have to be labeled as having to be used under medical supervision.

Manufacturing

License to Manufacture Drugs

All manufacturing of drugs in India requires a license. Manufacturing is defined by the DCA as including any process or part of a process for making, altering, ornamenting, finishing, packing, labeling, breaking up or otherwise treating or adopting any drug with a view to its sale or distribution. It does not include dispensing or packing at the retail sale level. A license is required for each such location at which drugs are to be manufactured, and also for each drug to be manufactured. The license has to be renewed periodically. It is also possible to obtain a license to manufacture a product in the factory premises owned by another party, a practice called "loan licensing."

The good manufacturing practices and requirements of premises, plant and machinery are provided in the DCR. The items covered are: locations and surroundings, buildings, water supply, disposal of waste, requirements for sterile products manufacturing areas (areas, access, surfaces), working space and storage areas, health clothing and sanitation of workers, medical services, equipment standards. The DCR also specifies rules for maintenance of raw materials and records, master formula records, and batch manufacturing records. Manufacturing operations and controls are also specified, including general controls, precautions against contamination and mix-up, reprocessing and recovery, product containers and closures, labels and other printed materials. Distribution records and records of complaints and adverse reactions are also necessary. Requirements for the quality control system are also provided, including the functions of the quality control department.

With respect to plant and machinery, the DCR provides for recommended equipment for all product forms including syrups, elixirs, pills, compressed tablets, capsules as well as repacking installations.

The DCA also specifies other conditions for the grant or renewal of a license: competent technical staff including a pharmacy/pharmaceutical chemistry/science/chemical engineer/ chemical technologist/equivalent foreign qualification with experience in drug manufacture, requirements of the testing laboratory and qualifications of the head of the testing unit. The applicant must also show (in case of patent or proprietary medicines), that the medicines contain the constituent ingredients in the therapeutic/ prophylactic quantities as determined in relation to the claims or conditions for which the medicines are to be used, that the medicines are safe for use in the context of the vehicles, excipients, additives and pharmaceutical aids used in the formulation, are stable in the conditions of storage recommended, and contain such ingredients and in such quantities for which there is therapeutic justification.

Industrial Licensing

Besides the drug manufacturing license as above, for certain drugs there is need for a manufacturing license from the Central

Government, in accordance with the Drug Policy and the Industrial Policy. The legal basis for this is the Industries (Development & Regulation) Act, 1956 (IDR). However, the list of such drugs has been reduced substantially and the only drugs now requiring a license are: those involving use of recombinant DNA technology, those involving use of nucleic acids as the active principles and formulations based on use of specific cells/ tissue - targeted formulations. The applicant in these cases has to apply for an industrial license. If the application is in order, the applicant is granted a Letter of Intent (LOI) which is an in principle approval, subject to setting up the factory within a specified period. Once the factory is established to the satisfaction of the authorities, the LOI is converted into an Industrial Licence (IL).

The IL will specify various conditions, including the annual capacity up to which the unit can manufacture the licensed item. All other manufacturing units have only to file an Industrial Entrepreneur's Memorandum (IEM) with details of the proposed items to be manufactured, the capacity, the location, the source of technology, the raw material requirement, the process description and other details. However even items not requiring a license should not be manufactured within 25 kilometers of a city of more than 1 million residents, unless the item is manufactured in a designated industrial area, or is a non- polluting industry such as software, printing or electronics.

Other Approvals

The major other approvals / registrations / licenses regarding a manufacturing facility are:

- License for Capital Goods import (for items other than those freely importable under the Import Policy)
- License for raw materials import (for items other than those freely importable under the Import Policy)
- Factories Act registration
- Labor laws registrations
- Pollution Control Board clearance
- Electricity supply
- Building permission
- Water supply

- Land lease / purchase
- Excise duty registration
- Sales tax registration
- Explosives license
- Licenses to store petroleum products
- Registration under the Boilers Act
- Registration with the State Director of Industries
- Registration under Standards of Weights and Measures Act.

Except for the licenses to import (which are described below), the other formalities are to be complied with at the State or local government level, where the factory is located.

Imports of Capital Goods and Raw Materials

Most capital goods, raw materials and spare parts are generally permissible (under what is called Open General License - OGL) upon payment of the appropriate import duty. Certain specific items may require a license, however. The licensing authority is the Director General of Foreign Trade, under the Ministry of Commerce. In case the item to be imported is a drug and requires an import license, permission of the DCI must be taken.

Imports

Import Licensing

India does not permit the free import of all goods. While India is a signatory to the World Trade Organization (WTO), it has been given time to remove its quantitative restrictions on imports (QRs) in a phased manner, with QRs to be totally lifted by 2002 or earlier. At present most non-consumer goods items are permitted to be imported freely, while some consumer goods are permitted to be imported freely, and others are prohibited for import. Most items are classified under the International Harmonized System (IHS or BTN) and categorized for import accordingly. Imports and exports are regulated by the Foreign Trade (Development and Regulation) Act, 1992.

Pharmaceutical Imports

Most pharmaceuticals are freely importable under the foreign trade law. Certain drugs may not, however, be imported except under a license given by the Drug Controller of India. Such products cannot be imported after the date shown on the label as being that on which the potency would reduce or toxicity would increase beyond the standard permitted.

The foreign manufacturer would have to appoint an Indian agent to apply for the import license. The agent would be responsible for fulfilling all the terms of the license. An agent has to be an entity (individual, partnership or company) registered in India. A license is valid for a year, up to December 31st of the year following the year in which the license was granted, and has to renewed thereafter. The importer must have a license to stock and sell drugs. In case there is any repacking or labeling to be done, then the importer must also have a drug manufacturing license. A single license may be applied to all drugs imported from one manufacturer, provided that the drugs are manufactured at one factory or more than one factory functioning conjointly as a single unit. If the drugs are made in two separate factories, a separate license is required for drugs manufactured by each such factory.

In case the drug being imported is a "new" drug, i.e. not so far used in India or used for less than 4 years, it has to be approved by the DCI for sale or clinical trials in India before he will give an import license.

The license holder has several responsibilities including: maintaining detailed records of sales, permitting inspectors to enter his premises to take samples, to furnish samples to the DCI for examination when required, not selling any item of a batch until the sample is cleared (if so directed by the DCI), withdrawing or recalling sold items if the batch from which the sample is drawn does not meet the prescribed standards.

All license applications from the importer/agent have to be accompanied by an undertaking from the foreign manufacturer stating that the applicant is the authorized agent of the manufacturer, the date since when the manufacturer has been making drugs at the relevant factory premises, an undertaking that any change of location of manufacturing will be informed to the DCI, an undertaking that the drugs imported will comply with the Indian standards and other undertakings as to compliance with the DCA and the conditions of license.

Tariffs

Duty on Imports

The import duty structure depends on the classification for import tariff and excise duty (classification is more or less similar to the IHS/BTN). Import duties are prescribed by the Customs Tariff Act. Specified life saving products can be imported at zero duty. For most other pharmaceuticals, the duty structure would be roughly as below:

Rupies (Rs.)

* C.I.F. value of the imported item (say): Rs.10.00
* Basic duty: 30% of c.i.f value Rs.3.00
* Countervailing duty 16% of c.i.f. value plus basic duty plus surcharge Rs.2.08 (equal to the rate of excise duty if the item was made in India)
* Special additional duty 4% of the total of all the above Rs.0.60
* Total landed cost Rs.15.68
* Effective duty rate 56.8%

Note 1.: c.i.f. value is based on supplier's invoice, which if in foreign currency is converted to Indian currency at a standard rate.

Note 2.: duties are paid by Indian importer in Rupees. Supplier can be paid in foreign currency: US$ etc.

Duty on Local Manufacture

In case the product is manufactured in India, the primary tariff structure would be as below:

* Ex-factory sale price of the item (say) Rs.10.00
* Excise duty: 16% of the above value Rs.1.60
* Total ex-factory price Rs.11.60
* Effective duty rate 16%

Sales Taxes

For both imports and local manufacture, after this point, there is a further sales tax levied mainly at the point of sale from the retailer to the customer. This tax is a percentage of the sale price and such percentage is the same for domestic or imported items. It may vary depending on the type of product.

There may be other local duties which vary depending on the item and in which State of India the sale transaction takes place.

Sales and local taxes vary from 4 to 10% of the price depending on item and location. Sales tax is chargeable upon sale by manufacturer to stockist/ wholesaler, from stockist/ wholesaler to retailer and from retailer to customer. In some cases there are setoffs.

Pricing

Price Regulation

Drug prices in India are among the lowest in the world (and imports are therefore negligible). This is because of several reasons. The first is that only product patents and not process patents (for pharmaceuticals) are so far recognized under Indian law.

Therefore Indian manufacturers can make bulk drugs and formulations by "reverse engineering" of the overseas patented medicines, reducing R&D expenses and also avoiding royalty payments. Further, Indian labor costs are low compared to overseas levels. India also has a large pool of technical and managerial personnel and does not need management skills from overseas. Most of the plant and equipment required is made locally.

Most importantly a measure of statutory price control for bulk drugs and formulations operates in India. Certain drugs (known as scheduled drugs, as they are listed in the First Schedule to the DPCO), 76 in number and accounting for 50% of Indian retail sales), are under price control, and the prices for the bulk drugs and formulations thereof (whether imported or locally manufactured) are restricted by certain formulae prescribed by Government under the Drug Price Control Order, 1995 (DPCO). Non-scheduled drugs can be priced freely, subject to some restrictions.

The price control regime is administered by the National Pharmaceutical Pricing Authority (NPPA). The Government can exempt certain products from price control if they are new drugs discovered in India or bulk drugs produced from the basic stage by a new process discovered in India or drugs manufactured by small-scale industries (capital investment below a certain level) and sold under their own brand names. Price control does not apply to formulations under the Indian system of medicine or homeopathic medicines or items to which the DCA does not apply.

The Government of India announced in February 2002, the Pharmaceutical Policy 2002, in which it is proposed to make changes in the method of detaining price controlled drugs and also in the pricing formula. However, these changes have not yet been implemented through legal notifications.

Scheduled Drugs

Scheduled drugs have been selected as such based on a combination of certain criteria including: number of manufacturers, market share of a single formulator, and the value of annual turnover. The schedule is not fixed, and items can be added or deleted by the Government, depending on the criteria. Most of the other drugs are antibiotics. Scheduled drugs may be bulk drugs or formulations. Scheduled formulations are described as formulations containing any bulk drug specified in the First Schedule either individually or in combination with other drugs, including one or more than one drug or drugs not specified in the First Schedule except single ingredient formulation based on bulk drugs specified in the First Schedule and sold under the generic name.

Pricing of Scheduled Bulk Drugs

Scheduled bulk drugs are allowed prices (excluding local taxes) that result in a post-tax return of 14% on net worth (share capital plus free reserves less value of investments not related to the bulk drug business) or a 22% return on capital employed (fixed assets plus working capital). In respect of a new plant, an internal rate of return based on long term marginal costing is allowed.

For a bulk drug produced from the basic stage, a post-tax return of 18% on net worth or a return of 26% of capital employed is allowed. The prices have to be applied for to the NPPA before any sales take place, with detailed supporting calculations and thereafter officially sanctioned (NPPA may make changes), and cannot be revised without prior approval.

Pricing of Scheduled Formulations Manufactured in India

Scheduled formulations are priced based on the formula:

RP = (MC + CC + PM + PC) x (1+ MAPE/100) + ED

where RP is retail price, MC is material cost, CC is conversion cost, including labor and overheads, PM is packing material, PC is packing charges and MAPE is Maximum Allowable post-manufacturing expenses.

ED is excise duty. MAPE is intended to cover all costs incurred by a manufacturer after packing, i.e. transport, manufacturers profit, dealers / retailers profit, etc. MAPE/100 should not exceed 100%. Local taxes are added on at the wholesaler/retailers level, and are not part of the retail price as above.

The process for approval of prices is similar to that for bulk drugs. The price charged to a retailer is the approved retail price less 16% (as against the usual practice of 20%).

The margin to the wholesaler should not exceed 8% (as against market practice of around 10%). It should be noted that all the costs are not the actuals. In some cases the NPPA notifies standard prices for inputs, such as sugar. There are also norms for conversion cost, wastage, wages, etc.

Example

An example of pricing of a locally manufactured scheduled drug is provided below (assuming the actual costs are lower than or equal to the Government norms):

* Material cost Rs.3.25
* Conversion cost Rs.0.75
* Packing material Rs.1.53
* Packing cost Rs.0.12
* Total Rs.5.65
* Post manufacturing expense 100% above cost Rs.5.65 (to cover other costs plus profit)
* Total: Rs.11.30
* Add: excise duty 16% of sale price Rs.1.59 to wholesaler (9.96 as below)
* Retail price: Rs.12.89 + local taxes

* Price to retailer (84% of 12.89 above) Rs.10.83 + local taxes
* Price to wholesaler (92% of 10.83 above) Rs.9.96 + local taxes
* Less: manufacturing costs: Rs.5.65 excise duty 1.59 7.24
* Balance for marketing, transport, etc. and profit of manufacturer Rs.2.72 (27% of sales price)

Pricing of Scheduled Formulations Imported into India

In this case the formula for calculating the retail price is that the importer can add to the landed cost of the goods (cost plus inward freight plus clearing charges plus import duty) 50% more to cover distribution cost including trade margins and profit to arrive at the retail price. Sales taxes, if any, can be added on separately. The price to the retailer must be the approved retail price less 16%. The margin to the wholesaler should be 8%.

Example

The price build up for an imported price controlled drug would be roughly as below:

Rs.

* Landed cost as per para 5.1 above 15.68
* Clearing charges 2% of CIF value Rs. 10 0.20
* Total 15.88
* Add: 50% mark-up 7.94
* Retail price 23.82 + local taxes
* Price to retailer (84% of 23.82 above) 20.00 + local taxes
* Price to wholesaler (92% of 20.00 above) 18.40 + local taxes
* Less: total cost 15.88
* Balance for marketing, transport, etc and profit of importer 2.52 (13.7% of sales price)

Note: there is no restriction on the price the overseas manufacturer charges to the importer.

Procedure for Price Fixation

No person can sell or dispose of an imported scheduled formulation unless it has prior approval of the price from the

NPPA. Also, no manufacturer or importer can market a new pack, new formulation or new dosage form without obtaining the prior approval of its price from the NPPA. However, where a manufacturer introduces a formulation similar to an existing one in a new pack, he may rework the price thereof based on the norms that the NPPA may announce and intimate the new price to the NPPA. After 60 days the pack may be sold at the price intimated, unless the NPPA revises the price, in which case the revised price will hold. In other cases, the importer or manufacturer has to file details justifying the price in the appropriate form. The NPPA will have to give approval first. The approval may be the price applied for or a lower price. A similar procedure applies to price revisions.

The NPPA also has the power to fix the ceiling price of scheduled formulations, based on the cost structure or efficiency of the bulk drug manufacturers, and such ceiling price shall be the maximum for all such formulations. The ceiling price can be changed by the NPPA on its own or on application made by a manufacturer.

The NPPA has the power to fix the price of a non-scheduled or scheduled local or imported formulations, based on information it may call for from the manufacturer or importer. The price fixation may be done in such manner that the pre-tax return of such manufacturer or importer should not exceed the pre-tax return specified in the Third Schedule to the DPCO. This prescribes different rates of return, which depend on a number of criteria such as whether the manufacturer has basic drug manufacturing activity besides formulations, whether it conducts research activity, and the turnover level of the unit. The minimum return is 8% and the maximum is 13%. However, notwithstanding this, the NPPA has the power to fix or revise the price of any formulation, including a non-scheduled formulation. It also has the power to include any bulk drug in the First Schedule and fix or revise the prices of the bulk drug and the formulations thereof.

Filing of Price Lists

For scheduled formulations, the manufacturer has to file a price list of all the prices fixed and/or revised for with the State Drug Controllers, the dealers and the Government, giving reference of the official price notification by the NPPA. The price list has to be prominently displayed by each dealer in his premises. Similarly, for each non-scheduled formulation the circulation of price lists as above is mandatory.

Price labeling

All packages of formulations (the outer container as well as the minimum pack being offered for sale) must bear the retail price (whether fixed by the NPPA or otherwise) with the words "retail price not to exceed" preceding the price and the words "local taxes extra" after the price. In this regard the requirement is different from the usual method of price marking for other commodities specified by the SWM, where the price on the package should be the maximum price inclusive of all taxes.

Marketing and Distribution

This section deals with aspects of marketing: licensing of sales outlets/ stocking points, OTC and ethical drugs, advertising and promotion, packaging and labeling, distribution methods, brand names, restrictive trade practices and consumer protection.

Licensing of Sales Outlets and Stocking Points

Under the DCA, sales offices, pharmacies or any other sales outlet or stocking point for drugs must be licensed to do so by the State Government having jurisdiction over the office/ pharmacy. Where drugs are sold/stocked for sale at more than one place, a separate license is required for each such location. A license once issued would be valid till December 31st of the year following the year in which the license has been granted.

The requirements and conditions for a license to stock and sell drugs (other than on a wholesale basis) include:

- specified minimum area and equipment
- compounding of drugs on the premises should be done by a Registered Pharmacist
- sales of any drugs on prescription should be under the supervision of a Registered Pharmacist (qualification and experience profile are specified), and a prescription register (for compounded drugs) or cash or credit memo book (for other medicines) maintained

- prescription register or sale memo should contain the specified particulars of the sale (including batch number of manufacture in case of prescription drugs)
- no prescription drug is to be sold without a prescription

There are restricted licenses for outlets that do not need the services of a Registered Pharmacist (these are to be called "drugstores"), and those where no compounding takes place (to be called "chemists and druggists"). Outlets may use titles such as "Pharmacy," "Pharmacist," "Pharmaceutical Chemist," or "Dispensing Chemist" only if they use the services of a Registered Pharmacist and maintain a pharmacy for compounding.

Wholesale and retail outlets would also need registration under the:

- the Shops and Establishment Act
- the Standard of Weights and Measures Act
- labor legislation
- sales tax

These are all local registrations.

OTC and Prescription Drugs

There is no category of drugs legally specified as OTC drugs. The DCA specifies certain drugs to be sold only under prescription. The rest can be sold without prescription. However drugs can be sold in retail only by licensed outlets as described earlier. The list of prescription drugs is quite large and covers all antibiotics, a number of painkillers, etc. Prescription drugs cannot be advertised in the general media. The DCA also provides a list of ailments that no drug may purport to prevent or cure.

In practice, a large number of prescription drugs are sold without prescription. However, this does not mean that self-medication is common, except to some extent in the upper classes of society. Most people like to take medical advice, either of doctors or of pharmacists. Even in case of prescriptions, due to cost considerations, several customers buy less than the prescribed amount, or ask the chemist for a cheaper alternative. The pharmaceutical industry has requested the Government to review this issue, and the Government has set up a committee of officials to draw up a list of OTC items. This would require an amendment of the DCA. The OTC items would be allowed to be advertised in the general media. At present there are a few so-called OTC drugs (15-20 types) such as rubs and balms, pain relievers, antacids, etc. Health drinks are, of course, commonly advertised.

Advertising and Sales Promotion

In the above circumstances, the avenues for advertising are restricted. Presently, advertising, as such, is restricted to trade journals, such as chemists' guides and directories, and medical magazines. Another method of "advertising" is to sponsor conferences in India and abroad and have doctors attend, often at company cost. At these conferences, various pamphlets and other material are distributed to the doctors, as well as complimentary items.

At the pharmacy level, the advertising is in terms of point-of-purchase displays. However the major incentive to chemists is the free (bonus) supplies of drugs. This is also a method of overcoming the retail commission restrictions under the DPCO.

The most important method of sales promotion is of medical detailing. The doctor is extremely important, as it is he who recommends treatment. A large company could have as many as up to 200-250 medical representatives whose duty is to visit doctors and hospitals, provide them with (technically non-saleable) samples and literature and brief them on new products. The representatives are qualified in science/chemistry/pharmacy or experienced in the field. They are given sales targets and other objectives. They have to file field reports and provide market intelligence as well.

Advertising Standards and Self-Regulation

Apart from restraint on advertising of prescription drugs, and making claims to provide prevention or cure of certain diseases, there are no legal constraints on advertising. However, advertisements should not make unjustified claims, and complaints can be made to the Advertising Standards Council of India (ASCI), a self-regulatory body. The purpose of this body is to complement and not replace the law. It is meant to maintain high standards of advertising. The advertising profession has drawn up the self-regulation code, which is administered by the ASCI, and advertisers, agencies and associations accept the same. The code has the objectives of ensuring truthfulness and honesty of representations and claims, safeguarding against misleading advertising, ensuring that advertisements are not offensive to general standards of decency, safeguarding against the indiscriminate use of advertising for products that are regarded as hazardous to society or to individuals to an unacceptable degree, and ensuring that advertisements observe fairness in competition so that the consumer's need to be informed about products in the market are balanced with generally accepted competitive behavior in business. If there is a complaint brought to the ASCI, it may ask the advertiser to withdraw or modify the advertisement in question if it deems fit. This has no legal basis, and if either of the parties is not satisfied they may take up the case in the courts under the laws related to restrictive trade practice or under the laws related to public decency.

Packing and Labeling

While specific aspects of labeling have been described elsewhere in this report, the major legislation affecting the same is the SWM and the PCR. The purpose of the SWM is to regulate inter-state trade in weights and measures and other goods, which are sold by weight or number. The general requirements of SWM / PCR are that the package carry the necessary information for consumers in a proper manner. Some of the major provisions of this legislation are:

- the necessary declarations as to name of manufacturer, date of manufacture, commodity, contents, weight, price, etc should be made on all packs
- the principal display panel (the area of the label on which the consumer looks for information about the product) should be as per the rules (size, size of letters, etc)
- all declarations should appear at the positions specified
- declaration of quantity should be made as per the norms and in the prescribed manner
- the statement of units or weight, measures or numbers should be as per norms
- specified commodities should be packed in the prescribed pack size, and within the prescribed margin of error

Distribution

India is geographically a very large country, with the population located in both urban and rural areas. There is at present no system of national chains of supermarkets or drugstores/pharmacies, and small independent shops dominate retailing. A manufacturer or importer has to make its own arrangements for distribution to the retail level. Due to complications arising from different sales tax regimes in various states, as well as taxes on inter-state sales, operating a few centralized warehouses and distributing to the rest of the country from there is not a common practice. Further, there are very few national marketing agencies that market third party products throughout the country. The method of distribution is therefore from the manufacturer's location to local depots for stocking.

These depots are either run by the company or contracted out to so-called carrying and forwarding agents (C&F), who operate the depots on the company's behalf, but employ their own staff and premises. The practice of operating company owned depots is reducing over time in favor of the C&F system. The C&F is under the supervision of the company's regional office (usually at least four offices based in Mumbai, New Delhi, Calcutta and Chennai, representing the West, North, East and South regions). Each regional office looks after sales in four or five states.

The dispatch of goods takes place from the manufacturer's location to the C&F locations, but without invoicing at that stage, as it is only a transfer of goods and not a sale. The C&F sends goods to wholesalers who have stocking points. At this point the goods are invoiced by the company to the wholesaler, and the legal sale takes place. However the company also retains the responsibilities under the DCA as applicable to manufacturers. The wholesaler has to pay the company for goods supplied. Besides dispatch, the C&F agent also performs functions such as providing sales staff, invoicing and collection. The agent is remunerated at 2% of the goods sold, plus expenses, but this could vary depending on the volume and the services provided.

The wholesaler is responsible for sending the goods to the various retailers under his jurisdiction. He invoices the sales in his own name and collects the money. The wholesaler has his own sales/delivery staff that surveys stock levels, order collection and supply. The utility of the wholesaler is that he can deliver small quantities of material to a large number of outlets economically and in time. A wholesaler receives a commission of 8-10% of the sale price. The company's sales representatives co-ordinate with both the C&F agent and the wholesaler to expedite sales and dispatches. Usually sales representatives are paid a part of their salary as a fixed monthly amount and partly by commission on sales in their territories.

Brand Names

There is no restriction on the use of foreign brand names on products sold within the country, whether locally manufactured or otherwise. The brand names may even be licensed to an Indian party. Brand names should not, however, be covered by an existing Indian registered trademark, unless the trademark has been registered wrongly. The usual practice is for brand names to be used as part of an overall foreign collaboration (along with equity investment and/or technology transfer), though there is no restriction on having trademark agreements alone.

Restrictive Trade Practices

The Monopolies and Restrictive Trade Practices Act, 1969 (MRTP) was intended to curb monopolistic power of industrial groups and to prevent restrictive trade practices. In effect it sought to regulate business through Anti-Trust type legislation restricting expansion, merger, amalgamation and new projects of large industrial groups without Government permission. The restrictions have largely been deleted from the Act, and it is now recast in a manner to deal only with restrictive trade practices such as price fixing, restrictive clauses in dealership agreements, unfair promotions, misleading advertisements, promotions against consumer interest, etc. The Director General may institute "suo moto" (by himself) investigations into any such practice, or may investigate based on a complaint brought by any person, whether a consumer or a competitor.

Consumer Protection

The Consumer Protection Act (COPRA), 1986 was enacted to establish methods of protection of consumer interest. The

Act provides a method for consumer complaints against manufacturers, sellers and service providers to be made and redress obtained at nominal cost. Suitable compensation/damages would be awarded to the aggrieved customer, if the complaint is found justified. A complaint can be lodged by the consumer concerned or a "recognized" consumer association. The objective of the act is allow complaints to be lodged with specialized tribunals for consumer complaints outside the regular legal system, which is expensive and time consuming. Small value complaints can be made to local district forums. If the complaint is for more than Rs. 100,000 but less than Rs. 1 million, the complaint has to be lodged with a State level Commission. Above this level, complaints have to be made to the National Commission. Complaints are usually lodged against overcharging, defective goods, deficiencies in service causing loss, false claims and advertising.

Patents and Trademarks

Patents

Under the Indian Patents Act, 1970 (IPA), a patent entitles the holder exclusive rights to manufacture, sell and distribute the product in India. For foods, medicines, drugs and substances prepared or produced by chemical processes, only process patents are given. Any manufacturer in these product ranges can "re-engineer" a patented item (manufacture the same item with a different process) and sell it without legal challenge by the patent holder.

Patents are registered with the Controller General of Patents, Designs and Trade Marks. The head office is in Calcutta, with branch offices in Delhi, Bombay and Madras. Applications must be filed in the appropriate office, with a provisional specification (with complete specification within 12, extendable to 15 months thereafter) or a complete specification. The patent application and specifications are studied by the examiners (eighteen months time is given to examine). Once the specification is accepted, the notice of patent is advertised in the Government's official gazette. Three month's time is given for notice of opposition. The opposition is to be replied to by the patent applicant within a month. Thereafter, the application is accepted or rejected. If the application is accepted, the patent is sealed. A patent is dated as of the date the complete specification was filed. For items of food or medicine, the process patent is granted for five years from the date of sealing or seven years from the date of the patent, whichever is earlier. For other inventions, the patent is granted for fourteen years from the date of the patent. Patents can be legally assigned or merely licensed to other parties, for use in India or any part of the country.

Besides this process, the Government may, on a reciprocal basis, declare any other country as a "convention" country, for the purpose of fulfilling any treaty. In such a case if a patent holder abroad makes an application in India within 12 months of having applied for a patent abroad, his patent protection in India will start from the same date it starts in his own country. India is a signatory to the Patent Convention Treaty, 1970.

Recent Amendments to Legislation

Under the TRIPS provisions of the WTO agreement, to which India is a signatory, India had to implement the minimum specified standards of intellectual property protection with effect from 1st January 1995, with an additional period of five years being allowed before it extended product patents to areas of technology not covered so far. Further, WTO member countries that did not provide for product patents in the areas of pharmaceuticals and agricultural chemicals had to provide, with effect from 1st January 1995, a mechanism (mail box) for receiving patent applications for such products and also to grant exclusive marketing rights (EMRs), also known as the "exclusive right to sell or distribute," for a period of five years or until the patent was accepted or rejected, whichever the is shorter.

The issue of granting product patents for all foods, medicines, drugs and substances produced by chemical processes is still under discussion. At present the Government has, in 1999, passed an interim measure by an amendment to the IPA, providing for EMRs for items where only process patents are granted. This measure is effective through 31st December 2004. From 2005, India has to fully comply with the international standards on patents. However the revised patent law has not been drafted so far. The recent interim amendments are discussed below.

Product Patent Applications for Medicines and Drugs

Product patent applications for medicines and drugs will now be accepted by the Controller of Patents ("the Controller"), but will not be sent for examination until 31st December 2004. For this purpose, "medicine or drug" includes: medicines for use by humans and animals, substances used for diagnosis or prevention of disease in humans or animals, substances used for the maintenance of public health or prevention or control of epidemic diseases among humans or animals, and substances used for the protection and preservation of plants. Chemical substances used as intermediates in the preparation of the above substances have not been given product patent protection.

Application and Grant of EMR

Applications for EMR can accompany the application for patent and EMR may be granted if the item is deemed patentable under the general law of patent. EMR will not be given for items based on the Indian system of medicine (eg. Ayurvedic) if the items are already in the public domain.

EMR will be granted where a patent application has been made in India and where before the date of such application, the item has already been patented in a convention country (a country which is notified as such by the Indian Government as having reciprocal arrangements for dealing with patent applications; India is also a signatory to the Patent Convention Treaty, 1970) and approved for sale or distribution in that country (provided the application for patent was filed in that country on or after 1st January 1995), and also approved for sale and distribution within India by the appropriate authority. EMR will also be granted where the invention has been made in India, and a process patent has been applied for and granted on or after 1st January 1995.

EMR will entitle the applicant the exclusive right for himself, his agents or licensees to sell or distribute the item in India for a period of five years from the date of approval or till the grant or rejection of the patent application, whichever is earlier. If, however, the specifications of the item under EMR have already been recorded or the item already tried or used or sold by any person, before the date of claim for patent in India, then sale or distribution of the item by that person, after the date of claim for patent is not deemed to be an infringement of EMR. This does not apply where the details of manufacture were originally supplied by a person who held the exclusive right to sell or distribute the item.

Compulsory Licensing and Revocation of EMR

At any time after two years from the date of approval for EMR, any person may apply to the Controller alleging that the requirements of the public with regard to the EMR item have not been fulfilled or that the item has not been made available at a reasonable price, and may request for a compulsory license to sell or distribute the item.

The Controller may, if he considers the application justified, order the EMR holder to grant a license to the applicant for sale.

The Controller has to take into account, the time that elapsed since the date of EMR approval, the ability of the applicant to sell or distribute to the public advantage, and the capacity of the applicant to provide capital for the operation. The provisions for compulsory licensing are also applicable in the case of patents already granted (applications to be made only three years after the date of sealing the patent). The Controller also has powers to revoke an EMR in the public interest (as it has the power to do for patents already granted).

Powers of Central Government to order Sale or Distribution by itself or any other Person

The Central Government may, if it decides it is in the public interest, sell or distribute the item reserved for EMR by itself or through any other person (other than the EMR holder). The Central Government may also, if it decides it is in the public interest, direct that the EMR item be sold at a price determined by an authority to be nominated by the Government.

Permission for Residents to Apply for Patents Outside India

Under the previous law, residents of India were not permitted to make patent applications abroad without written permission of the Controller. This requirement has now been removed, and any resident of India can apply for patents in overseas countries.

Trademarks

The law on trademarks is the Trade and Merchandise Marks Act, 1958 (TMMA). The TMMA provides for registration of trademarks for a period of 7 years at a time, renewable after each such period. Presently only goods, and not services, can have registered trademarks. For any item, trademarks should not be objectionable from religious or social points of view. They should not contravene the Emblems and Names (Prevention of Improper Use) Act, 1950. They should also not be already registered or applied to be registered in India. The trademark can be registered even if the item is not produced or sold in India at present.

Applications have to be made separately for trademarks for each class of goods to be covered. These applications are to be filed with the Trade Mark Registry at either Delhi, Bombay (Head Office), Madras, Calcutta and Ahmedabad depending on the location of the applicant's principal place of business. There is first an application for "search" to determine whether the proposed registered trademark is already registered by someone else, or whether an application for the same is already pending. After the search, the applicant is then given a registration number (which may take over a month), and then the examination process begins. The law specifies one year for this process. If the examiners clear the trademark, then the notice inviting objections has to be published in the Trademark Journal, a Government publication. Objections must be filed within 3, extendable to 4, months. After objections, the applicant has two months to reply, failing which it will be assumed that he has abandoned the application. After this the Registrar will decide whether to grant registration or otherwise. Thereafter it takes about six months to receive the certificate of registration. However when registration is granted, the effective date of start is the date of the original application.

Besides this process, the Government may determine "convention" countries, in pursuance of treaty obligations, whereby a person, after making an application in his home country, may within 6 months apply to register in India, and he would be deemed to have been registered in India as of the date of his home country application. As in patents there can be assignment of a trademark and also licensed use for a fee.

A foreign trademark can be used without any restriction. It can also be registered. A trademark can also be used without registration or used before registration or after expiry of the registration, but this use would not have protection of the TMMA. Recently Indian courts have held, that copying of international names (even in products that are not made in India by the international trademark holder) is not permissible. Several international companies are engaged in trademark litigation in India, including IBM, Apple, Microsoft, Dunhill, Whirlpool, Sony and Cartier.

Market Entry and Investment

Entry Strategies

Three entry strategies are available for entering the Indian pharmaceutical market. In some cases all three strategies are followed sequentially as the overseas party becomes more familiar with the Indian market:

- imports through agent
- manufacture under license
- investment in joint venture / subsidiary company

Imports Through Agent

Imports of formulations to India are negligible due to the price disadvantage arising from imports due to tariffs and local manufacturing cost advantages. The lack of patent protection has also contributed to this. Further, the product approval process can be difficult. Price controls are also an added negative factor. However, assuming that the market proves to be adequately substantial and remunerative, then this strategy could be employed. Under current policy, a foreign manufacturer is unlikely to be allowed to set up a 100% subsidiary in India only for imports. In case the company is prepared to do some exports from India, then it can be allowed to invest up to 51% equity (the balance to be held by Indian resident individuals or companies) in a trading company that is primarily involved in exports (it can import as well). India exports a large number of bulk drugs and formulations to several countries.

Manufacture Under License

In order to avail of the lower manufacturing costs available in India, a foreign manufacturer can have the product made in India by an Indian manufacturer (multinational company or otherwise) under license. The foreign entity can charge a one-time technology transfer fee of up to US$2 million and receive royalties of 5% on local sales and 8% on export sales, with the post facto approval (known as "automatic approval") of the Reserve Bank of India (RBI). Higher royalty payments require the approval of the Foreign Investment Promotion Board (FIPB). A foreign company can also invest in the equity of the company manufacturing the product as described in the following paragraph. Even in this situation, it could continue to receive royalty and technology transfer fees as above. The foreign company can also charge for the use of trademarks at the rate of 1% of domestic sales and 2% of export sales. However, the "automatic approval" route is not available to foreign companies that either have or have had in the past a joint venture/ technical collaboration/ trademark agreement for the same or allied product. In such a case the foreign investor will have to apply for specific approval to the FIPB.

Investment in Joint Venture / Subsidiary Company

Foreign investment in a new or existing Indian registered company in the pharmaceutical manufacturing business (up to 100% of the equity through an issue of new equity shares) is permitted under the "automatic approval" route, prescribed by the Foreign Exchange Management Act 2000 (FEMA). Under this procedure there is no necessity to take prior approval for foreign investment. The RBI has to be informed only after the capital has been remitted into India. Automatic approval is not allowed in cases where industrial licensing is mandatory. Further, "automatic approval" route is not available to foreign companies which either have or have had in the past a joint venture/ technical collaboration/ trademark agreement for the same or allied product. In such a case the foreign investor will have to apply to the (FIPB). A foreign investor may also acquire the whole or part of an existing company by buying out existing shareholders. For this, prior permission will be needed from the FIPB and thereafter the RBI. If the company to be taken over is not listed on the stock exchange, the formalities are fewer. If the company is listed, then there are formalities to be complied with in terms of announcement of acquisition of substantial shareholding, public offer to buy out other shareholders at the same price, etc. and other formalities required by the Securities and Exchange Board of India (SEBI).

FIPB

The FIPB functions under the Ministry of Industry. The Board receives investment and collaboration proposals (other than those for which the automatic approval route is available) and recommends the same or disapproves by rejection or requiring amendments or asks for further clarifications. Rejection is not necessarily the end of the process. The applicant can apply again at a later point in time. The approvals must be signed by the Industry Minister to be effective. The Minister can clear all recommended projects up to Rs. 6 billion. For projects of value above this level, approval has to be given by the Cabinet Committee on Foreign Investment. The approval is communicated by the Secretariat for Industrial Assistance (SIA) of the Ministry for Industry. The FIPB consists of the Secretary, Industrial Development, who is the Chairman as well as the other permanent members: Finance Secretary, Commerce Secretary, and Secretary (Economic Relations) to the Ministry of External Affairs.

For specific investment proposals, other officials from the concerned ministries would attend the FIPB meeting. For example, officials from the Ministry of Chemicals and Fertilisers, Department of Chemicals and Petrochemicals), and from the Ministry of Health and Family Welfare would attend if the application pertained to pharmaceuticals. The Board usually meets every Saturday. Decisions are normally taken within one month after all papers are submitted and all queries raised by the FIPB are answered by the applicant.

Procedurally, an application to the FIPB is simple and can be made in a letter form. The enclosures are the annual report, corporate profile and product profile. The application should be made in fifteen copies. The application is circulated to the concerned administrative ministry (eg. the Ministry of Chemicals and Petrochemicals and the Ministry of Health and Family Welfare for pharmaceuticals) and other ministries that may have some opinion on the application.

The FIPB provides single point clearance for foreign investment level, definition of item to be made / marketed, industrial license if required and foreign collaboration terms. It is not, however, meant for getting certain specific licenses and clearances which are given under various other legislation (import licenses, state level licenses for manufacture of drugs, municipal licenses etc). These have to be dealt with separately.

The FIPB may issue the approval letter with any conditions it deems fit. These include: restrictions on activities, or dilution of foreign equity percentage, over a period of time.

FIPB was set up originally to consider investment proposals without concern for the existing parameters for permitting foreign investment. However, it has some published guidelines as to the issues it will consider for allowing various levels of foreign equity in each sector. The FIPB considers aspects such as technology brought in, employment to be created, exports, foreign exchange implications, social benefits, the amount of capital to be brought in, and also the image conveyed to other countries / investors.

New procedure for applications from foreign companies which have/ had joint ventures in the same or allied industry.

In December 1998, the Government came out with specific rules for applications for foreign investment/ collaboration/ trademark contracts, which either have current joint ventures or collaborations in India or have had such ventures at any time in the past in the same or allied industry. "Same or allied industry" is defined by the National Industries Classification (NIC), 1987 list of industry codes.

In such cases, the "automatic approval" route is not permitted. The application has to be made to the FIPB, and the applicant has to give detailed justification for the new arrangements/ joint venture.

The applicant has to give justification as well as proof that the new venture will not hurt the interests of the existing collaborators/ partners. "Proof" is usually given by obtaining a resolution form the Board of Directors of the current / former collaborator that they have no objection to the proposed investment/ arrangement. Hence an applicant in who had a had a previous venture, however long ago, and even if terminated legally or by mutual consent, would have to go through the same process.

Legal Entity

Doing business in India by a foreign investor can involve several possible types of legal entity:

- a branch
- a liaison / representative office
- an Indian company with varying levels of foreign shareholding

Branch Office

Branch status was normally permitted only for banks, airlines, shipping companies and companies carrying out contracts in India. The RBI may permit branch status for carrying out the following activities:

- export/import of goods
- rendering professional or consultancy services.
- carrying out research work, in which the parent company is engaged.
- promoting technical or financial collaborations between Indian companies and parent or overseas group company.
- representing the parent company in India and acting as buying/selling agent in India.
- rendering services in information technology and development of software in India.
- rendering technical support to the products supplied by parent/group companies.
- foreign airline/shipping company.

In practice this is not an option usually used for any substantial level of activity, except in service industries as above. A branch is also taxed at a higher rate of income tax compared to an Indian company, assuming it earns income.

Liaison / Representative Office

A liaison or representative office is a non- commercial office mainly for studying economic and market trends, disseminating information on overseas products of the parent, searching for Indian partners, etc. No commercial activity, not even giving quotations or making invoices should be undertaken and the expenses of the office (salaries, etc.) should be met by remittances from abroad. This status is used in the early days of the pre-investment period, before an Indian company is established. Permission from the RBI is needed for this status and is usually routinely given in 30-45 days.

A branch or a liaison office is bound by all the laws of India. In practice the branch is different from an Indian company in that it has to comply with fewer rules of the Companies' Act, and, without the permission of the RBI, there are restrictions on its business activities and its acquisition of immoveable property in India. The branch must file its annual accounts with the Registrar of Companies (ROC) and register themselves with the ROC within 30 days of start up. A branch or liaison office can, through its contractual or other actions, bind the overseas company including claims against the overseas assets and its liability is not restricted to the assets held in India.

Indian Company

The usual form of business entity is through establishing an Indian company. This is a company limited by shares (mainly equity shares, with a right to participate in profits, and to the extent of which the liability of shareholders is limited). A limited company is registered and regulated under the Companies' Act, 1956, as amended from time to time. A comprehensive amendment is about to be introduced in the near future. The Companies' Act is a central legislation administered by the Ministry of Law, Justice and Company Affairs. An Indian company is very similar to a company in the U.S.A. or the U.K.

There are two types of company: private limited and public limited, distinguished by several factors such as capital, turnover, maximum number of shareholders, restrictions on rights to transfer shares, restriction on obtaining funds from the public etc. The distinction between the two is in certain areas such as documents to be filed with the ROC and capital raising and other formalities. It should be noted that "public" does not imply that the shares have to be compulsorily listed on a stock exchange. All laws and tax rates are applied uniformly to all companies, regardless of the percentage of foreign ownership. It should be remembered that generally the limited company structure restricts the liability of the members to the share capital. However, there have been cases where foreign majority companies' parents have been sued for acts of the subsidiary, and the courts have permitted the so-called corporate veil to be pierced.

In any type of company, shareholders' rights are governed by the Companies' Act, 1956, and there are two types of resolution - ordinary and special - that must be passed at shareholders' meetings.

Ordinary resolutions are passed by a simple majority of the members present and voting (including proxies) and special resolutions need to be passed by a three- fourths majority.

Some resolutions (such as those for inter- corporate investment in excess of specified limits, or changing main objects of business) have to be approved by the Government and some resolutions have also to be approved by the High Court (merger, amalgamation, etc.)

Examples of matters requiring ordinary resolutions are:

- adopting the annual accounts
- declaration of dividends
- appointing directors in place of retiring directors

Matters requiring special resolutions include:

- altering the provisions of the Memorandum of Association (the basic charter of the company) with respect to the main objects of the company or the location of the registered office
- altering the Articles of Association (the internal rules governing the company, shareholders and directors)
- reduction of share capital
- commencing a new business or disposing off an existing business

In practice a company can be controlled effectively with 51% of the shares, and comprehensively with 75% of the shares. Many foreign companies operate with 40% and above.

The Board of Directors is appointed by the shareholders and may do the acts and carry out the activities that the company is authorized to do.

The Board cannot, however, exercise any power which, either by the Companies' Act or by the Memorandum or Articles of Association of the Company, is required to be exercised by the company in general meeting. The Board of Directors may include foreign citizens, but permission of the Government and of the Reserve Bank (for receiving salary from which they are to make remittances overseas) is required.

Company Formation

The formation of a company requires submission of various documents to the ROC of the State in which the company is to be incorporated. The main documents to be submitted are:

- Application for name of company (one month before the other documents)
- Memorandum of Association
- Articles of Association
- Directors consent to act as such
- Notice of situation of registered office

The ROC will, after scrutiny of the documents, issue a certificate of incorporation.

If the company is a public company, it must then file a prospectus or statement in lieu of prospectus. Thereafter the ROC will issue a certificate to commence business, after which business activity may commence. In case the company uses names of overseas collaborators, the ROC will require a letter of no objection from the parent company to the use of the name in the Indian subsidiary.

Once a company is formed and its bank account opened, the foreign investor can remit in foreign exchange its share of capital from abroad, in accordance with the "automatic" or FIPB approval.

Dividends on capital are payable in foreign exchange. Similarly, the capital and profits thereon in case of sale of the whole or any part of the foreign holding can be remitted overseas in foreign exchange, after payment of Indian taxes.

However prior permission of the RBI is required for selling these shares. Royalty and technical service fees are also payable in foreign exchange (subject to Indian taxes), though they may be paid net of taxes (taxes being borne by the Indian company) if the collaboration agreement so provides.

FOREIGN LABOR TRENDS REPORT: INDIA 2006

KEY LABOR INDICATORS INDIA 2006

	Indicator	2005	2006	% Change
1.	Per capita GDP, current prices (US$)[2]	3,100	3,400	9.7
2.	Consumer prices (inflation rate, est.) (%)	4.2	4.6	9.5
3.	GDP generated in agriculture (%)	23.6	20.6	-12.7
4.	—, in industry (%)	28.4	28.1	-1.1
5.	—, in services (est. %)	48.0	51.3	6.4
6.	Population, total (millions, est.)	1.080	1.095	1.4
7.	— by major ethnic groups (%) (2000 est.)			
	Indo-Aryan	72	72	0.0
	Dravidian	25	25	0.0
	Mongoloid and others	3	3	0.0
8.	—, in major urban areas (%)[3]	28	28	0.0
9.	Population beneath the poverty level (est. %)	25	25	0.0
10.	Birth rate (per thousand population)	22.23	22.01	-1.0
11.	Life expectancy at birth, total (year)	64.35	64.71	1.0
12.	—, male	63.57	63.90	0.6
13.	—, female	65.16	65.57	0.6
14.	Adult literacy rate (%)	59.5	64.8	8.9
15.	Labor force, civilian, total (millions, est.)	482.2	496.4	2.9
16.	—, agriculture (%)	60	60	0.0
17.	—, industry (%)	17	17	0.0
18.	—, services (%)	23	23	0.0
19.	—, in the informal economy (%)	93	n/a	~
20.	Employment, civilian, total (millions)	200418.6	n/a	~
21.	—, in industry (%)	11.7	n/a	~
22.	—, in special economic zones (est.%)	0.1	n/a	~
23.	—, in agriculture (%)	7.2	n/a	~
24.	—, in services (%)	81.0	n/a	~
25.	—, in government (%)	n/a	n/a	~
26.	Unemployment rate (2004 & 2005 est.%)	20059.2	9.9	7.6

Contd...

	Indicator	2005	2006	% Change
27.	Underemployment rate (%)	n/a	n/a	~
28.	Level of unionization of workforce (2003 est. %)	7	n/a	~
29.	Labor productivity, manufacturing (2003 & 2004 est.%)	6.0	7.4	23.3

n/a = not available

Exchange rate: US$ = 45.01 rupees (April 2006); 44.101 rupees (2005) 45.8692 rupees (2004)

Please Note: The labor force figure relates to the formal sector in India - defined by law - it does not include all industries. Authentic figures for all industries are not available and the Government provides figures only for the formal sector - as defined by it. Informal economy includes the booming software industry and other services not included in the formal sector.

8

Major Developments in Industrial Sector

GOVERNMENT

The Government is a federal republic made up of three branches at the federal level: the Executive Branch, consisting of the President (Chief of State), the Prime Minister (Head of Government), and the Council of Ministers (Cabinet); the Legislative Branch, which has a bicameral Parliament, consisting of a lower house (Lok Sabha) with 545 members and an upper house (Rajya Sabha) with no more than 245 members; and the Judicial Branch, which is independent.

At the state level, each of India's 28 states and 7 union territories has its own state assembly, council of ministers, and court system.

In 2004, India held national parliamentary elections that resulted in a change of government. A United Progressive Alliance (UPA) government led by the Congress Party under Prime Minister Dr. Manmohan Singh took office in May 2004 replacing the Bharatiya Janata Party (BJP) led National Democratic Alliance (NDA) government.

The BJP is now the main opposition party, with 131 seats. A group of regional and communist parties does not belong formally to the UPA but supports the UPA government from the outside.

The UPA depends on the cooperation of these outside parties to maintain its control of Parliament, a situation that has sometimes produced tension between Congress and its allies, particularly over economic and labor policies.

ECONOMY

India's economy encompasses traditional village farming, modern agriculture, handicrafts, a wide range of modern industries, and a multitude of support services. The agricultural sector employs the largest percentage of the workforce, although it generates only 20.6 percent of GDP. Major crops include wheat, rice, coarse grains, oilseeds, cotton, jute, and tea. Major industrial products include textiles, processed food, steel, machinery, transportation equipment, cement, aluminum, fertilizers, mining, petroleum, chemicals, and computer software. India is capitalizing on its large numbers of well-educated people skilled in the English language to become a major exporter of software services and workers.

India's impressive growth rate is largely attributable to increased agricultural production, robust merchandise exports, a booming stock market, and the steady pace of reforms. The Government would like to increase the growth rate, but most economists believe it will not be possible without further structural reforms. Wages and benefits kept pace with inflation.

WORKFORCE

In 2006, there are an estimated 496.4 million workers in the Indian economy. Only seven percent of the work force is in the formal, organized sector. Growth in this sector remains sluggish. Employer organizations attribute this to the presence of labor laws that restrict downsizing. To circumvent such laws, private sector companies continue hiring workers on a contract basis. The informal sector, where the workforce generally does not enjoy legal protection, has witnessed more growth. Official statistics put the unemployment rate at 9.9 percent, but unofficial estimates suggest it could be as high as 20 percent.

HIV/AIDS in the Workplace

According to the National AIDS Control Organization (NACO), a government agency under the Ministry of Health and Family Welfare, nearly 90 percent of the 5.13 million Indians currently estimated to be infected with HIV/AIDS are in the 15-49 age group, the prime of their working years. HIV/AIDS has a negative impact on individual workers and their families as well as on the economy as a whole. NACO and the

International Labor Organization (ILO) [with funding from USDOL], in conjunction with industrial, workers' and employers' organizations, are collaborating to respond to the problem of HIV/AIDS in the workplace, using the ILO Code of Practice on HIV/AIDS as a guideline.

The code includes the following: recognition of HIV/AIDS as a workplace issue, non-discrimination, gender equality, social dialogue, no screening of HIV/AIDS at the workplace, confidentiality, continuing the employment relationship, prevention, and care and support.

The Steel Authority of India, the Employees State Insurance Scheme, and Indian Railways are among the organizations and associations that NACO has worked with to implement HIV/AIDS programs in the workplace. In addition, the Confederation of Indian Industries (CII) founded an "Indian business trust" to combat HIV/AIDS in the workplace and has begun programs in its 22 branches across India. The Lawyers' Collective, an NGO, has successfully defended workers who lost their jobs due to their HIV/AIDS status.

DESCRIPTION OF THE LABOR SCENE

The central and state governments share jurisdiction over labor issues. Both may enact legislation concerning the following: trade unions, industrial and labor disputes; social security, insurance, employment, and unemployment; and welfare of labor, including conditions of work, provident funds, pensions, and maternity benefits. Only the central government may enact legislation concerning regulation of safety in mines and oil fields, industrial disputes concerning central government employees, and central government agencies and institutions for vocational training.

The Ministry of Labor, a Cabinet-level ministry, is the lead central governmental agency on labor issues. The Ministry is headquartered in New Delhi and has subsidiary offices throughout the country. The Main Secretariat of the Ministry consists of eight divisions: social security, emigration, industrial relations, child and women labor, labor welfare, economics and statistics, international labor affairs, and labor conference. Each state government also has a labor ministry that may implement labor laws within its jurisdiction.

The Labor Bureau, created in 1946 as part of the Ministry of Labor, is responsible for the collection, collation, and publication of statistics and related information on wages, earnings, productivity, absenteeism, labor turn-over, industrial relations, and working and living conditions. It also tracks important economic indicators like the Consumer Price Index, data concerning industrial, agricultural and rural laborers; wage rate indices; and data on industrial relations and socio-economic conditions in the organized and unorganized sectors of industry.

In April 2000, USDOL signed a Memorandum of Understanding with the Indian Ministry of Labor to provide technical assistance in five areas: the elimination of child labor, prevention of HIV/AIDS in the workplace, improvement in mines safety, provision of decent employment for women, and labor market information systems. A subsequent agreement between the two governments resulted in the INDUS project, a U.S.-India partnership to eliminate hazardous and exploitative child labor, towards which each government has contributed 20 million dollars. The project is focused on removing children from 10 specific industries in India: bidi cigarettes, brassware, bricks, fireworks, footwear, bangles, locks, matches, quarried stones and silk. Thus far, the joint project has enrolled more than 71,000 child laborers and at-risk youths in education and training programs. The only area of the MOU without a funded technical assistance program is labor market information systems. This was originally due to U.S. sanctions after India's 1998 nuclear tests, but now reflects a lack of resources.

Employers

The Council of Indian Employers (CIE) is a confederation of three smaller employer organizations: the All India Organisation of Employers (AIOE), the Employers' Federation of India (EFI), and the Standing Conference of Public Enterprises (SCOPE). The CIE is not registered under any Act of the Government, but AIOE, EFI, and SCOPE are all registered as individual organizations. Total membership in AIOE and EFI consists of 80 regional associations of employers or chambers of commerce and 322 public and private companies. SCOPE covers 240 public sector undertakings (PSUs).

The CIE's primary objective is to interact with the government in formulating labor, economic, and social welfare policies that concern workers and employers. It also aims for increased cooperation between employers' and workers' organizations and holds regular meetings with the trade union centrals to accomplish this. The CIE is represented on almost all Government Advisory Boards, is affiliated with the International Organization of Employers, and represents India at the ILO.

Employers in some industries have taken steps to combat child labor. The Carpet Export Promotion Council (CEPC), a quasi-governmental organization that receives funding from the Ministry of Textiles, has a membership of 2,500 exporters who subscribe to a code of conduct barring them from purchasing hand-knotted carpets knowingly produced with child labor. The CEPC conducts inspections to insure compliance and allows members to voluntarily use a government-originated label to signify adherence to a code of conduct. However, the CEPC has stated that even with its programs, it is impossible to ensure that a carpet has been produced without child labor, given the difficulties of monitoring a decentralized and geographically dispersed industry. A private sector research and consulting firm conducts the inspections, which cover only 10 percent of registered looms. The inspectors have had difficulty locating unregistered looms.

Trade Unions

Approximately 496.4 million persons constitute India's active work force. Approximately seven percent of these workers are employed in the formal, or organized, sector. The rest are overwhelmingly agricultural workers, and to a lesser extent, urban non-industrial workers. While some trade unions represent agricultural and informal sector workers, the majority of India's estimated 13-15 million union members are part of the formal sector.

Of these 13 to 15 million unionized workers, some 80 percent are members of unions affiliated with one of the five major trade union centrals. These include the Bharatiya Mazdoor Sangh, Indian National Trade Union Congress, Center of Indian Trade Unions, Hind Mazdoor Sabha, and the All India Trade

Union Congress. By U.S. standards, all of these major trade union centrals are "politicized," i.e., they are either directly linked or ideologically associated with a political party. However, since many Indians now view party identification as detrimental to trade union interests, all centrals stress their independence and in some cases are attempting to reduce or sever previously tight party control.

Total membership in unions affiliated with the national centrals has remained essentially static in the face of an annual growth in the work force of seven to eight million. Union members account for approximately two percent of the overall work force. Unions remain concentrated in the public sector, and although labor leaders have tried, they have been unable to organize workers in the new Indian and foreign companies in the private sector. Although a few significant examples exist, independent unions are not a major factor.

All five major trade union centrals participate in ILO activities. In addition, local unions participate in ILO programs such as Organizing in the Informal Sector, Campaigns on Eradication of Child Labor, Tripartite Response on Discrimination at the Workplace on HIV, and Promotion of the Core Labor Standards in Enterprises.

Regional Reviews

Industrial and employment growth in the northern region of India has been sluggish, due primarily to the absence of reforms in the agricultural sector. Infrastructure shortfalls and concerns regarding effective governance have kept investment low in the region, particularly in Uttar Pradesh, India's most populous state. The Delhi state government has relaxed working conditions for women in the IT sector by permitting them to work night shifts. Punjab and Haryana have subsequently adopted the same measure.

Barring Assam, where there is public sector investment in the oil sector, state governments continue to be the biggest employers throughout the northeast region.

West Bengal has continued its ongoing process of selling government-owned assets by privatizing 16 ailing public sector units. The West Bengal State Government estimates that children make up 3.1 percent of the state's total workforce, with about 11 percent, or 1.2 million, of the children in the 5-14 age group. With the help of UNICEF, the Government has developed an Action Plan to address the problem. In West Bengal and elsewhere in the region, children continue to be employed in brick making, "bidi" (tobacco) binding, and agricultural labor. In the urban areas, they are employed as domestic workers, in shops and offices, in the large informal service sector (tea stalls, wayside restaurants and kiosks), or in hazardous jobs such as scavenging and rag picking. The U.S. is giving financial support to leading NGOs such as Child-in-Need Institute (CINI), Asha, and Tiljala Shed to provide these children with preparatory coaching and to enroll child laborers and potential child laborers in school. All states in the region have strict laws banning the use of child labor, but enforcement remains poor.

The Center of Indian Trade Unions (CITU) — the trade union wing of the Communist Party of India (Marxist) — has been subdued in recent years, as West Bengal Chief Minister Buddhadeb Bhattacharjee has discouraged "aggressive unionism" to create an industry-friendly atmosphere. Although CITU membership has increased in West Bengal, CITU noted a 10 percent decline in its Calcutta membership.

The South Indian states have experienced a generally peaceful labor situation with no major prolonged strikes in any sector. Home to leftist parties and trade unions, Kerala, the smallest southern state, experienced several general strikes in 2005. Although courts have declared general strikes to be illegal, activists have sometimes paralyzed economic activity by organizing work stoppages under other names.

Regional state governments have initiated some significant labor reform measures. In Tamil Nadu, Karnataka and Kerala, state governments have implemented provisions allowing women to work night shifts, particularly in the IT industry. In Andhra Pradesh and Tamil Nadu, new provisions allow industries to hire contract labor even in core areas for temporary periods to meet market demand.

Although achievement of this goal seems unrealistic, the international community, particularly the ILO, is supporting the efforts of the southern states to end all child labor by 2007, in hopes that this will set an example for other states. As part of their programs to combat child labor, the southern states are increasing education programs for working children, particularly those in the informal sector.

The Tamil Nadu Government hopes to eradicate child labor in non-hazardous employment by 2007. It prepared an Action Plan, established a state authority on the eradication of child labor headed by the Chief Secretary, is reviewing proposals submitted by district collectors, and has allotted $333,332 (Rs. 15 million) in funds.

Tamil Nadu has created an additional Commissioner position in its Labor Department to head a Child Labor Monitoring Cell. It also has organized a Child Labor Monitoring System Workshop in collaboration with the ILO, demonstrated a web-based monitoring system, and observed an "Anti Child Labor Day." The state is also considering an incentive scheme to encourage village-level administrators to establish child-labor-free areas, and it introduced a state award for the district collector who operates the best program for the rescue and rehabilitation of child laborers. The Women's Development Corporation also formed about 1,000 self-help groups for mothers of child laborers.

The Government of Maharashtra has established a new labor policy for the IT industries which permits 24-hour-a-day operations, forbids the closure of units employing up to 1,000 workers without prior government permission, and allows self-certified reports of compliance with labor laws.

LABOR LAWS AND SYSTEM

India is a founding member of the ILO and has ratified a total of 39 ILO Conventions. Of the eight core ILO Conventions, India has ratified four: the Conventions on Forced Labor (No. 29), Equal Remuneration (No. 100), Abolition of Forced Labor (No. 105), and Discrimination (Employment and Occupation) (No. 111). India has not ratified the remaining four core conventions on Freedom of Association and Protection of the Right to Organize (No. 87), Right to Organize and Collective Bargaining (No. 98), Minimum Age (No. 138), and Worst Forms of Child Labor (No. 182).

Industrial Disputes Act: The Industrial Disputes Act (1947) regulates reductions in force (RIF) and plant closures. It requires state approval 90 days before large firms (more than 100 employees) lay off employees. Likewise, no plant employing more than 100 employees can shut down without obtaining approval 90 days before the closure date. Laws also prohibit firms from employing contract laborers for extended periods of time without extending permanent employment.

Labor Law Reforms: Many observers believe that India's labor laws are antiquated and in need of reform. The second National Labor Commission (NLC), established by the government in September 1999, submitted its report in June 2002.

It recommended reviews of Indian labor laws and the social security system and the strengthening of governmental programs to eradicate child labor. Although the NLC recommendations are not binding on the government, the Ministry of Labor has begun consulting various social partners on their possible implementation. Unlike the previous NDA government, the UPA has not made labor law reform a top priority. Considering the lack of consensus within and outside the government to reform, most observers do not expect large-scale changes to existing labor legislation.

LABOR STANDARDS AND WORKER RIGHTS

The Right to Association

The Constitution provides for the right of association, and the Government generally respects this right in practice. Workers may establish and join unions of their own choosing without prior authorization.

In practice, legal protections of worker rights are effective only for the organized industrial sector. Outside the modern industrial sector, laws are difficult to enforce. The authorities generally prosecute and punish those persons responsible for intimidation or suppression of legitimate trade union activities when the victims are members of nationally organized unions. Unaffiliated unions are not able, in all instances, to secure for themselves the protections and rights provided by law.

The Trade Union Act prohibits discrimination against union members and organizers, and employers are penalized if they discriminate against employees engaged in union activities.

The Right to Organize and Bargain Collectively

The law provides for the right to organize and bargain collectively. Collective bargaining is the normal method used to set wages and settle disputes in unionized plants in the organized industrial sector. Trade unions vigorously defend workers' interests in this process. Although a system of specialized labor courts adjudicates labor disputes, there are long delays and a backlog of unresolved cases. When the parties are unable to agree on equitable wages, the Government may establish boards of union, management, and government representatives to determine wages. The legislation makes a clear distinction between civil servants and other workers. Public service employees have very limited organizing and collective bargaining rights.

Trade unions often exercise the right to strike, but public sector unions are required to give at least 14 days notice prior to striking. Some states have laws requiring workers in certain nonpublic sector industries to give notice of a planned strike.

The Essential Services Maintenance Act allows the Government to ban strikes in government-owned enterprises and requires conciliation or arbitration in specified essential industries; however, essential services never have been defined in law. Legal mechanisms exist for challenging the assertion that a given dispute falls within the scope of this Act. The Act thus is subject to varying interpretations from state to state. State and local authorities occasionally use their power to declare strikes illegal and force adjudication. The Industrial Disputes Act prohibits retribution by employers against employees involved in legal strike actions, and this prohibition is observed in practice.

The Supreme Court has upheld a Kerala High Court verdict that all general strikes are illegal and protest organizers are liable for losses caused by shutdowns. The verdict is drawing attention to the difference between a complete closedown of all activities and a general strike. While it is likely that the ruling was aimed at discouraging political strikes, unions have stated that it remains a potential threat to their activities. Other court rulings have also declared such strikes illegal and made striking workers pay damages to consumers and the public who suffered due to the strikes. In August 2004, the Supreme Court declared all strikes by government employees illegal; however, in practice this has not been enforced.

Prohibition of Forced or Compulsory Labor

The Bonded Labor System (Abolition) Act (1976) prohibits all bonded labor by adults and children; however, such practices remain widespread primarily among the agricultural and rural unorganized workforce. Offenders may be sentenced up to three years in prison, but prosecutions are rare. Enforcement of this statute, which is the responsibility of state and local governments, varies from state to state and often is not effective due to inadequate resources and societal acceptance of bonded or forced labor. On the occasions when inspectors have referred violations for prosecution, long court backlogs and inadequate funding for legal counsel have frequently resulted in acquittals.

The Government does not publish official statistics on bonded labor, but it claims to have identified, rescued and rehabilitated about 266,000 bonded laborers since the advent of the Act. Many NGOs, however, claim that these numbers do not reflect the actual magnitude of the problem. They estimate that there are 20 to 65 million bonded laborers in the country, including a large number of children. According to a Government report, more than 85 percent of bonded laborers belong to scheduled castes and scheduled tribes.

Female bondage, forced prostitution, and trafficking in women and children for the purpose of prostitution are widespread problems. According to press reports from 2004, *Devadasis*, defined as prepubescent girls given to a Hindu deity or temple as "servants of God," were taken from their families and required to "work" for priests and high caste Hindus.

Status of Child Labor Practices and Minimum Age for Employment

The Government prohibits forced and bonded child labor; however, this prohibition is not effectively enforced, and forced child labor continues to be a problem. The law prohibits the exploitation of children in the workplace. However, National Human Rights Commission (NHRC) officials have admitted that implementation of existing child labor laws is inadequate, that administrators are not vigilant, that children are particularly vulnerable to exploitation, and that the Commission is focusing on the adequacy of existing legislation.

There is no overall minimum age for employment. However, work by children under 14 years of age is barred completely in "hazardous industries," which include passenger goods and mail transport by railway, and in factories and mines. Work in some other hazardous industries, as defined by the Child Labor Act of 1986, is regulated. Such industries include glass, brassware, locks and carpet weaving, among others. The NDA government has resolved to end child labor in hazardous industries by the year 2007, and the UPA government is working towards that goal. In occupations and processes in which child labor is permitted, work by children is permissible only for 6 hours between 8 a.m. and 7 p.m., with one day's rest weekly and two hours of education provided by the employer.

Estimates of the number of child laborers varies widely. The 2001 national census puts the number of child workers at 12.7 million. However, the ILO has estimated the number at 44 million and Global March Against Child Labor, an NGO, claims there are 60 million.

The Government has submitted their commitment to eliminate all forms of child labor starting with hazardous occupations. This is identified under the Child Labor (Prohibition and Regulation) Act, 1986. The Government notes that their scheme of intervention was extended in 2004 from 100 to 250 districts, across 21 states. Over 320,000 working children have been mainstreamed into the formal education system in approximately 4,000 special schools for child workers. The government plans to increase these special schools to about 10,000, providing funds to voluntary organizations and non-governmental organizations. The Government also plans to combine various poverty alleviation and income generation programs to raise income levels of families of working children.

Through the Child Labor (Prohibition and Regulation) Act, 1986, the Government convicted 1,799 offending employers in 2001-02, 325 in 2002-03 and 3,910 in 2003-04. Most, if not all of the 87 million children not in school did housework, worked on family farms alongside their parents as paid agricultural workers, or worked as domestic servants. In 2000, the Government issued a notification prohibiting government employees from hiring children as domestic help. However, this did not prevent non-government employees from hiring children as domestic help.

The working conditions of domestic servants and children in the workplace often amount to bonded labor. Children are often sent away to work because their parents cannot afford to feed them or in order to pay off a debt incurred by a parent or relative. There is evidence that child labor is used to produce hand-knotted carpets, gemstone polishing, leather goods, sari weaving, beadwork and sporting goods. In addition, there is reasonable basis to believe that industries such as brassware, explosive fireworks, hand-blown glass bangles, hand-broken quarried stones, hand-spun silk thread and cloth and hand-made bricks among others exposed children to particularly hazardous conditions.

The Government does not provide free, compulsory, and universal primary education. Government statistics from 2003 claim that 165 million of the 200 million children between the ages 6-14 attend school. However, UNICEF has reported that approximately 120 million of the primary school-age population of approximately 203 million attended school. The Government launched its ambitious universal elementary education program — Sarva Shiksha Abhiyan — in 2000. The program aims to provide elementary education to all children in the age group 6-14 by the year 2010.

The enforcement of child labor laws is the responsibility of the state governments; however, enforcement is inadequate and uneven among states, especially in the informal sector in which most children are employed. The continuing prevalence of child labor is attributable to social acceptance of the practice, the failure of the state and federal governments to make primary school education compulsory, ineffective state and federal government enforcement of existing laws, and economic hardships faced by families. In addition, over-worked and ill-trained local magistrates have many competing responsibilities, many of which receive greater priority and attention than child labor enforcement.

The INDUS project — jointly funded by the U.S. Department of Labor and the Government and implemented by the ILO — is designed to complement the National Child Labor Program and States programs. It hopes to remove 80,000 children from hazardous work situations in 21 districts of the country by September 2007.

The Government also cooperates with UNICEF, the United Nations Educational, Scientific and Cultural Organization (UNESCO), the United Nations Development Program (UNDP), and the ILO in their efforts to eliminate child labor. The Government participates in the ILO's International Program on the Elimination of Child Labor (IPEC). Approximately 145,000 children have been removed from work and received education and stipends through IPEC programs since they began in the country in 1992. The NHRC, continuing its own child labor agenda, has organized NGO programs to provide special schooling, rehabilitation, and family income supplements for children in the glass industry in Firozabad. In addition, employers in some industries have taken steps to combat child labor.

Acceptable Conditions of Work

Occupational safety and health (OSH) remains a problem area in India. Extensive legislation covering various aspects of OSH notwithstanding, industrial accidents continue to occur frequently due to lack of proper enforcement. The chemical sector is the most prone to accidents. The lack of awareness regarding occupational health has resulted in many deaths throughout the country. OSH in the state-controlled mining industries is of significant concern. The USDOL has funded an approximately US$ 1.5 million project to improve safety standards in selected public sector mines and to provide training to mine inspectors. The project has improved working conditions in five selected pilot mines and drastically reduced accident rates. In addition, the project has helped the Indian Directorate General of Mines Safety establish for the first time a computerized mine inspection system that significantly reduces the time needed by mine inspectors to inspect a mine.

The Factories Act (1948) mandates an 8-hour workday and 48-hour workweek, as well as minimum working conditions.

Workers are to be paid twice their regular wage rate for working overtime. State government laws set minimum wages, hours of work, and safety and health standards. These standards are generally enforced and accepted in the modern industrial sector, but are not observed in less economically stable industries. However, the large number of industries covered by a small number of factory inspectors and the inspectors' limited training and prevalence of bribery result in lax enforcement.

Minimum wages vary according to the state and sector of industry. Such wages are inadequate to provide a decent standard of living for a worker and his/her family. Most workers employed in units subject to the Factories Act receive more than the minimum wage, including mandated bonuses and other benefits. The state governments set a separate minimum wage for agricultural workers but do not enforce it effectively. Some industries, such as apparel and footwear, do not have a prescribed minimum wage in any of the states in which they operate.

Safety conditions are better in the Special Economic Zones (SEZs) than in the manufacturing sector. Legal foreign workers (but not illegal foreign workers) are protected under the law. The law does not provide workers the right to remove themselves from work situations that endanger health and safety without jeopardizing their continued employment.

Discrimination in Employment

The Constitution prohibits discrimination on the basis of a person's race, sex, religion, place of birth, or social status. Government authorities work to enforce these provisions with varying degrees of success. Despite laws designed to prevent discrimination, social and cultural practices as well as other legislation have a profound discriminatory impact, and discrimination against women, persons with disabilities, indigenous people, homosexuals, and national, racial, and ethnic minorities is a problem. The traditional caste system, as well as differences of ethnicity, religion, and language, deeply divide the society.

Women: The participation of women in the formal labor force is much lower than that of males (33 percent vs. 67 percent). The rate of promotion of women to managerial positions within businesses often is slower than that of males. The Equal Remuneration Act of 1976 mandates that men and women performing the same job receive the same payment; however, enforcement is often weak, especially in rural areas where traditions encouraging discrimination against females are deeply rooted. In both rural and urban areas, women are paid less than men are for the same job. Women experience economic discrimination in access to employment and credit, which acts as an impediment to women owning businesses. In a positive development, state-supported microcredit programs for women have begun to have an impact in many rural districts.

Sexual harassment is common, with a vast majority of cases unreported to authorities. In June 2004, the National Commission for Women (NCW) and the Press Institute of India jointly released a report that found that a majority of women experienced gender discrimination at their workplaces. Often, attempts by women to report harassment have resulted in further problems or dismissal. In 2004, the Supreme Court determined that a victim of sexual harassment could be awarded compensation based on the findings of an internal departmental report or investigation of the case.

Dalits, Scheduled Castes, and Scheduled Tribes: The Constitution and the 1955 Civil Rights Act outlaw the practice of untouchability, which discriminates against Dalits (formerly called "untouchables") and other people defined as Scheduled Castes. According to the 2001 census, scheduled castes, including Dalits, make up 16 percent of the country's population, and scheduled tribes (members of indigenous groups outside the caste system) comprise 8 percent of the population. Despite longstanding efforts by the Government to eliminate the discriminatory aspects of caste, discrimination based on the caste system still occurs throughout the country.

The Government uses a system of "reservations," similar to affirmative action programs in the U.S., in an attempt to decrease employment-based discrimination towards these scheduled castes and scheduled tribes. The Anti-Untouchability Act of 1955 and the Prevention of Atrocities Act of 1989 give further protection; however, Dalits are often relegated to the most menial of jobs. Employment discrimination against Dalits is widespread in rural areas; many rural Dalits work as agricultural laborers for upper caste landowners without remuneration. The majority of bonded laborers are Dalits. Those who attempt to change the status quo regularly face violence. Low caste Hindus who converted to Christianity lost their eligibility for affirmative action programs. Some states reserved government jobs for Muslims of low caste descent.

Persons with Disabilities: Although the Persons with Disabilities Act provides equal rights to all persons with disabilities, advocacy organizations admit that its practical effects have so far been minimal, in part due to a clause that makes the implementation of programs dependent on the "economic capacity" of the Government. Widespread discrimination occurs against persons with physical and mental disabilities in employment, education, and in access to health care.

SOCIAL SAFETY NET

India lacks a comprehensive social security system. In the informal sector, which employs the vast majority (93 percent) of Indian workers, there is no social security protection for unemployed or retired workers.

The Employees' State Insurance Corporation (ESIC) provides social protection to workers (and their dependents) in the organized sector in case of sickness, maternity, and death or disablement due to an employment injury or occupational hazard. In most states, employees in the following classes of establishments are eligible for coverage: non-seasonal factories using power and employing 10 or more persons; non-seasonal and non-power using factories, shops, hotels, restaurants, cinemas, preview theatres, motor transport undertakings and newspaper establishments employing 20 or more persons.

Employees covered under the scheme are entitled to medical facilities for themselves and their dependents, as well as cash benefits in the event of specified contingencies resulting in loss of wages or earning capacity. Insured women are entitled to maternity benefits to cover the period of confinement. When an employment injury causes the death of an insured employee, the dependents are entitled to a family pension.

The ESI Scheme is financed by contributions from covered employees and their employers. The State Governments bear one-eighth of the share of expenditure on medical benefits within the per capita ceiling of Rs. 600 ($14) per year and all additional costs beyond the ceiling. Employee contributions are tied to a fixed percentage of the workers' wages, but benefits are provided according to individual needs regardless of employee contributions.

FOREIGN INVESTMENT POTENTIAL

Tariffs and poor infrastructure present the biggest obstacles to foreign investment and growth, but India's infrastructure requirements also present trade and investment opportunities for American companies. Although the average level of Indian tariffs has declined significantly since the early 1990s, India's economy remains among the most protected in the world. India's average non-agricultural tariff is about 22 percent, compared to the 11 percent median for other emerging markets, according to the World Bank. India controls foreign investment with limits on equity and voting rights, mandatory government approvals, and capital controls. Although the Government has gradually relaxed some of these constraints, foreign direct investment is still prohibited in some sectors or sub-sectors.

The communist and socialist parties that support the UPA government oppose the privatization of state-owned companies and increasing foreign direct investment, and have blocked or slowed UPA attempts to relax restrictions in these areas. Other factors that inhibit an otherwise "business-friendly" environment include India's vast and still largely unreformed bureaucracy and various forms of social tension (some manifested violently) in a huge and extremely diverse population, much of which suffers from extreme poverty and the burdens of underdevelopment.

Sectoral Issues: Labor management relations have been calm in the government owned airlines, with pilots in both government run carriers — Air India (international) and Indian Airlines (domestic) — receiving pay and benefit increases. The Government initially planned to offer low equity participation to private partners, with restrictions on foreign investment, which would have deterred private partners from bidding for the national carriers. Now, the Government has changed its policy and is no longer planning to sell equity in the airlines.

The banking and insurance sectors are highly unionized and predominantly state owned.

Special Economic Zones: In 2000, the Government converted India's seven government-controlled Export Processing Zones to Special Economic Zones (SEZs), and the private sector set up an eighth SEZ. All SEZs must follow labor laws. While SEZ workers enjoy freedom of association and collective bargaining, trade union activity in the zones has been negligible. Entry into the SEZs ordinarily is limited to employees, and union organizers claim that such restrictions make it difficult for them to organize workers. In addition, unions have not vigorously pursued efforts to organize private-sector employees since SEZs were established. Women constitute the majority of the work force in the SEZs. The International Confederation of Free Trade Unions has reported that industries in the SEZs have compelled their workers to work overtime, often employed them on temporary contracts with fictitious contractors, and have threatened dismissal to those that complained about substandard working conditions.

9

Special Economic Zones in India

INTRODUCTION

India was one of the first in Asia to recognize the effectiveness of the Export Processing Zone (EPZ) model in promoting exports, with Asia's first EPZ set up in Kandla in 1965.

With a view to overcome the shortcomings experienced on account of the multiplicity of controls and clearances; absence of world-class infrastructure, and an unstable fiscal regime and with a view to attract larger foreign investments in India, the Special Economic Zones (SEZs) Policy was announced in April 2000.

This policy intended to make SEZs an engine for economic growth supported by quality infrastructure complemented by an attractive fiscal package, both at the Centre and the State level, with the minimum possible regulations.

SEZs in India functioned from 1.11.2000 to 09.02.2006 under the provisions of the Foreign Trade Policy and fiscal incentives were made effective through the provisions of relevant statutes.

To instill confidence in investors and signal the Government's commitment to a stable SEZ policy regime and with a view to impart stability to the SEZ regime thereby generating greater economic activity and employment through the establishment of SEZs, a comprehensive draft SEZ Bill prepared after extensive discussions with the stakeholders.

A number of meetings were held in various parts of the country both by the Minister for Commerce and Industry as well as senior officials for this purpose.

The Special Economic Zones Act, 2005, was passed by Parliament in May, 2005 which received Presidential assent on the 23rd of June, 2005.

The draft SEZ Rules were widely discussed and put on the website of the Department of Commerce offering suggestions/comments. Around 800 suggestions were received on the draft rules.

After extensive consultations, the SEZ Act, 2005, supported by SEZ Rules, came into effect on 10th February, 2006, providing for drastic simplification of procedures and for single window clearance on matters relating to central as well as state governments.

The main objectives of the SEZ Act are:

(*a*) generation of additional economic activity

(b) promotion of exports of goods and services;

(c) promotion of investment from domestic and foreign sources;

(d) creation of employment opportunities;

(e) development of infrastructure facilities;

It is expected that this will trigger a large flow of foreign and domestic investment in SEZs, in infrastructure and productive capacity, leading to generation of additional economic activity and creation of employment opportunities.

The SEZ Act 2005 envisages key role for the State Governments in Export Promotion and creation of related infrastructure. A Single Window SEZ approval mechanism has been provided through a 19 member inter-ministerial SEZ Board of Approval (BoA).

The applications duly recommended by the respective State Governments/UT Administration are considered by this BoA periodically. All decisions of the Board of approvals are with consensus.

The SEZ Rules provide for different minimum land requirement for different class of SEZs.

Every SEZ is divided into a processing area where alone the SEZ units would come up and the non-processing area where the supporting infrastructure is to be created. The SEZ Rules provide for :

- Simplified procedures for development, operation, and maintenance of the Special Economic Zones and for setting up units and conducting business in SEZs;
- Single window clearance for setting up of an SEZ;
- Single window clearance for setting up a unit in a Special Economic Zone;
- Single Window clearance on matters relating to Central as well as State Governments;
- Simplified compliance procedures and documentation with an emphasis on self certification

APPROVAL MECHANISM AND ADMINISTRATIVE SETUP OF SEZS

Approval Mechanism

The developer submits the proposal for establishment of SEZ to the concerned State Government.

The State Government has to forward the proposal with its recommendation within 45 days from the date of receipt of such proposal to the Board of Approval.

The applicant also has the option to submit the proposal directly to the Board of Approval.

The Board of Approval has been constituted by the Central Government in exercise of the powers conferred under the SEZ Act. All the decisions are taken in the Board of Approval by consensus.

The Board of Approval has 19 Members. Its constitution is as follows:

(1)	Secretary, Department of Commerce	Chairman
(2)	Member, CBEC	Member
(3)	Member, IT, CBDT	Member
(4)	Joint Secretary (Banking Division), Department of Economic Affairs, Ministry of Finance	
(5)	Joint Secretary (SEZ), Department of Commerce	Member
(6)	Joint Secretary, DIPP	Member
(7)	Joint Secretary, Ministry of Science and Technology	Member
(8)	Joint Secretary, Ministry of Small Scale Industries and Agro and Rural Industries	Member
(9)	Joint Secretary, Ministry of Home Affairs	Member
(10)	Joint Secretary, Ministry of Defence	Member
(11)	Joint Secretary, Ministry of Environment and Forests	Member
(12)	Joint Secretary, Ministry of Law and Justice	Member
(13)	Joint Secretary, Ministry of Overseas Indian Affairs	Member
(14)	Joint Secretary, Ministry of Urban Development	Member
(15)	A nominee of the State Government concerned	Member
(16)	Director General of Foreign Trade or his nominee	Member
(17)	Development Commissioner concerned	Member
(18)	A professor in the Indian Institute of Management or the Indian Institute of Foreign Trade	Member
(19)	Director or Deputy Sectary, Ministry of Commerce and Industry, Department of Commerce	Member Secretary

(b) Administrative set up

The functioning of the SEZs is governed by a three tier administrative set up. The Board of Approval is the apex body and is headed by the Secretary, Department of Commerce. The Approval Committee at the Zone level deals with approval of units in the SEZs and other related issues. Each Zone is headed by a Development Commissioner, who is ex-officio chairperson of the Approval Committee.

Once an SEZ has been approved by the Board of Approval and Central Government has notified the area of the SEZ, units are allowed to be set up in the SEZ. All the proposals for setting up of units in the SEZ are approved at the Zone level by the Approval Committee consisting of Development Commissioner, Customs Authorities and representatives of State Government. All post approval clearances including grant of importer-exporter code number, change in the name of the company or implementing agency, broad banding diversification, etc. are given at the Zone level by the Development Commissioner. The performance of the SEZ units are periodically monitored by the Approval Committee and units are liable for penal action under the provision of Foreign Trade (Development and Regulation) Act, in case of violation of the conditions of the approval.

Incentives and facilities offered to the SEZs

The incentives and facilities offered to the units in SEZs for attracting investments into the SEZs, including foreign investment include:-

- Duty free import/domestic procurement of goods for development, operation and maintenance of SEZ units
- 100% Income Tax exemption on export income for SEZ units under Section 10AA of the Income Tax Act for first 5 years, 50% for next 5 years thereafter and 50% of the ploughed back export profit for next 5 years.
- Exemption from minimum alternate tax under section 115JB of the Income Tax Act.
- External commercial borrowing by SEZ units upto US $ 500 million in a year without any maturity restriction through recognized banking channels.
- Exemption from Central Sales Tax.
- Exemption from Service Tax.
- Single window clearance for Central and State level approvals.

- Exemption from State sales tax and other levies as extended by the respective State Governments.

The major incentives and facilities available to SEZ developers include:-

- Exemption from customs/excise duties for development of SEZs for authorized operations approved by the BOA.
- Income Tax exemption on export income for a block of 10 years in 15 years under Section 80-IAB of the Income Tax Act.
- Exemption from minimum alternate tax under Section 115 JB of the Income Tax Act.
- Exemption from dividend distribution tax under Section 115O of the Income Tax Act.
- Exemption from Central Sales Tax (CST).
- Exemption from Service Tax (Section 7, 26 and Second Schedule of the SEZ Act).

SEZ Approval Status

Consequent upon the SEZ Rules coming into effect w.e.f. 10th February, 2006, Twenty-one meetings of the Board of Approvals have since been held. During these meetings, formal approval has been granted to 439 SEZ proposals. There are 138 valid in-principle approvals. Out of the 439 formal approvals, 195 SEZs have been notified.

Land requirements for approved Special Economic Zones:

The total land requirement for the formal approvals granted till date is approximately 59685 hectares out of which about 97 approvals are for State Industrial Development Corporations/ State Government Ventures which account for over 20000 hectares. In these cases, the land already available with the State Governments or SIDCs or with private companies has been utilized for setting up SEZ. The land for the 195 notified SEZs where operations have since commenced involved is approximately over 26072 hectares only.

Out of the total land area of 2973190 sq km in India, total agricultural land is of the order of 1620388 sq km (54.5%). It is interesting to note that out of this total land area, the land in possession of the 195 SEZs notified amounts to approximately over 260 sq km only. The formal approvals granted also works out to only around 596 sq km.

SEZs- leading to the growth of labour intensive manufacturing industry:

Out of the 439 formal approvals given till date, 150 approvals are for sector specific and multi product SEZs for manufacture of Textiles & Apparels, Leather Footwear, Automobile components, Engineering etc.. which would involve labour intensive manufacturing. SEZs are going to lead to creation of employment for large number of unemployed rural youth. Nokia and Flextronics electronics hardware SEZs in Sriperumbudur are already providing employment to 9645 and 2069 persons, majority of which are women.

Hyderabad Gems SEZ for Jewellery manufacturing in Hyderabad has already employed 2000 persons, out of which 1200 are women, majority of whom are from landless families, after providing training to them. They have a projected direct employment for about 30,000 persons. Apache SEZ being set up in Andhra Pradesh will employ 20, 000 persons to manufacture 10,00,000 pairs of shoes every month. Current employment in Apache SEZ is 4500 persons. Brandix Apparels, a Sri Lankan FDI project would provide employment to 60,000 workers over a period of 3 years. Even in the services sector, 12.5 million sq meters space is expected in the IT/ITES SEZs which as per the NASSCOM standards translates into 12.5 lakh jobs. It is, therefore, expected that establishment of SEZs would lead to fast growth of labour intensive manufacturing and services in the country.

Benefits Derived from SEZs

Benefit derived from SEZs is evident from the investment, employment, exports and infrastructural developments additionally generated. The benefits derived from multiplier effect of the investments and additional economic activity in the SEZs and the employment generated thus will far outweigh the tax exemptions and the losses on account of land acquisition. Stability in fiscal concession is absolutely essential to ensure credibility of Government intensions.

Exports from the functioning SEZs during the last three years are as under:

Year	Value (Rs. Crore)	Growth Rate (over previous year)
2003-2004	13,854	39%
2004-2005	18,314	32%
2005-2006	22 840	25%
2006-07	34,615	52%

Projected exports from all SEZs for 2007-08: Rs. 67088 crores

(b) Investment and employment in the SEZs set up prior to the SEZ Act, 2005:

At present, 1277 units are in operation in the SEZs. In the SEZs established prior to the Act coming into force, there are 998 units providing direct employment to over 1.83 lakh persons; about 40% of whom are women. Private investment by entrepreneurs in these SEZs established prior to the SEZ Act is of the order of over Rs. 7104 crore.

(c) Investment and employment in the SEZs notified under the SEZ Act 2005:

Current investment and employment:

- o Investment: Rs. 67347 crore
- o Employment: 61015 persons

Impact of the scheme

The overwhelming response to the SEZ scheme is evident from the flow of investment and creation of additional employment in the country. The SEZ scheme has generated tremendous response amongst the investors, both in India and abroad, which is evident from the list of Developers who have set up SEZs:

- Nokia SEZ in Tamil Nadu
- Quark City SEZ in Chandigarh
- Flextronics SEZ in Tamil Nadu
- Mahindra World City in Tamil Nadu
- Motorola, DELL and Foxconn
- Apache SEZ (Adidas Group) in Andhra Pradesh
- Divvy's Laboratories, Andhra Pradesh

- Rajiv Gandhi Technology Park, Chandigarh
- ETL Infrastructure IT SEZ, Chennai
- Hyderabad Gems Limited, Hyderabad

SPECIAL ECONOMIC ZONES: AN INDIAN PERSPECTIVE

As "SEZ" is a geographical region that has economic laws that are more liberal than a country's typical economic laws. An SEZ is a trade capacity development tool, with the goal to promote rapid economic growth by using tax and business incentives to attract foreign investment and technology. Today, there are approximately 3,000 SEZs operating in 120 countries, which account for over US$ 600 billion in exports and about 50 million jobs. By offering privileged terms, SEZs attract investment and foreign exchange, spur employment and boost the development of improved technologies and infrastructure.

There are 13 functional SEZs and about 61 SEZs, which have been approved and are under the process of establishment in India.

Most developing countries in the world have recognized the importance of facilitating international trade for the sustained growth of the economy and increased contribution to the GDP of the nation. As part of its continuing commitment to liberalization, the Government of India has also, since the last decade, adopted a multi-pronged approach to promote foreign investment in India. The Government of India has pushed ahead with second-generation reforms and has made several policy changes to achieve this objective.

The SEZ policy was first introduced in India in April 2000, as a part of the Export-Import ("EXIM") policy of India. Considering the need to enhance foreign investment and promote exports from the country and realizing the need that level playing field must be made available to the domestic enterprises and manufacturers to be competitive globally, the Government of India in April 2000 announced the introduction of Special Economic Zones policy in the country deemed to be foreign territory for the purposes of trade operations, duties and tariffs. To provide an internationally competitive and hassle free environment for exports, units were allowed be set up in SEZ for manufacture of goods and rendering of services. All the import/export operations of the SEZ units is on self-certification basis. The units in the Zone are required to be a net foreign exchange earner but they wouldl not be subjected to any pre-determined value addition or minimum export performance requirements. Sales in the Domestic Tariff Area by SEZ units is subject to payment of full Custom Duty and as per import policy in force. Further Offshore banking units are being allowed to be set up in the SEZs.

The policy provides for setting up of SEZ's in the public, private, joint sector or by State Governments. It is also being envisaged that some of the existing Export Processing Zones would be converted into Special Economic Zones.

Accordingly, the Government has converted Export Processing Zones located at Kandla and Surat (Gujarat), Cochin (Kerala), Santa Cruz (Mumbai-Maharashtra), Falta (West Bengal), Madras (Tamil Nadu), Visakhapatnam (Andhra Pradesh) and Noida (Uttar Pradesh) into a Special Economic Zones. In addition, 3 new Special Economic Zones were approved for establishment at Indore (Madhya Pradesh), Manikanchan – Salt Lake (Kolkata) and Jaipur and have already commenced operations.

India is one of the first countries in Asia to recognize the effectiveness of the Export Processing Zone (EPZ) model in promoting exports. Asia's first EPZ was set up in Kandla in 1965. With a view to create an environment for achieving rapid growth in exports, a Special Economic Zone policy was announced in the Export and Import (EXIM) Policy 2000. Under this policy , one of the main features is that the designated duty free enclave to be treated as foreign territory only for trade operations and duties and tariffs. No licence required for import. The manufacturing, trading or service activities are allowed.

To provide a stable economic environment for the promotion of Export-import of goods in a quick, efficient and hassle-free manner, Government of India enacted the SEZ Act, which received the assent of the President of India on June 23, 2005. The SEZ Act and the SEZ Rules, 2006 ("SEZ Rules") were notified on February 10, 2006. The SEZ Act is expected to give a big thrust to exports and consequently to the foreign direct investment ("FDI") inflows into India, and is considered to be one of the finest pieces of legislation that may well represent the future of the industrial development strategy in India. The new law is aimed at encouraging public-private partnership to develop world-class infrastructure and attract private investment (domestic and foreign), boosting economic growth, exports and employment.

The Ministry of Commerce and Industry lays down the regulations that govern the setting up and administering of the SEZs. The Central Government isfunctioning, while the State Governments play a significant lead role in the development of SEZs in their respective States by stipulating the conditions to be adhered to by an SEZ and granting the necessary approvals. The policy framework for SEZs has been enacted in the SEZ Act and the supporting procedures are laid down in SEZ Rules.

The Special Economic Zone Act 2005 came into force with effect from 10th February 2006, with SEZs Rules legally vetted and approved for notification. The SEZs Rules, inter-alia, provide for drastic simplification of procedures and for single window clearance on matters relating to central as well as state governments.

Investment of the order of Rs.100, 000 crores over the next 3 years with an employment potential of over 5 lakh is expected from the new SEZs apart from indirect employment during the construction period of the SEZs. Heavy investments are expected in sectors like IT, Pharma, Bio-technology, Textiles, Petro-chemicals, Auto-components, etc. The SEZ Rules provides the simplification of procedures for development, operation, and maintenance of the Special Economic Zones and for setting up and conducting business in SEZs. This includes simplified compliance procedures and documentation with an emphasis on self-certification; single window clearance for setting up of an SEZ, setting up a unit in SEZs and clearance on matters relating to Central as well as State Governments; no requirement for providing bank guarantees; contract manufacturing for foreign principals with option to obtain sub-contracting permission at the initial approval stage; and Import-Export of all items through personal baggage.

With a view to augmenting infrastructure facilities for export production it has been decided to permit the setting up of Special Economic Zones (SEZs) in the public, private, joint sector or by the State Governments. The minimum size of the Special Economic Zone shall not be less than 1000 hectares. Minimum area requirement shall, however, not be applicable to product specific and port/airport based SEZ. This measure is expected to promote self-contained areas supported by world-class infrastructure oriented towards export production. Any private/public/joint sector or State Government or its agencies can set up Special Economic Zone (SEZ).

This paper explores the Indian policy framework for an SEZ, it further discusses the various incentives available to an SEZ and an SEZ Unit, and the recent legal and regulatory developments pertaining to SEZs in India.

ADMINISTRATIVE SET UP FOR SEZS:

SEZs is governed by a three tier administrative set up

a) The Board of Approval is the apex body in the Department,

b) The Unit Approval Committee at the Zonal level dealing with approval of units in the SEZs and other related issues, and

c) Each Zone is headed by a Development Commissioner, who also heads the Unit Approval Committee.

APPROVAL MECHANISM OF SEZS

Any proposal for setting up of SEZ in the Private/Joint/ State Sector is routed through the concerned State government who in turn forwards the same to the Department of Commerce with its recommendations for consideration of the Board of Approval. On the other hand, any proposals for setting up of units in the SEZ are approved at the Zonal level by the Approval Committee consisting of Development Commissioner, Customs Authorities and representatives of State Government.

Approval given for Setting up new SEZs in Private/Joint/ State Sector

Approvals have so far been given for setting up of 117 new Special Economic Zones (including 3 Free Trade Warehousing Zones) spread over 15 States and 2 Union Territories in the Private/Joint Sector or by the State Governments and its agencies. Of the 117 SEZs approved for establishment, 7 SEZs have already become operational, 6 SEZs are now getting ready for operation and the other are at various stages of implementation.

Indian Textile Industry: A Fact Sheet

In the post-quota regime, the Indian textile industry is poised to become a major player in the US $395 billion global textile and clothing market. With the global retailing industry exploring opportunities for outsourcing, Indian exports are expected to surge from the current levels of $14 billion to $50 billion by 2010. ICFDC.com presents an analysis of the sector, the key drivers and the opportunities for Indian players.

India is fast emerging as a key player in the $395 billion global textiles and clothing market. Clothing accounts for roughly 60 per cent of the market while textiles constitute the balance 40 per cent. The dismantling of the quota regime has brought the entire market at an interesting stage with players like China and India beginning to make their presence felt. On 1 Jaunary 2005, the WTO Agreement on Textiles and Clothing (ATC) came into operation replacing the earlier Multi-Fibre Agreement (MFA). The phasing out of the MFA is expected to trigger exponential growth for global textile trade.

Currently the US imports nearly 85 per cent of its clothing needs while the EU imports 60-70 per cent. In 2004, the US imported $76 billion of textiles from across the world. China at $18.2 billion was the frontrunner in meeting this demand with a 24 per cent share of the market, a little less than the total share of Mexico, India, Canada and Indonesia. In the first quarter of 2005, India's textile exports to the US has risen by an estimated 22 per cent.A key driver of global textile trade is low cost sourcing of textiles and clothing. Global retailing industry is exploring opportunities for outsourcing to deal with pricing pressures. As a result outsourcing budgets of retail giants like Wal-Mart, JC Penny, Tommy Hilfiger, Marks and Spencer, K-Mart and Tesco are on the rise. China is expected to get a bulk of the advantage due to its economies of scale and superior infrastructure. India too will be a major beneficiary, thanks largely to its low cost labour, its skilled manpower and the fact that it is a low cost sourcing base for cotton. What's more, the anti-surge initiatives launched against Chinese exports will benefit the Indian industry and experts believe that India could emerge as the second largest textile outsourcing hub. Indian exports are estimated to grow from the current levels of $14 billion to $50 billion by 2010. And its share of the global textile trade is expected to double from 3.5 per cent currently over the next five years.

Textile Sector in the Post-MFA Regime

	2004	2010 (estimated)
Global Textile Trade	$395 billion	$600 billion
China's Exports	$97 billion	$220 billion
India's exports	$14 billion	$50 billion

The key advantages of the Indian industry are:

- India is the third largest producer of cotton with the largest area under cotton cultivation in the world. It has an edge in low cost cotton sourcing compared to other countries.
- Average wage rates in India are 50-60 per cent lower than that in developed countries, thus enabling India to benefit from global outsourcing trends in labour intensive businesses such as garments and home textiles.
- Design and fashion capabilities are key strengths that will enable Indian players to strengthen their relationships with global retailers and score over their Chinese competitors.
- Production facilities are available across the textile value chain, from spinning to garments manufacturing. The industry is investing in technology and increasing its capacities which should prove a major asset in the years to come.
- Large Indian players such as Arvind Mills, Welspun India, Alok Industries and Raymonds have established themselves as 'quality producers' in the global market. This recognition would further enable India to leverage its position among global retailers.
- India has gathered experience in terms of working with global brands and this should benefit Indian vendors.

GOVERNMENT POLICY

Recognising the immense potential of the textile industry to spur economic growth and drive exports, the Indian government has taken initiatives to encourage investment and enhance global competitiveness of the sector. In the recent Budget reforms the textile sector has been given some major concessions. Prominently, the government has removed the disparity in excise duty structures between organised and unorganised sector. Reduction of custom duty on textile machinery, polyester, viscose, and garment making machinery further acted as an impetus to the industry. The excise duty on polyester has also been reduced from 24 per cent to 16 per cent, which has brought the duty structure in line with ASEAN countries, providing filament yarn processors with optional excise duty of nil or 8 per cent excise duty with cenvat credit.

Challenges for Indian Companies

While Indian exports to the US has risen 22 per cent in the first quarter of 2005, profits are sliding as prices have dropped 8-20 per cent and the industry is on the verge of a shakeout. With importers preferring suppliers that have 'vertical' production systems rather than dispersed production facilities, Indian exporters need to shore up their mass production techniques. Of the 1,500 Indian exporters only 15 have turnovers of $50 million-plus. Infrastructure development is the need of the hour. Power and water contribute to nearly 37 per cent of total production costs. In contrast, in China, this cost comprises just 24 per cent. India also has to deal with inefficient port handling facilities.

Labour laws also comprise a stumbling block in the growth of Indian textile companies. Political considerations have prevented successive governments from instituting an exit policy. As a result, manufacturers cannot employ short duration labour as they cannot lay them off when the global trade cycle turns. Low labour productivity is also another constraint.

On the technology front, the Technology Upgradation Fund Scheme has been instituted by the government in an effort to encourage manufacturers to go in for enhanced technology. The grant during the current fiscal has been enhanced to nearly two-and-a-half times the amount that was granted the year before. But this does not get utilised in the appropriate manner as the technology imported is obsolete and virtually no new technology is developed indigenously.

While China is clearly the leading exporter in the world of textiles and clothing, China and India are not direct competitors. While China mainly uses man-made fibre and serves mass markets, India essentially produces natural fibre and caters to niche markets. India is now the No. 1 producer of man-made fibre, thanks to Reliance Industries, but is only No. 3 in cotton. A garment-driven and export-led strategy is expected to help the Indian industry to grow to a $85 billion industry by 2010, according to a CRISIL report. The focus should be on moving up the value chain instead of exporting intermediate stage products, say industry analysts.

The investments needed to make the Indian industry a dominant player in the global textile market is estimated to range between $15 and $30 billion. Increase in foreign direct investment will benefit the industry but this is largely dependent on the reforms process.

Growth Segments for Indian Players

The domestic market is expected to boom with demand for high value branded items and household items showing a sharp increase. Not surprisingly, yarn manufacturers are shifting away from exports and focusing on domestic markets. The industry is ready to utilise high quality yarn in the domestic market, which was earlier meant exclusively for exports.

The global home textiles market, estimated at US $ 70 billion offers tremendous opportunities for Indian players. The US and EU imports nearly $30 billion worth of home textiles. The US market is growing at 5 per cent per year while the EU market is growing at an estimated rate of 9-10 per cent. Japan, Australia, New Zealand are also large consumers of home textiles. McKinsey estimates that the global trade in home textiles will grow from $8.6 billion to $23 billion in 2010. India's presence in the US home textile market is growing. India is the largest supplier of terry towels, bed linen and second largest vendor of cotton made-ups to the US markets. China, Pakistan, Bangladesh and Vietnam are major competitors for India in this segment. In the post-quota regime, India's share of US imports has grown (between January and August 2004) for sheets (20%) terry towels (21%), pillowcases (19%) and total made-ups (11%).

While China is slated to be the biggest beneficiary in terms of market share in US apparel imports, India and Pakistan are expected to benefit substantially as well. China's share in total US apparel imports is 16 per cent compared to India's 3.5 per cent. In cotton apparel imports, China's share is 10 per cent while India's is 5 per cent, in wool apparel, the shares are 9 per cent for Chinese products and 6 per cent for Indian. In man-made fibre apparel, China's share is 15 per cent compared to India's 2 per cent.

Another segment in which India is a strong player is the embroidery market. The Indian market for embroidery is valued at Rs 7.5 billion and is growing at 18 per cent per year. This is a highly fragmented market with the organised sector constituting 40 per cent of the industry. Demand for embroidery is on the rise and export to countries like the US, UK, Africa, Middle East offers a huge market for embroidery products.

Key Indian Players:

- Welspun India is Asia's largest terry towel manufacturer and fourth largest in the world. It supplies to leading global retailers, meeting 15 per cent of Wal-Mart's terry towel requirements, 85 per cent of Tom Hilfiger's and 100 per cent of Shopko's. It has plans to double its terry towelling capacity to 23830 TPA, enhance yarn capacity by 25000 spindles and introduce bed linen with a 35 million metres capacity and has earmarked a Rs 6 billion budget for its expansion plans.
- Alok Industries has the largest processing capacity in India and offers fully integrated facilities for yarn texturising, weaving, knitting, processing, made-ups and garments. It has initiated plans to expand capacities across all segments by investing Rs 10 billion. It is focusing on home textiles and garments, which will contribute to nearly 50 per cent of its revenues by 2007. It has already got an impressive client list that includes brandnames such as JC Penney, Tommy Hilfiger, TARGET, Wal-Mart and international buying houses

such as Britannica Home Fashions, Elite Home Products, etc.

- Arvind Mills boasts of a wide product range in value added fabric, from fabric to garments in denim, shirting and knits. It is a supplier to brands such as GAP, Marks & Spencer, Levis, Tommy Hilfiger and Nike and is upgrading its garment capacities to 14.3 million pieces per annum. Arvind Mills dominates the.Indian denim market with a 72 per cent share of the estimated 80 million metres denim market.

Future Outlook

The future prospects for the Indian industry are bright, particularly in the post-quota regime. The industry is in an expansion mode and is likely to benefit from growing demand both in the domestic as well as global markets. Further, the anti-surge mechanism which the WTO has imposed on Chinese exports is expected to benefit India. Turkey is the first country to set quotas on textile and apparel imports from China. The EU is also in the process of adopting measures to avoid surge in imports from China. China has announced exports tarriff on textile and clothing with effect from January 2005 that will last until 2007 as measures to avoid penal duties. Even though these tarriffs are nominal, it will increase export prices and curb demand for low priced Chinese goods in world markets. This should enable Indian industry to offer competitive products to global markets and increase its share in US and EU markets.

BUILDING ECONOMIC STRENGTH SHOULD BE OUR TOP PRIORITY

Innovation can make India a Super Power

Knowledge is the new currency of international trade and commerce. Neo-classical economic theory attributed growth in output to increase in the factors of production, namely, labour and capital. The new paradigm is that the economic power, increasingly seen as the basis of new political clout, arises out of a strong technology muscle of the nation.

A nation's advantage in trade no longer flows merely out of its natural endowments, e g, raw materials, labour, capital and land. Over-whelming empirical evidence shows that the per capita economic growth of the industrialised countries has been driven by innovation resulting in technological progress, and not by aggregate capital investment per se. Recent experience of nations shows that the contribution of raw materials, and in many cases of labour, has steadily declined in providing the competitive edge to the products.

This is perhaps best exemplified in micro-processor technology where the raw material content has steadily fallen to an insignificant proportion of its price. The big strides of the Asian 'tigers' is not because of their natural resources. Malaysia's prosperity is no longer based on tin and rubber. Countries rich in natural resources, on the other hand, for example oil producing countries of Middle East, are not great economic powers. Technology supremacy is the key to success. Increasingly, the contribution comes from value addition through technology. While the market for capital is becoming freer with nearly $400 billion moving across the globe every day, technology is highly guarded and hardly ever transferred.

A dramatic example of how nations compete on their technological edge is given by the well-established Swiss watch industry . The base of their technical excellence was rendered obsolete virtually overnight with the advent of the electronic quartz watches. The precision of the quartz watches could not be met by that of the best mechanical watches. They were also cheaper to produce. The irony in this case is that the concept of new technology of quartz watch had emanated from Switzerland itself!. They were unable to identify its potential. Many Swiss watchmaking companies were forced out of market. Faced with technological threat, several ailing companies of this industry got together and subsequently used technology as a competitive weapon. The new firm, ETA, created "Swatch". The revolutionary product design was backed by an unconventional manufacturing and assembly process. They resorted to new technologies such as the micro-injection of plastic under pressure, the use of polymethylemetracrylate to obtain an extremely resistant glass, a new technique for welding the glass and case together to make the watch totally water-proof, etc.

We will witness similar examples in a number of our industries. The traditional sports goods industry in Jalandhar, for example, faces threat as new materials and manufacturing processes lead to improved quality at lower costs. The tennis racket industry in Sialkot has faced extinction with the advent of carbon fibres and vastly improved production engineering.

A large number of industries, particularly the Small and Medium Enterprises (SMEs) in the country face growing technological obsolescence. Punjab, for example, has the the highest intensity of SMEs in the country – some 2,00,000. Their technological upgradation is not even on the state government,s agenda. Regional R&D institutes, once at par with world standards, have run down in quality. They have become simply irrelevant to industry. In agriculture, too, productivity has plateaued at levels 30-50 per cent below world standards. Indian industry is far too dependent on imported technology. Even very large companies which enjoyed market dominance and economies of scale in the protective, truly 'Swadeshi', days, did not upgrade their products. When they need even marginal improvements on earlier technologies, they fall back on import of further knowhow. The position has hardly changed. They are happy to walk on the crutches of foreign technology.

There is a certain degree of inevitability in the change process relating to technology. Four broad phases of economic development can be identified : Phase I witnesses gradual liberalisation to integrate the country's insulated economy with that of the world's. This phase is marked by hesitation and advocacy of protectionism from certain sectors of industry in the name of giving more time to 'adjust'.

While many forge ahead to take advantage of emerging technologies to meet with global competition, some seek protection behind high fences of tariffs. In India there are repeated calls again of 'level playing field' 'Swadeshi', and now 'calibrated globalisation'. Clearly, economic liberalisation is not an unmitigated advantage. This phase witnesses extensive restructuring take-overs and mergers and selective privatisation. 50 years after independence, we are still in Phase I.

Phase II is marked by accelerating changes and institution building. The emphasis is on generating knowledge and creating manpower skills. The emphasis is away from import substitution and on developing technology which is contemporary.

In Phase III economy is fully liberalised, high growth rates are witnessed and the country becomes a global player.

Phase IV is marked by sustained generation and creating wealth and exploiting new knowledge.

The need for indigenous technology development at the national level and in our companies is going to be a greatly pressing one. Much of the impact of recent changes on technology is actually not visible. How?

Firstly, liberalisation has led to low tariff walls, freer imports and liberal foreign direct investment regime. Companies abroad, therefore, now prefer to export finished goods to India rather than transfer technology to manufacture them locally.

Secondly, it is lot easier now to manufacture by setting up companies with majority foreign equity holding, often 100%. Rather than give the know-how to partners, technology will come 'sealed' in 100% equity companies. This has been witnessed in a number of sectors.

Thirdly, as India grows competitive and as the industrial muscle grows, we shall increasingly be perceived as a threat. We have witnessed growing restrictions on export of products and technologies to India. This is just the beginning. Its full implications have not been grasped.

The new technological order leaves India with no choice but to create and improve on technologies. There is no other way to survive in an environment where commodity prices decline and factors of production, such as labour and raw materials, face a rapidly reducing advantage. It is no surprise that nations invest heavily in their R&D. The distribution of global R&D is highly concentrated in the developed economies. About two-thirds of the world-wide R&D efforts are found within the Triad of the US, Japan and Western Europe. The Third World, by the most generous estimates, accounts for only about 5% of global R&D and it is declining, especially in the heavily indebted countries. Only in the "four tigers" (South Korea, Taiwan, Singapore, Hongkong) and also in China and some other East Asian countries is there a rapid rise of R&D. Their R&D expenditures have been growing rapidly. Taiwan and Singapore now have a level of R&D intensity comparable to that of many european countries.

There is a new urgency to technology development by the Indian industry. It is time our Chief Executives in industry, Research Laboratories and the Government took charge of the cycle that embraces improving design competence through innovation and invention, right to the point of commercialising. New products are not created at a single point. They follow the well-recognised process of (A) basic research when no applicable technology is right (B) Developmental work where possible end use is visible (C) Proto-typing and testing. Commercial feasibility at this stage is not clear. (D) Full scale installation of new process. Technological risks are minimum. (E) Commercial launch. Business risks dominate. The driving force in technology is desire to excel.

Mere market forces do not supply the motivation. Technology development does not evolve by itself. It is not a natural law. It has to be willed. Societies everywhere have shown that technological achievements are driven by strong social economic and political commitments. When the Egyptians built pyramids, they created the tallest structures : 400,000 people employed for 20 years moving 4 million tonnes of sandstone. That was the state-of-art technology then. They created the tallest structures in the world.

They remained unchallenged for next 4000 years, even though the knowledge and skills existed to surpass them, till the new masts and skyscrapers, cathedrals and Eiffel Tower came. That happened not because the technology was simply waiting to be converted into structures. Materials were available, joining techniques were known. The real feat of Eiffel Tower is that there was a will to do it. When the societies lose will, when industries lose interest, technology development declines. There is no such thing as a technology base from which developments spring up on their own.

When the US pride was hurt by launch of the 'Sputnik' by the Soviet Union in 1956, it took them 10 years and as many workers as the Egyptians did for Pyramids to put man on the moon in 1968. In both cases, the accomplishments grew out of a 'will to do'. Where is our will?

Let us, therefore, put technology on our agendas and make it an area of concern. We have to reward engineering knowledge-making sure it is no less remunerative than marketing or finance. Design and manufacturers must find a preference with our youth. The excitement with chartered accountancy and commercial courses must be matched with that of science and technology. We have to change salary structures in our companies to help improve the contribution of technology in industry.

All changes require champions. The freedom movement needed a Gandhi. But great ideas also require their singers and poets to carry the message, to enthuse people. The freedom movement also needed a Tagore. The message of technology has to spread.

India's might will, in the end, come from its economic strength. A nuclear test here and there, even build-up of an arsenal and a delivery system cannot bring India the stature and its rightful role in the world affairs. It has to be backed by a strong industrial base. It is essential that we pursue science which is contemporary, not second rate, and develop technology which answers the social and economic needs of the country. To change this into reality, we need champions.

We need them to carry the message across, enthuse people with technology and make them believe that not only it is within our reach but that, without it, we are not going to be able to have our voice heard. Technology cannot stay a neglected agenda much longer.

An Economically Strong India can Dictate Terms

INDIA of the next century should be an economically strong nation, with the quality of life of all its people comparable to the one in the developed societies.

How can we quantify 'quality of life'? The United Nations has a methodology to quantify the quality of life of the people of a country in terms of what they call the Human Development Index (HDI), and they base this on per capita GDP, literacy rate and life expectancy at birth. The UN Human Development Report, 1995, ranked India, with an HDI of 0.439, at the 134th position in the world.

It has been our feeling for many years now that better measures of HDI in a developing country are per capita electricity consumption and female literacy, and both need to be raised substantially for India to be rated as a "developed" country in the world community. The per capita electricity consumption in India should go up by a factor of at least 8 to 10 for this to be achieved.

Electrical energy is an essential ingredient of social development and economic growth. Argentina and Brazil had per capita electricity consumption figures of 1636 and 1547 kv per year, respectively, in 1992. Thus, to be able to reach even a reasonable level of development the Indian per capita electricity consumption should be about 1500 kv per year. It may be noted that the corresponding world average figure even now is 2400 kv per year which is higher than the modest target indicated here. For achieving this target by the year 2020, and assuming that the Indian population will level off beyond this year, we will need to have an installed electrical generation capacity of about 450 GWe by the year 2020. Making slightly different sets of assumptions, one may have somewhat different projections, but the basic point sought to be established through this assertion does not get altered. Having an installed capacity of 450 GWe by the year 2020 and beyond, is surely a desirable objective.

Our annual rate of growth of GDP during the past few years has been about 5.5 per cent. An analysis of past trend indicates that for each one per cent rise in GDP the per capita electricity consumption has to increase by about 1.25 per cent. This, in turn, implies that even to sustain the current rate of growth of the Indian economy, with the existing rate of population growth, it is necessary to have a rate of growth of installed electrical capacity of at least about eight per cent per annum.

Let us now consider the requirements for working out an optimum mix of energy resources needed to achieve the aforementioned desirable objective. Remembering that we are still talking about reaching a less than optimum goal, we should consider only our currently known economically exploitable resources and technologies which are available to us today. Based on available information we can assume that the total renewable and hydro potential available in India, economically convertible to electrical energy through established technologies, amounts to 104 GWe. Let us also assume that this maximum potential can be reached by the year 2020. We have already done an exercise to assess the potential growth of nuclear power up to the year 2020 and came to a conclusion that by the year 2020 it should be possible to reach an installed capacity of 20 GWe using nuclear energy, at the currently envisaged rate of growth, which averages to about 12 per cent of nuclear generation capacity addition per year during the forthcoming 22 years. The balance of about 320 GWe required in the year 2020 will need to be, therefore, provided by using fossil fuel based thermal power stations. Essentially it amounts to a growth of thermal based electricity generation capacity at the rate of about seven per cent per year up to the year 2020. With our meagre reserves of oil and natural gas, and expected rise in the cost of their import in the years to come, we can also assume that by the year 2020 practically all the thermal power stations will be based on coal.

With an installed capacity of 320 GWe, the annual consumption of the Indian coal used for power generation purposes would be such that our currently estimated economically mineable reserve of coal available for power generation purposes, would be fully consumed a couple of decades before the end of the next century. Surely, there is a possibility of using advanced technologies in future for exploiting the remaining, currently not economically mineable, reserves of coal. We may also probably locate some additional reserves of coal. Even if it is so, one must take into account increasing concern about global warming due to CO_2 emission, the need for conserving coal as a basic industrial raw material in steel and other such industries, and the increasing utility of coal to serve as a source of generating fluid fuels for transport application. For India, with a heavy dependence on oil imports draining its economy and making it potentially vulnerable to external pressures, the last factor has to be given a serious consideration in a short term time frame itself. With these economic as well as strategic considerations, it does not seem to be wise to contemplate a continued growth in the use of coal for power generation in India after we reach a level of about 450 GWe installed capacity. If this objective is met by 2020 then during the post-2020 era, the installed capacity in coal- fired stations should progressively get depleted as the older stations are taken out of service.

With the renewable and hydro having reached maximum potential in the year 2020, the deficit arising out of the progressive retirement of coal-fired stations will need to be made up by other sources of energy. There is no other choice other than nuclear energy.

This will require the nuclear power generation capacity to continue increasing beyond 20 GWe from 2020 AD onwards. With some additional renewable resources becoming economically exploitable, technological advances leading to increased efficiency in energy conversion processes becoming available, and adoption of energy conservation measures, some part of the burden on nuclear energy may get reduced, but the bulk of the future requirements will still need to be borne by nuclear energy. Unforeseen commercial development of new sources of energy including fusion, which is another form of nuclear energy, along with the aforementioned other possible developments may lead to a better prospect of reaching beyond the modest goal without reducing our dependence on fission-based nuclear energy.

It must be remembered that we are not discussing whether the target is realistically achievable or not at the currently envisaged rate of growth of nuclear energy. We are at a crucial juncture today, and our decisions and actions today will determine the feasibility or otherwise of achieving the desired objectives in time.

Generation of electricity through application of nuclear energy has been our main priority so far. We must, however, also plan for the scenario when the indigenous reserves of fossil fluid fuels will get depleted and their import will become unaffordable for our economy. This situation may manifest in the early decades of the next century. Conversion of low-grade coal reserves to fluid fuels, and extraction of low quality petroleum reserves requires high temperature steam. Most of the potential hydrogen generating processes also demand heat at high temperature. Nuclear energy seems to be the only viable means to provide such process heat in a medium to long term time frame. Thus, apart from its application for electricity generation purposes, India also requires nuclear energy for meeting its long term non-electricity application needs.

To summarise, it can be stated that while we must exploit the renewable and hydro-potential to the fullest in the quickest possible time, and we should utilise our fossil fuel resources to achieve an accelerated economic growth in the short term; it is only nuclear energy which can provide us the essential long term energy security.

In view of the foregoing, the R&D challenges in nuclear technology have been and are directed towards providing the required energy services for the Indian population while avoiding any unacceptable environmental impacts. These challenges have been defined considering the indigenous nuclear fuel resources. India has a modest reserve of uranium and a large reserve of thorium. Most of the other nations in the world, who are advanced in nuclear technology, have access to sufficiently large quantities of uranium reserves. Hence, the technologies required for exploitation of thorium have a much higher priority for India than that accorded in most of these other nations. Therefore, the R&D challenges involved in pursuing the thorium path, have to be necessarily met head-on by the Indian R&D teams without much benefit from the knowledge base available elsewhere.

This perception was the basis of planning an indigenous nuclear energy programme in India way back in the mid-fifties by our policy-makers. The indigenous R&D has led to our developing self sufficiency in all the important technological areas important for our current programmes. It has also led to creation of an R&D infrastructure which can take up, and has been taking up, any challenges for the future development of next generation nuclear energy production systems, undeterred by the technology control regimes sought to be imposed on us.

Uranium-235 is the only naturally occurring fissile isotope constituting about 0.7 per cent of natural uranium. The balance mostly comprises uranium-238, a 'fertile' material which gets partially transmuted to fissile plutonium-239 on absorbing neutrons during operation of a nuclear reactor. Thus, during the operation of a nuclear reactor, while the original fissile material gets converted to fission fragments and energy, the fertile inventory gets partially converted to transmuted fissile materials. Progressively, on account of the neutron absorbing character of most of the fission fragments, the capability of the fuel to generate additional energy reduces and the fuel has to be discharged. There are two ways of dealing with this spent fuel.

The first one, termed 'open cycle', consists of treating the entire spent fuel inventory as waste and dispose it as such. This has been the approach being followed by several advanced nations of the world. With this approach, for a uranium fuelled reactor, along with the fission waste products, the plutonium content in the spent fuel, and the balance uranium-238 which constitutes almost 98 per cent of the spent fuel is also disposed. In other words, with this approach only about two per cent of the energy potentially exploitable from nuclear fuel is utilised.

To avoid this colossal waste, a closed fuel cycle has to be pursued. It is possible to remove the plutonium and uranium-238 from the spent fuel in a reprocessing stage and use these two valuable nuclear materials once again in a recycling mode. Thorium is a fertile material which cannot be used as a fresh fuel alone. However, like uranium-238, thorium also gets partially converted to a fissile material uranium-233 when used as a part of nuclear fuel mix. Thus, utilisation of thorium is possible only if a closed nuclear fuel cycle is adopted.

Right from the inception of the Indian nuclear power programme, the Indian strategy has been to reach closed nuclear fuel cycle stage based on utilisation of plutonium and thorium based fuels in a planned manner at the earliest.

On the basis of the above mentioned strategy, three phases of Indian nuclear power programme have been identified. In the first phase, natural uranium dioxide based fuel is used in heavy water moderated and cooled Pressurised Heavy Water Reactors. The indigenous resources can support about 10,000 MWe of installed capacity through use of PHWRs without plutonium recycling. In a subsequent stage, the fissile plutonium contained in the spent fuel of the PHWR is separated in fuel reprocessing plants. This plutonium serves as the main fissile element for fuelling the Fast Breeder Reactors (FBRs), with plutonium-uranium mixed fuel and fertile depleted uranium and thorium in blanket regions, where plutonium can be efficiently used to not only generate power but also to convert non-fissile uranium-238 and thorium to fissile plutonium-239 and uranium-233 respectively.

Using FBRs an energy output of 350 GWe can technically be sustained using indigenously available fuel resources. In parallel, as a part of the second stage of Indian nuclear programme, it has been planned to use thorium based fuel along with a small feed of plutonium based fuel in Advanced Heavy Water Reactors (AHWRs).

The AHWR would help in reaching the stage of large-scale thorium utilisation sufficiently early. In the third stage, dedicated breeder reactors based on uranium-233 and thorium are planned to be constructed. These reactors would serve as the main stay of the final, thorium utilisation stage, of the Indian nuclear programme. The currently known Indian thorium reserves amount to more than 200,000 GWe-year of electrical energy and can easily meet the Indian requirements during the next century and beyond.

10

Global Competitiveness of Indian Industries: Strategies and Innovation

INTRODUCTION

Time and again, corporate, big and Small, have been perplexed by the very definition of innovation, and there is no dearth of business gurus. Corporate honchos, scholars speaking on this subject of importance. Rather than offering yet another definition to this already confused space, I would try to substantiate with success stories from innovation leader. Let me start with the latest red hot offering by Microsoft Inc windows XP Media center PCTM. This is what I would truly call can innovation, but would you call box from the same company an innovation? May be not workman TM from Sony inc. Was an innovation at that point in time from Apple inc today's innovation, but would the hundreds of " me-too " products that come a these years n between , quality for innovation ? May be not so what is / are the lament(s) in a product or process or strategy, that makes a few truly innovative and others "me -too"

SYSTEMIC PROCESS OF INNOVATION

The name of game is to convert concept in to reality it is not creativity it's not event immolation, but it is the rare ability to make a product see the light of the day and eventually make success out of it. The process discussed is generic one exact steps may vary from company to company depending upon the product life-cycle, market trends, skill-sets availability and the degree of novelty amongst others.

The process that innovation goes through is discussed along with the elements, which will fall into place. Indian Business has been undergoing, liberalization process since July-1991. In order to survive in the cut - throat competitive age of zest century, Indian business units and houses have to face local as well as global competitions proof. Dhaval Mehta has rightly coined a new term "Global Competition "in respect.

Liberalization aims at freeing business, trade and industry from the clutches of control Entire world has been converted onto global village.

The term "Business" implies "Global Business "and nothing else survival and developments of Indian business depend on its ability to compete with other Indian firms and multinationals. Ability to maintain high quālity and maximize productivity determines the competitive ability pf Indian firms competitive advantage ultimately depends on quality and commitment of human resources Innovation implies something new, something different and something better.

Shift from labor management to personnel management was an innovation. Similarly, shift from PM to Human Resource Management was also an innovative practice. How current shift from Human Resource Management (HRM) to Human Capital Management (HCM) is also an entirely new and innovative HR Practice Recent concept of Human Resource Management (HRM) implies following innovative HR practices in the field of HRM.

Innovative Strategy for Indian Business for the Future

The elements in the outer ring as well as in the inner ring of chakravyuha require immediate attention and creative insight of business men. Businessmen should try to adopt themselves at the earliest face the battle.

Quality

As reported by CEOs of Japanese firm's quality is not something which should be provided separately in a product or service. It should become part and parcel of complete business process. Quality is an important weapon in the firm's armory to face the competition. Quality, however, should not exploit consumers through undue price rise.

Innovation

Sustained innovation coupled with nourishment of factors is the road to glorious success. Innovation should be continuous in nature so that fresh air enters the organization. Innovation, to be successful, should start at the lowest levels and in microscopic dimensions. It is necessary to face the cut-throat competition and to lower the capital out pure Ratio.

Customer - Commitment

Customer case should be assured. If innovation and quality are given by other firms, customers may switch towards their product. A satisfied customer is our best canvasser is an ever lasting principle.

Change Acceptance

Indian businessman should anticipate the change, bring forth the change, conceptualize the change, design the change and lastly, equip for the change enough case should be taken in the sense that change could not be forced or imposed form above it should involve from within. Change is change it is not turbulence. This positive will make Indian businessmen strategically stronger, powerful and competitive at global level.

Globalization

Globalization is not a problem, it is an approach to stay ahead, and Globalization may not be only in terms of products or services. It should be in terms of global financial markets and management styles, too.

Marketing Innovation

It is now common knowledge that the era of anything sold is well on its way out consumers have become more discerning and demanding. We are seeing the demonstration effect at work, with our people getting greater exposure to international trends and demanding that the very best be made available here at terms acceptable to them. The challenge before the marketer, therefore, is to innovate on a continuous basis in every aspect of its offering viz. the product, the packaging, the distribution, the advertisements, the promotion teal. The idea of creativity for sheer survival is an idea whose time has come simple as it may seem, interesting ideas in marketing have emerged simply by asking the right questions. Few also use a well known technique of high utility and simplicity called as the combination technique.

There is, in the words of Edward De Bono. A need for us to come up with a technique of idea generation that involves breaking out of the well trodden path of logic and analysis Lateral thinking is one such technique that may assist companies in exploring the by lanes of the territory as it were. The khushboowalla pen was born out of the advertent or inadvertent application of this technique. A lesser known application of creativity in the marketing arena is in respect of sales goals setting. The following marketing innovations might prove to be useful to better retain its target customer.

BRAND MANAGEMENT AND INDIAN COMPETITIVENESS

Nothing can be taken for granted for a product. A strong or a weak marketer can succeed if they manage to create a difference. If they don't, failure is the only outcome unless lack of product differentiation is made up through significant price differentiation. It is better to act proactively, thinking of the worst. Else, when things start going the other way, enough time and even money may not be available to differentiate. It is essential that a product has a reason for being purchased which is different from other available products. The days of just being a good product is over. Among a range of good products one with a difference will survive. At the market place it is the survival of the differentiated. On the other hand manufacturers eventually learn market power lies with building their own brands. Japanese and South Korean companies spent liberally to build up brand names such as Sony, Toyota, Gold star, and Samsung. Even when these companies can no linger afford to manufacturer their products in their homelands, the brand manes continue to command customer loyalty. Branding is a major issue in product strategy. On the one hand, developing a branded product requires a great deal of long-term investment companies' subcontract manufacturing to other companies.

What Is Brand?

Perhaps the most distinctive skill of professional marketers is their ability to create, maintain, protect, and enhance brands. Marketers say that "branding is the art and cornerstone of marketing." The American Marketing Association defines a brand as follows:

A brand is a name, term, sign, symbol, or design, or a combination of them, intended to identify the goods or services of one seller and to differentiate them from those of competitors.

In essence, a brand identifies the seller of marker. It can be a name, trademark, logo, or other symbol. Under trademark law, the seller is granted exclusive rights to the use of the brand name in perpetuity. Brands differ from other assets such as patents and copyrights, which have expiration dates.

A Brand is a Promise

First and foremost, a brand is a promise. It says 'you know the name, you can trust the promise'. As all promises, it is trusted only as far as those promises are met. Trust is a critical first step and brands aim to accelerate that step leveraging the implied promise of the brand.

A Brand is an Associated Image

Most brands have a logo which acts as a short-cut to remind us of the brand promise. The logo uses color, shape, letters and image that is designed both to catch our eyes and to guide our thoughts in the rights direction. The brand may also be associated with tunes, celebrities, catchphrases and so on. All parts of the brand image works as a psychological trigger or stimulus that causes an association to all other thoughts we have about the brand.

Everything and Everyone is a Brand

If you get down to the detail, everything is a brand, because we build our understanding of the world by creating associations about. Even words are brands. When I say 'speed', you will conjure up image of fast cars, etc. People are brands, too. When people see you, or even hear your name, they will recall the image they have of you. In a company where people are visible to customers, such as a service business, the people are very much a part the brand. But a brand is an even more complex symbol. It can convey up to six level of meaning:

1. Attributes: A brand to mind certain attributes. Mercedes suggests expensive, well-built, well-engineered, durable, high-prestige automobiles.

2. Benefits: Attributes must be translated into functional and emotional benefits. The attribute "durable" could translate into the functional benefits "I won't have to buy another car for several years." The attribute "expensive" translates into the emotional benefits "The car makes me feel important and admired."
3. Values: The brand also says something about the producer's values. Mercedes stands for high performance, safety, and prestige.
4. Culture: The brand may represent a certain culture. The Mercedes may represent German culture: organized, efficient, high quality.
5. Personality: The brand can project a certain personality.
6. User: The brand suggests the kind of consumer who buys or uses the product. We would expect to.

Why A Brand?

Strong brands are important to both marketers and customers. These are wanted by marketers, as they:

- o Provide relatively higher return on sales,
- o Have higher loyalty than their weaker competitors,
- o Provide opportunities for brands extension,
- o Can bounce back after a mistake,
- o Recover fast from aggressive price promotion by its competitors,
- o Have longer life,
- o Are important to customers,
- o Create entry barriers for others into the category,
- o Facilitate entry into related categories to which the brand can be extended, and
- o Can command a price premium.

They are important to customers as they:

- o Are seen to be performing through it or with its help,
- o Find it easy to choose,
- o Use it to define/project themselves,
- o Have a perceived consistent quality about it which acts as a benchmark for brand consideration/choice.

The importance of strong brands as highlighted above makes the need for a process of building a brand all the more important. And this has to structured and implemented as part of the overall marketing process. Marketing, as we understand, is continuous process of making customers continue to prefer to but a particular product or service, in the form of a brand. A brand is a combination of the basic products or service, and aspect not overtly specific to the basic product or service, and aspect not Product/Service + /other aspects. A brand provides a specific product/service an identity and differentiation. It does not just exist as a mark on the pack outside of the product but as something with in it.

* Is It Enough To Be Strong At '4ps' To Build A Strong Brand?

The process of marketing, which includes 'product, pricing, promotion, and place' helps define 'product/service' and 'other aspects'. Each of these four activities includes the process of brand formation, i.e. Branding. However, none of these in isolation of together define the complete branding process. It is just not enough to:

- o Develop a product based on customer need,
- o Develop an attractive packing,
- o Decide on a brand name,
- o Design likeable and relevant advertising,
- o Arrive at an appropriate price,
- o Run consumers offer,
- o Implement efficient sales and distribution plan,
- o Keep tab on competition,
- o Contact market research to ascertain effectiveness of marketing initiatives,
- o Market segmentation,
- o Undertake billed brand position,
- o Redress customer's complaints tactfully, etc.

All the above are important activities and have a role to play in branding. But this does not provide a structured and complete process. The process of branding is too critical, not to have its own identity, structure, and distinct place in a marketer's 'things to do'. Unless it is done, 'product, price, promotion, and place,' may happen, but brand formation may not happen. Enough of such cases exit at the market place. Once the process of branding is understood and planned for a brand, other activities, Vis, 'product, price, promotion, and place need to be tuned around it. These together will go a long way in building strong brand.

What is Brand Management?

Brand management is the application of marketing techniques to a specific products, product line, or brand. It seeks to increase the product's perceived value to the customers and thereby increase brand franchise and brand quality. Marketers see a brand will continue with present and future purchases of the same product. This may increase sales by making a comparison with competing product more favorable. It may also enable the manufacturer to change more for the product. The value of the brand is determined by the amount of profit it generates for the manufacturer. This results from a combination of increased sales and increased price.

The annual list of the world's most valuable brands, published by inter brand and Business Week, indicates that the market value of companies often consists largely of brand equity. Research by MeKunsey & Company, a global consulting firm, in 2000 suggested that strong, well-leveraged brands produce higher returns to shareholders than weaker, narrower brands. Taken together, this means that brands seriously impact shareholder value, which ultimate makes branding a CEO responsibility.

Branding/Manageable Elements of the Brand

Consumers are human beings. They know brands, express about brands think brands, feel brands, compare brands, choose brands, recommend brands, reject brands, buy brands, and do not buy brands through a combination of :

- o Brand name
- o Brand associations
- o Brand attitude
- o Brand looks
- o Brand personality, and

o All these are not just a matter of semantics. These are specific manageable concepts, born and brought up on the minds and hearts of the consumers, linked to each other in more ways than one. These, if 'added' to a product, lead to creation of brand.

As per the branding model, this in a way is a branding process:

* Brand Relationship is the ultimate achievement need of branding. All other aspects (e.g. Brand Positioning) might happen but if this does not happen the job is not complete. Brand Relations happens of 'image' and 'attitude' for a brand exits. It is the resultant effect of these two aspects of a brand.
* Brand Attitude defines what the brand thinks about the consumer, as per the consumer. A brand may have 'attitude' on one or more aspects.
* Brand Image includes two aspects of a brand its associations and its personality. A brand may have image on one more aspects.
* Brand Associations includes all the linked up in memory about the brand. It could be specific to attributes, features, benefits or looks of the brand. A brand may have a range of associations. But the one association that stands out in memory and differentiates it becomes the 'positions' of the brand. A brand may have one or more associations but no 'positions'.
* Brand Looks, which have a role to play in forming/ reinforcing brand associations are facilitated by two key properties of a brand its name and its symbol. While brand name is a necessary condition for existence of brand relationship, the same is not true for brand symbol. However, if the latter exists it helps the process of brand relationship and reinforces it.
* Brand symbol includes two visual signals of a brand its character (e.g. Amul girl. Pillsbury doughboy) and its logo.
* 'necessary' aspects for brand relationship to exist are:
  o brand name,
  o brand associations, and

- o brand attitude
- * 'Highly desirable' aspects for brand relationship to exist are (excluding the 'necessary' aspects):
  - o brand position, and
  - o Brand symbol.

Conclusion

The above mentioned elements of the Brand are manageable. A firm has to adapt all the elements with its target segment and with proposed positioning of the Brand. As we discussed earlier that today is the era of branding. So, it's very obvious that Brand management at global level becomes very crucial and important. At global level starting from Brand name to Brand Relationship all the elements should be adopted with the culture and environment of the concerned country.

CONCEPTUAL STUDY OF OPPORTUNITY FOR RURAL INDIA

Introduction: The Indian nation is on the move. The Indian are astir. Agriculture is blooming. Industry is booming. The legacy of self-deprecation and self-doubt inherited from the colonial period has given way to a new-found dynamism, confidence and sense of self-determination. No longer harping critically about its past, the country has come to recognize its commendable achievements and become aware of the tremendous opportunities which the future holds for even more rapid progress. This change in attitude and this emerging consciousness of opportunity are the most essential ingredients for accelerating development.

Strategy Applied by the Indian Firm to Become Global Competitor

Strategy to Complement the Economic Liberalization

The international community has noted with some amazement India's impressive gains over the last five years in recovering from the severe economic problems brought on by high rates of inflation, high budget deficits, and falling foreign exchange reserves. Today the country enjoys a very low inflation rate, comfortable reserves of hard currency and an industrial growth rate approaching 12%. Exports are growing at a phenomenal rate of 24%. Employment generation has risen from an average of 4.8 million new jobs per annum in the 1980s and a low of 3 million just five years ago to a record 7.2 million last year.

These gains are remarkable and beyond the expectations of even the most far-sighted analysts. However, even if the most optimistic targets are achieved, it will not ensure that rising incomes and employment opportunities will be available to all who presently live in poverty. The problem with the economic reform package is not that it is stimulating the rapid growth of some sectors, especially industry and exports, but that it is not doing enough for the 70% of the population residing in rural areas, of which 65% are engaged in agriculture. India needs a new strategy to complement the economic reforms, a strategy designed to take full advantage of the country's agro-climatic advantages, huge tracks of cultivable land, and large internal market to stimulate a rapid development of the rural economy.

Agriculture as an Engine for Industrialization

Rising productivity and profitability from agriculture was a primary cause of the Industrial Revolution in England during the early 19th Century. It raised the purchasing power of the rural population, stimulated greater demand for manufactured goods and led to the growth of industries. In America too, rising productivity in agriculture was a strong spur to the development of the manufacturing sector at the turn of the century. The rapid development of South Korea, Taiwan, and Malaysia provides ample evidence that an agriculture-driven strategy can act as a powerful engine for raising rural incomes, industrialization and employment generation. More recently, commercial agriculture has been a powerful engine for economic development in Thailand, where 70% of the population is still employed in the farm sector.

India's Competitive Advantage in Agriculture

India possesses four outstanding competitive advantages in agriculture comparable to those of any other country in the world. First, it has regions which are climatically favorable for cultivation of every commercially-important plant species grown in other parts of the world – ranging from temperate orchard crops such as almonds and apples to tropical mangoes and pineapple. Second, the country already possesses the largest acreage of irrigated land in the world with 40% of the potential still to be tapped. Third, the gap between present productivity and proven technological potential is very large for most crops; yet even so, the country is already among the world's top three producers of tea, cotton, sugar, food grains, groundnut, coffee, eggs and milk. Fourth, the country has an abundance of available skilled, educated, technical and scientific manpower.

From Minimum Needs to Maximum Potentials

During the colonial period India suffered from food deficits and severe famines. Thus, in the early days of India's Independence, it was natural for the Government to focus its attention on production of sufficient food grains to meet the minimum dietary needs of a rapidly expanding population. As a result of the Green Revolution, India defied the dire predictions of international experts by doubling its food grain production within a decade and achieving self-sufficiency in cereal crops. Since then, the agricultural sector has ceased to receive the attention it deserves. Combating the threat of famine is no longer a pressing priority, but that does not mean agriculture has fulfilled its mission.

Creating Rural Jobs as a Counter to Urban Migration

Agriculture is the key to generating full employment in the country. This sector not only provides on-farm employment but also generates employment opportunities in processing industries, manufacturing, food distribution and the transport sector. Although less than 3% of the US population is currently engaged in farming, one out of every three jobs in America is related to the production, processing, distribution or export of agricultural produce.

Growing Domestic Demand

Achieving nutritional security for the Indian masses will require a significant increase in daily intake of calories, protein, vitamins and minerals. The present nutritional gap represents a vast pent-up demand for more and better quality foods while can be translated into commercial opportunities for India's farmers. Indians consume an average of 40 grams per day of horticulture products compared to a normal nutritional demand of 90 grams. As incomes rise, the domestic market for horticulture products is projected to increase by 60% over the next six years. Overall, there is scope for placing an additional 1 million acres under horticulture crops. This will generate demand for 100 new commercial hybrid seed production units in the country.

Tremendous Export Opportunities

India has the potential to become a global leader in agriculture. Already agriculture exports, including textiles, have risen from Rs 10,000 crores to Rs 40,000 crores over the past five years. Grape and mango exports to Western Europe are rapidly increasing. Floriculture is a $40 billion global industry that is projected to reach $70 billion by year 2000, of which international trade in cut flowers accounts for $6 billion. India's exports of cut flower have risen from $2 million to $10 million annually over the past five years, but the potential is 100 fold greater. New floriculture projects are already springing up around the country.

Creating Rural Entrepreneurs

With the rights technology and management practices, agriculture offers lucrative for entrepreneurs. A ten acre farm growing a combination of cash crops such as sugar, cotton, fruits, vegetables and flowers can earn Rs. 5 lakh or more per annum for a rural family. Although it is widely believed that the problem of educated unemployment cannot be solved, a shortage of agricultural graduates is actually developing due to the rapid development of commercial agriculture. A single agri-business enterprise has recruited more than 250 agricultural graduates within the past two years.

Need for New Organizations

The technology and capital required to bring about a second revolution in Indian agriculture are readily available and well within the country's means. But another critical ingredient is needed to galvanize the rural sector for rapid growth – organization. Indian agriculture can benefit immensely from an induction of professional management and marketing capabilities to handle processing and distribution in the post-harvest phase of agri-business. The division of the agricultural sector into 100 million small holdings has long retarded the emergence of effective rural enterprises. Baring a few bright exceptions such as the dairy and sugar industries in some states, the cooperative sector has been too encumbered by bureaucratic regulations to generate dynamic agricultural firms.

Rural Aquaculture Estates

Fresh water fish and prawn culture can be a highly remunerative undertaking for rural farmers, provided that they have access to appropriate technology, feeds, processing and marketing facilities. One approach is for Government to establish rural aquaculture estates and lease out small production ponds to farmers and landless labor. Each estate could consist of 20 to 25 acres of ponds, each pond .25 acres in size and equipped with machinery for aeration and drainage. Each estate should have a centralized source of pure water, power, feed and processing plant, cold storage and marketing facilities. Utilizing fast growing varieties, each pond can generate a minimum of Rs 50,000 per acre net profit per annum.

India's Unique Opportunity

Never before has India been poised for such rapid economic progress. Never before have the opportunities been so great or the country so ready. Now what is needed is to generate a widespread awareness of the potentials at all levels of the society – among political leaders, administrators, farmers and the corporate sector. It took the leaders of India's Freedom Movement more than half a century to achieve Independence largely because it took that long to convince the Indian elite and masses that such a goal was achievable. It has taken another half century for the Indian nation to cast off the oppressive legacy of colonialism and to rediscover its own inherent dynamism and resourceful. It need not take another half century to convert this rich capacity into material accomplishments. What is needed now is a national Prosperity Movement to realize the goal of Indian economic accomplishment. If pursued with confidence and determination, India can achieve widespread prosperity within a decade.

CONCLUSION

The dream runs of Indian growth continuous. With economy growing at over 8% , foreign exchange reserve of over $170bn ; booming IT-industry Service sectors, rapidly growing domestic markets, buoyant stock markets, and Indian companies buying companies abroad, things have never looked better for India. The Indian story is indeed for real, the World Economic Forum's Global Competitiveness Index has placed India at 43rd position out of 125 countries ahead of China, Russia, and Brazil. India's share of global services exports too has doubled in just last two years to 2.5%. The overall export growth is averaging 25% per annum over last three years. As per the latest figures, industry has locked a growth of 14.4% during November-2006 – the highest since February-1996. This has been backed by manufacturing sector, which has logged 15.7% growth. Recognizing the intrinsic worth of our strong macro-economic fundamentals, international investors are making a beeline for India.

11

Strategies of Various Industrial Sectors

STRATEGIES, TRENDS AND OPPORTUNITIES

Retail is India's largest industry, accounting for over 10 per cent of the country's GDP and around eight per cent of the employment. Retail industry in India is at the crossroads. It has emerged as one of the most dynamic and fast paced industries with several players entering the market. But because of the heavy initial investments required, break even is difficult to achieve and many of these players have not tasted success so far. However, the future is promising; the market is growing, government policies are becoming more favorable and emerging technologies are facilitating operations.

Retailing in India is gradually inching its way toward becoming the next boom industry. The whole concept of shopping has altered in terms of format and consumer buying behavior, ushering in a revolution in shopping in India. Modern retail has entered India as seen in sprawling shopping centers, multi-storied malls and huge complexes offer shopping, entertainment and food all under one roof. The Indian retailing sector is at an inflexion point where the growth of organized retailing and growth in the consumption by the Indian population is going to take a higher growth trajectory. The Indian population is witnessing a significant change in its demographics. A large young working population with median age of 24 years, nuclear families in urban areas, along with increasing working-women population and emerging opportunities in the services sector are going to be the key growth drivers of the organized retail sector in India.

WHAT IS "STRATEGY"?

* Consists of competitive moves & business approaches to produce successful performance
* Management's "game plan" for
  - Running the business
  - Strengthening firm's competitive position
  - Satisfying customers
  - Achieving performance targets

THINKING STRATEGICALLY: THREE BIG STRATEGIC QUESTIONS

1. Where Are We Now?
2. Where Do We Want To Go?
   * Business positions management wants to stake out
   * Financial outcomes to achieve
   * Strategic outcomes to achieve
3. How Will We Get There?

FIVE TASKS OF STRATEGIC MANAGEMENT

1. Defining business, stating a mission, & forming a strategic vision
2. Setting measurable objectives
3. Crafting a strategy to achieve objectives
4. Implementing & executing strategy
5. Evaluating performance, reviewing new developments, & initiating corrective adjustments

DEVELOPING A VISION & MISSION

* Begins with thinking strategically
  - About firm's future makeup &
  - Forming vision of firm's future in 5-10 years
  - Task is to
  - Inject sense of purpose into firm's activities
  - Provide LONG-TERM DIRECTION
  - Decide "WHO we are, WHAT we do, & WHERE we are headed"
* Give firm STRONG ID SPECIFIC QUESTIONS THAT HELP FORM STRATEGIC VISIONS

* What business are we in now?
* What business do we want to be in?
* What will our customers want in future?
* What are expectations of our stakeholders?
* Who will be our future competitors? Suppliers? Partners?
* What should our competitive scope be?
* How will technology impact our industry?
* What environmental scenarios are possible? ENTITY

WHY A SHARED VISION MATTERS

* A strategic vision widely shared among all employees functions similar to how a magnet aligns iron filings
* When all employees are committed to firm's long-term direction, optimum choices on business decisions are more likely
  - Individuals & teams know intent of firm's strategic vision
  - Daily execution of strategy is improved

EXAMPLES: MISSION / VISION STATEMENTS AVIS RENT-A-CAR

Our business is renting cars. Our mission is total customer satisfaction.

McCormick & COMPANY

The primary mission is to expand our worldwide leadership position in the spice, Seasoning, and flavoring markets.

SATURN DIVISION OF GM

To market vehicles developed and manufactured in the U.S. that are world leaders in quality, cost, and customer satisfaction through the integration of people, technology, and business systems and to transfer knowledge, technology, and experience throughout GM.

* *Innovative strategies in Indian corporations for a dynamic economy*

The current business environment in India is marked by staggering contrast. The country represents one of the world's largest market opportunities, yet it is also one of the most complex and demanding regarding management and execution. Achieving breakthrough business success in India requires overcoming a host of challenges— infrastructure, recruitment, bureaucracy—by deploying proven management strategies and leveraging the latest technological innovations in enterprising ways.

In this program, renowned professors from Stanford's Graduate School of Business and School of Engineering apply their latest research to the unique dynamics of Indian business. In addition, both Mr. Narayana Murthy (Chairman and Chief Mentor, Infosys Technologies) and Mr. Mukesh Ambani (Chairman, Reliance Industries Limited) will deliver keynote addresses, and interactive panel discussions will showcase the opinions of multiple thought leaders regarding how the future of global competition and information technology will affect Indian business.

* *Do talk on strangers; encouraging per formative ties to get competitive advantage.*

Imagine the following situation: You are a consultant who has just been assigned to a new project at your firm, and your first major presentation is in a week. Unfortunately, your client's problem isn't something you have any expertise in. Chances are, according to research by Sheen S. Levine, a professor at Singapore Management University who earned his PhD from Wharton; you would pick up the phone and make a call.

In a recent study, Levine has found that often, what gives firms competitive advantage isn't just their repository of knowledge, but their use of "per formative ties" — those impromptu communications made by colleagues who are strangers in which critical knowledge is transferred with no expectation of a quid pro quo. Levine and others explain how per formative ties function in daily practice and — more importantly — how managers can go about encouraging them.

* *Innovative retention strategies for Indian BPOs.*

Retention of Key employees is critical to the long term health and success of any organization. It is a known fact that retaining your best employees ensures customer satisfaction, increased product sales, satisfied colleagues and reporting staff, effective succession planning and deeply imbedded organizational knowledge and learning. Employee retention matters as organizational issues such as training time and investment; lost knowledge; insecure employees and a costly candidate search are involved. Hence failing to retain a key employee is a costly Proposition for an organization various estimates suggest that losing a middle manager in most organizations costs up to five times of his salary.

The BPOs in India face an enormous challenge in reducing attrition rate and this being a nascent industry needs to Draw parallels, examples from other industry practices as well as develop innovative Employee Relation Initiatives As highlighted below. This has been classified into three groups:

1. The Corporate level
2. Managerial/supervisory levels
3. Employee Recognition Initiatives

* 10 Key Benefits of a Strategic Management System

Which of these benefits are still missing in your organization?

1. Taking an organization-wide, proactive approach to a changing global world
2. Building an executive team that serves as a model of cross-functional or horizontal teamwork
3. Having an intense executive development and strategic orientation process
4. Defining focused, quantifiable outcomes measures of success
5. Making intelligent budgeting decisions
6. Clarifying your competitive advantage
7. Reducing conflict; empowering the organization
8. Providing clear guidelines for day-to-day decision making
9. Creating a critical mass for change
10. "Singing from the same hymnal" throughout the organization

**** Assessing Overall Industry Attractiveness***

- Industry's market size & growth potential
- Whether industry will be favorably or unfavorably impacted by driving forces

* Potential for entry/exit of major firms
* Stability/dependability of demand
* Will competitive forces become stronger or weaker
* Severity of problems facing industry
* Degree of risk & uncertainty in industry's future

To review overall situation & develop conclusions about relative attractiveness or unattractiveness of the industry, both near- and long-term a firm uniquely well-suited in an otherwise unattractive industry can, under certain circumstances, still earn unusually good profits.

CORPORATE CROSSROADS

Ram was a flamboyant and proved to be the most creative chap in his college. When students started attending the campus interviews, he won the highest compensations among the others. He was excited and his expectations soared very high while entering into the company.

James Software Inc. seemed to be a cavern of wonders. It had a huge auditorium, a library, technical training centre and a professional work block. Ram was given a laptop, wi-fi enabled packages with a fully furnished cabin. He was part of the five member team and his team leader was a very nice gentleman. His creativity was at its peak and he started imagining about the career growth and recognitions he was about to achieve.

Everything was going well but only for a year. His collegeaus were comfortable in not taking some complex projects that could make them learn a lot. It was something like a "Bench Post". Ram was very disappointed and, his excellences started to diminish, he started to sulk. Whenever he suggested to start an innovative project or assignment his colleagues started to resist. On the other hand, the leader of his team had a fear that Ram might professionally overtake him and for that fact, he did not inform Ram about the programs and techniques that might enhance him and his team.

The team was assigned only short term easy projects. It dawned on Ram that he had no career growth in the company. If he quits the job and went to another company, the same scenario might prevail there, in accordance to the proverb that says "Known devil is better than unknown angel".

At this point of time the organization organized a get together and collected suggestion for improvements from the employees. What should Ram suggest?

WORK LIFE BALANCE OF WOMEN EMPLOYEES

Times have changed. From the time the husband earned, and the wife stayed at home. To the time now when the husband earns and the wife earns too. But the wife still cooks and washes and runs the house. So, how does she balance her work with life at home?

Although, over the years women in India have struggled to establish an identity & create a mark in the social as well as in the organizational platforms, but with educational institutions training more and more women to enter professional careers, have drastically changed the scenario.

Infact, between 1991 and 2001 female employment in India on the whole, have increased by 3.6% per annum. Within the professional world, which reflects India's small but growing middle class more than the country as a whole, the phenomenon of Indian women "breaking through the glass ceiling" is perhaps more muted. Even, despite legal provisions made by acts like those of the Equal Remuneration Act of 1976 (which promulgates equal payment for equal work, regardless of gender & prohibits gender discrimination in hiring practices), the so-called "glass ceiling" is perhaps still very prevalent within organizations.

This article would highlight the various values, attitudes & beliefs of women regarding job anxiety in their formal work organizations & particularly balancing their work & personal life. Work Life Balance (WLB) is not a new concept.

Let's first define what work-life balance is not. Work-Life Balance does not mean an equal balance. Trying to schedule an equal number of hours for each of your various work and personal activities is usually unrewarding and unrealistic. Life is and should be more fluid than that. Your best individual work-life balance will vary over time, often on a daily basis. The right balance for you today will probably be different for you tomorrow.

The right balances for you when you are single will be different when you marry, or if you have children; when you start a new career versus when you are nearing retirement. There is no perfect, one-size fits all, balance you should be striving for.

The best work- life balance is different for each of us because we all have different priorities and different lives. However, at the core of an effective work-life balance definition are two key everyday concepts that are relevant to each of us. They are daily Achievement and Enjoyment, ideas almost deceptive in their simplicity. Engraining a fuller meaning of these two concepts takes us most of the way to defining a positive Work-Life Balance.

The change in the pattern of work and the concept of the workplace after the industrial revolution in the second half of the 18th century gave a new dimension to the concept of WLB. As time progressed, nuclear families increased. A later change was the fading away of the "ideal home" in which the earning member's spouse took care of the home.

With improved education and employment opportunities today, most homes are ones in which both parents work, because of necessity and the desire to augment incomes.

The need to create congenial conditions in which employees can balance work with their personal needs and desires became a factor that companies had to take note of both to retain them as well as to improve productivity. It was a compulsion that they couldn't afford to ignore. Having realized that, companies started introducing schemes to attract and retain employees and improve their productivity.

Why Work Life Balance is Important to Women? Today's career women are continually challenged by the demands of full-time work and when the day is done at the office, they carry more of the responsibilities and commitments to home. The majority of women are working 40-45 hours per week and 53% are struggling to achieve work/life balance.

Women reported that their lives were a juggling act that included multiple responsibilities at work, heavy meeting schedules, business trips, on top of managing the daily routine responsibilities of life and home. "Successfully achieving work/life balance will ultimately create a more satisfied workforce that contributes to productivity and success in the workplace."

Employers can facilitate WLB with many schemes that can attract women employees and satisfy their needs.

Some of these are

* Facilities for child care
* Financial planning services for employees who need them
* Flexi-timings
* Work sharing
* Part time employment
* Leave plans - both paid and unpaid - to suit employee's needs
* Subsidized food plans
* Insurance plans
* Counseling services for problems like managing work and the home
* Rest rooms, food preparation services
* Jobs with autonomy and flexibility
* Realistic work loads
* Review of work processes to see if the burden on employees can be lightened Maintaining dialogue with the employees and considering their suggestions on a continuous basis

Work-life Balance

Can women be both sharers and careers Often, working women drop out of the work force when they are doing well, simply because they wanted to stay at home with their children, or care for an ageing parent. Or for both reasons. And then there are women who have children later in life because they want to work for reasons of personal satisfaction or for the money. So, can a woman have it all? The working woman should refuse to take on too much. She should adopt a sense of priorities.

If she has children, she should teach them to share responsibilities. But what about the husband? Has he changed at all anywhere in the world?

Surprisingly, a survey in the UK revealed that a majority of men want a 50/50 partnership with their wives both at work and home. They no longer see themselves as macho men. They want to spend more time with their children. Has the Indian man kept pace with the times? Can women achieve a work-life balance?

The changing Equations of New Era The Changing Equations The Machine Age The Industrial Age The Networked Age Stress High Higher Highest Work- Life balance You went to work-life started only when you go home Not only are people working at work, but also at home 24-hour workdays split into compartments dedicated for 'life' Women and Work The men worked and women tended the house Both men and women worked, and women still tended the house Both men and women work and tend to the house.

Framework for successful Work-Life Balance in organizations

* Identify the key need or reason for introducing Work-Life Balance policies
* Build the commitment to Work-Life Balance Policies into the organization ' s vision or value statement
* Set up a Work-Life Balance Task Force Examine current practices in the organization
* Hold joint discussions with employees to evolve policies, while also identifying possible barriers
* Communicate policies through handbooks, newsletters, Intranet and other forms of communication
* Hold workshops to help Managers implement and manage policies
* Begin with a few "quick win" policies

Monitor implementation and put feedback systems into place In India, there is a starting point in that organizations have recognized the need for and value of Work-Life Balance policies.

An integral part of our lives is our profession. Just as there is responsibility and opportunity in life, our careers are also guided by opportunities and responsibilities. We must ensure that these two factors don't work at cross purposes. Quality of life is something we all covet, every profession affects life in general and every profession has a duty towards life.

Top 5 Strategies to Strike a Balance

* Budget your time both in and out of the office - Schedule your time efficiently at work. Put yourself on your calendar and take some time for you and your family/ friends. Leave work on time at least three days per week - There are times when working late just can't be helped, but schedule your time to leave on time three days per week.
* Control interruptions and distractions - Stay focused while in the office, and budget your time effectively. Try to schedule a block of time during the day without meetings when you can focus on your tasks with minimal interruptions.
* Explore the availability of flex-time - Research flex-time options within your organization. If available, it may be a helpful solution.
* Seize the weekend - Plan your time off as you plan your work week.
* Schedule activities with family and friends, a weekend trip, or just something fun. Make your time away from work count!

Conclusion for working women, getting caught in the work/ life balance trap will continue to be an ongoing challenge. Careful planning and personal effort is the advice from those who have found balance in both career and home life. As one respondent summarized, "Plan, prioritize and schedule as efficiently as possible... and don't be afraid of hard work!" Work-life balance is a person's control over the conditions in their workplace. It is accomplished when an individual feels dually satisfied about their personal life and their paid occupation. It mutually benefits the individual, business and society when a person ' s personal life is balanced with his or her own job. The work-life balance strategy offers a variety of means to reduce stress levels and increase job satisfaction in the employee while enhancing business benefits for the employer. In our increasingly hectic world, the work-life strategy seeks to find a balance between work and play. A sentence that brings the idea of work life balance to the point is: "Work to live. Don't live to work."

LONG LINTED ARBOREUM COTTON FOR FUTURE INDUSTRY REQUIREMENTS

Cotton continues to remain the most sought after raw material for the Indian textile industry, contributing about 57 per cent to the total fibre basket. The predominance of this 'white gold' prevails, despite a severe onslaught by polyester with its steeply expanding production base. This commercial crop retains its hold in the Indian economy by providing employment directly or indirectly to 60 million people and contributing to about 4 per cent of GDP. Cotton-based textile exports have been showing significant gains with the export earnings in rupee terms crossing Rs 60,000 crore in the current year. But this impressive scenario seems to end here.

In the post-quota regime, the Indian textile industry being all along protected with an assured domestic market of 1 billion populace, is bound to face unprecedented threat from textiles originating from South East Asian countries. While it is feared that cheap imports would flood the market making the survival of the domestic industry difficult, at the same time the Indian textile industry can convert the challenge into a golden opportunity to increase its exports from the current level of 3 per cent if the necessary strategy and action plans are put in place. It is the cotton sector that is expected to face stiff challenge from cheap imports of uncontaminated, least trashy quality cotton from China, Australia, USA, Africa, Africa and CIS in the years to come.

Cotton Scenario

Indian cotton is in an unenviable position besieged with competition from polyester on the one hand and imported cottons on the other. The foreign influx has become so strong that today 15 per cent of the mill consumption constitutes imported lint. While favourable international prices and credit facilities have been the motivating factors for this preference by the industry, certain quality deficiencies in the Indian growing and the mostly fraudulent adulteration in different qualities in the trade have contributed in good measure to the current situation.

The ITMF biennial surveys consistently labelling Indian varieties/hybrids as the most contaminated have worsened the situation further. It is high time that the Indian industry and trade should come forward to make a realistic assessment of the status of contamination in the trade varieties so as to project the true picture of the Indian cotton. Institutions like CIRCOT would always be ready to play their part in this worthwhile endeavour.

India's standing in textile exports particularly of yarns is well known. About 25 per cent of the yarn produced is being sold abroad realising sizeable foreign exchange. However, a recent report from ministry of commerce contained an interesting statistics about raw cotton. India's imports of raw cotton of about 2.12 lakh MT in 2000-01 valued at Rs 1,185 crore seems to be dismally low if looked at the export of raw cotton from this country to the tune of 15.34 lakh MT worth Rs 2,943 crore with the import forming only 1/7 of the exports.

However, the disturbing news is that the lint value realised in export is only 1/3rd of that expended in import of raw cotton. This brings to fore the poor value fetched by Indian cotton in the international market owing to its being in the lower end of the quality spectrum. This fact needs a strong attention. Serious efforts need to be made to enhance the unit value realisation in the export.

Constraints in Cotton Cultivation

Over the years, cotton cultivation has become less remunerative with the economic viability becoming a question mark. Although Technology Mission on Cotton - Mini Mission I, is justifiably proud that due to its concerted efforts the pesticide consumption has significantly reduced; still about 45 per cent of the pesticide produced in the country is being used up only in the 5 per cent of the total cultivable land that is occupied by this crop. The severe drought during the last three-four years affecting one or the other cotton areas, has also made an impressionable dent on the profitability of this commercial crop. As 55 per cent of the area under cotton is occupied by hybrids and since hybrid cultivation is input-incentive and pest and disease prone, the economic viability gets further eroded, compounded by a very meagre productivity of 300-325 kg per hectare.

Several ways could be thought of by which the production cost could be conserved. Apart from increasing the productivity and minimising on inputs; a situation should be created in which farmer gets benefit on commercial terms from by-products and crop residues as well. This is feasible only by promoting the use of cotton crop as a whole by adopting a realistic approach to the utilisation of its by-produces by adding value. To reduce production cost, there is need to look for eco-friendly production practices, organic cultivation and also promotion of genetically-modified cotton. Another plausible alternative is to promote extensively cultivation of 'Desi cottons' that require minimum inputs and are largely pest free.

Desi cottons

At present desi cottons are cultivated in about 22-25 lakh hectares accounting for about 17-20 per cent of the cotton crop in the country. The relative merits of Desi cottons vis-à-vis the new world cottons in textile applications are many as follows:

- Unlike hirsutum and barbadense varieties, desi cottons (arboreums and herbaceums) show inherent resistance to pests, diseases and drought.
- Since the requirements are minimal, the net gain for the farmer is often higher with Desi cottons than with many hirsutums.
- Desis are eminently suitable for organic cultivation which is becoming a promising area of activity.
- Many desi varieties have yields comparable with or superior to that of hirsutum varieties.
- Desi cottons unlike many hirsutum varieties have superior fibre maturity which makes them easy to process on spinning and preparatory machines and which ensures uniform colour shades in dyed fabrics.
- An outstanding feature of desi cottons particularly arboreums is the low propensity to shed seed coat bits during ginning. The seed coat bits are extremely small in size and very few in number unlike in hirsutum cottons and their hybrids. Seed coat trash that leads to 50 per cent of yarn imperfections is a major cause of export rejections.
- Extensive researches in evolving new varieties of desi cottons in many centres have yielded positive results.

Several varieties with superior medium to long staple (26-30 mm); medium fineness (3.7-4.5 mic. value) and reasonably high strength (22-24 g/tex in HVI ICC mode) are now available.

- In arboreum cottons, neps considered as prominent components of yarn imperfection are relatively few.
- Desi cottons have micropores smaller in size. Structural reversals are fewer and fibrils are better oriented. These features ought to have provided enhanced mechanical strength but offset by the presence of structural weak links. This warrants a thorough look and remedial measures need to be taken.

Promising Desi Cottons

As already pointed out, the All India Coordinated Cotton Improvement Project (AICCIP) under the Indian Council of Agricultural Research system has developed several promising high quality G. arboreum cottons with yield levels matching the conventional hirsutum varieties and their hybrids.

CONCLUDING REMARKS

With the inherent positive fibre attributes and minimal input requirements, Desi cottons particularly long-linted quality arboreums are eminently suitable for large scale cultivation and processing. It is high time that these cottons are adopted by quality conscious mills for regular use. CIRCOT's promotional efforts with some export-oriented units for some of the promising varieties have yielded positive results. The yarn produced using an improved arboreum variety was found to be at par with that from foreign cotton used by the mill and in certain aspects like yarn neps, thick and thin faults, feel and appearance even superior. Indian industry should note this and come forward to take advantage of the indigenous raw material.

How do we make quality arboreums available to the Indian industry? This is a crucial issue needing urgent attention. Rather than waiting for our production system to supply this raw material that would any day be cheaper than either conventional hirsutums or imported cotton. The industry should come forward to adopt any one of the several modes identified for raw material promotion and utilise the same for its own use.

The 'village adoption' model or the 'backward integration' approach would be ideally suited in a region like Central India where the cottons are found to be well adopted for cultivation. The 'Integrated Cotton Cultivation' scheme that seems to be picking up in our country is another intervention worth trying by a ginner or textile mill with adequate 'buy back system' in place to rope in farming community to realise benefits of these desi cottons.

Utilisation of quality desi cottons by the industry would not only help the Indian farmer to keep his hold on the cultilvation of this cash crop but also save the precious foreign exchange. Time has come to use these cottons for production of quality yarns for the export market by our renowned enterprising industry.

12

Bright Future for Indian Industries

It has been ten years since it was recognised that the banking industry cannot continue to drive the economy by merely collecting deposits and lending to predetermined borrowers at predetermined rates. Over the past decade it has also come to be recognis ed that banks have to become profitable entities to function in an economy getting increasingly integrated with the world at large.

FUTURE OFINDIAN PETROLEUM INDUSTRY

The future ofIndian petroleum industry has good potential but it needs developmental activities in this sector to strengthen itself.

The world at present is experiencing a lot of changes of mammoth proportions. The Petroleum Industry inIndia is one of the harbingers of huge economic growth. The arena for business has now gone global since trade boundaries are fast dissolving. These developments presentIndia with tremendous opportunities in the future to be one of the major players in the export of petrochemical intermediaries.

Today,India imports more than 70% of its oil requirements. The search for more oil ledIndia to sift through the international markets comprising of the emerging energy-trading countries - China, Russia, and Iran.India has made new partnerships with Venezuela, Burma, Middle East nations, and Pakistan.

The long-term energy strategies ofIndia have to emphasize on the methods of using energy effectively and efficiently, and to enhance energy self-sufficiency. To lift theIndian economy to enhanced economic standards innovation, diplomacy, creativity, and vision are the need of the hour.

India has to compete for conventional energy sources and for that there must be developmental activities for energy efficient buildings and vehicles. The main problems with the Petroleum Industry inIndia are related to infrastructural developments. The lack of proper storage facilities, enhancements in refining capacities, and fluctuating import prices plays important role in the development of the sector. The target of improvement for the growth of the economy forIndia should be in the area of the petrochemical sector. The need for intermediary products for the manufacturing of the end use products is an important sector to tap in. With the per capita consumption for the petrochemical products inIndia being low and the production of these products being high,India may become one of the leading exporters of such intermediary products.

The future of Indian petroleum industry depends on:

- Demand for petroleum is growing in leaps and bounds
- Shifting focus to more production of olefin - ethylene, propylene, butadiene,
- Price and availability of crude oil and gas as feedstock would still be critical factors
- The demand of the end products would affect the demand of the intermediary products

COMPETITIVENESS OF INDIAN MANUFACTURING

This paper reports the findings of a survey to study the competitiveness of Indian manufacturing sector. The paper conceptualizes these findings in terms of priorities of Indian manufacturing firms, the programmes that they undertake to reach their objectives, and the outcome or the performance of these firms. We also present some international comparisons based on a similar study done in the USA. The paper highlights the role of innovation and supply chain management, as a part of any robust manufacturing strategy, in developing world class operations.

How competitive are Indian manufacturing firms? What are some of the key manufacturing issues that leaders of Indian manufacturing are concerned about? What kinds of initiatives are being taken by these firms to improve their competitiveness?

How do these leaders perceive their own strengths and weaknesses? What will make Indian manufacturing world-class? These were some of the many questions we have been seeking to answer through the 1997 Manufacturing Futures Survey. While changes have been numerous at the firm level we wanted to examine to what extent they have achieved their objectives and met the emerging competitive needs. Another key question we address is whether our industry is gearing up to realise its full potential or whether firms are satisfied with limited success. The survey measures broad trends in the Indian manufacturing sector and assesses its competitiveness through a variety of self-answered questions in a sample survey. Appendix 1 describes the metnodology. The larger purpose of this study is to disseminate good practices across the industry and to help firms to benchmark their performance. An closely related issue is our standing vis-à-vis the best in the world. In this report, we also present some of the key practices and characteristics of world class plants.

The cost structure of Indian plants shows that materials constitute 66 percent of total costs, direct labour 10 percent and overheads 24 percent. This implies that initiatives to control manufacturing costs may need to focus on reduction in material costs and overheads. However, traditionally the focus has been on managing labour costs. Efforts to control material related costs may need to address several issues including rejects and rework on the shop floor, identifying alternative materials, and better materials management and sourcing. An underlying implication is that all sources of uncertainty to materials need to be eliminated or reduced. Otherwise costs of high inventories would go up. Interestingly, the break-up of the manufacturing cost for USA was 55 percent, 31 percent and 14 percent for the three factors respectively. The emphasis on labour cost is therefore hard to explain.

In the following sections, we describe the findings of a nation-wide survey of top executives in manufacturing organizations. In the next section we describe the new competitive challenges that Indian firms face followed by the manufacturing strategies that these leaders have devised for their firms in order to face the competition. We then examine how effective these strategies have been in the past, compare these strategies with those of US firms, look at the future in term of efforts needed to improve manufacturing and effectively manage the entire supply chain, and finally, present conclusions of the study.

New Competitive Challenges

Today, Indian firms are facing a very different competitive scenario as compared to the past. They are facing competition from imports and from MNCs in the domestic markets. Several firms also have to compete as new entrants in global markets. Earlier, firms would segregate these two markets and serve them with different quality products and services, while perhaps compromising on quality in the home market. This is no longer possible. Therefore, many strategies that may have worked in the past are not likely to succeed in the future.

The new competition is in terms of reduced cost, improved quality, products with higher performance, a wider range of products, and better service - all delivered simultaneously. A lot has already been written the in business press about many of these issues. However, Indian firms have quite often followed an opportunistic approach to growth as opposed to a capability driven approach that seeks to strengthen key aspects of manufacturing. Consequently, firms have paid very little attention to their shop floors in the last few decades. There have no doubt been notable exceptions to this and some firms have systematically built up their capability in the recent past. Firms have also started paying attention to quality, but it is not clear whether enough is being done about faster throughput and delivery, introduction of a wider range of products, and better service. It would not be incorrect to say that we are still struggling to get the "quality" right and that firms will perhaps focus on other issues at a later date.

The Indian market place has been witnessing a quiet revolution where old products are being substituted by better ones. In fact, for the first time, products and services are being introduced to meet certain customer needs that were only partially met in the past. One implication of this rapid introduction of new products is the pressure on manufacturing facilities to profitably produce a larger variety in smaller volumes. Firms have to search for new processes, new materials, new vendors, new shop floor layouts, new ways of reducing cycle times, new designs, new channels etc. to deliver these products and services.

In addition, manufacturing firms are being increasingly required to integrate services with products to meet customer needs. The real challenge is therefore to improve substantially on several dimensions, including quality, technology, shop floor practices, supply chain coordination, and new product introduction over a short period of time.

Manufacturing Strategies

The 1997 survey shows that to improve their competitive position, Indian firms will give the highest priority to quality improvement in the next five years. Figure 1 shows the relative importance given to four sets of issues by Indian firms on a 7 point scale, with higher scores indicating higher priority. These are Quality, Operations, Structural Changes, and Innovation & R&D. Quality for purposes of this research, comprises *conformance* quality or adherence to specifications, *performance* quality of products, product reliability and product durability. Operations related practices were those that improved the distribution network and performance, on-time delivery, ability to handle production volume changes, product support, and after-sales service. These practices can usually be changed or improved without fundamental changes in the manufacturing system. For instance, production volumes can often be increased by the use of overtime, or by operating an additional shift. On the other hand Structural Changes, which include fast delivery capabilities, low prices, and ability to change product mix, often require major changes in manufacturing. For instance, to substantially improve delivery performance of a wide variety of products, firms would need to cut down on production throughput times, reduce set up times, improve scheduling, and in some cases, change the manufacturing system or bring in new equipment. These changes require much greater effort and often take time to implement. Innovation and R&D included new product introduction, broadening the product line, making design changes and customizing the product. Quality is the number one competitive priority, followed by Operations, Structural Changes and finally, Innovation & R&D.

However, there is a close link between Quality and Structural change, and between Quality,

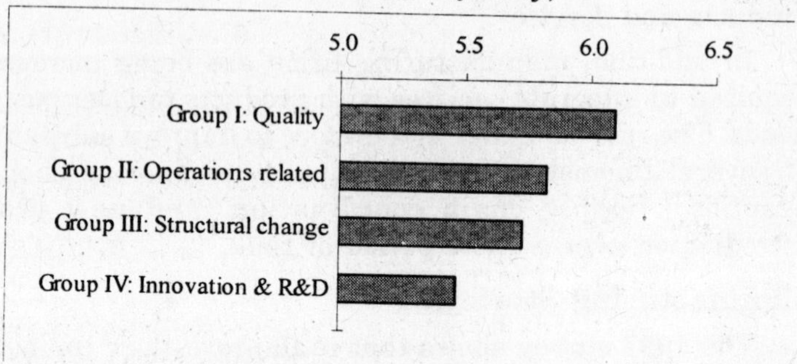

Figure: Competitive priorities of firms: group averages

Innovation and R&D. For instance, quality often cannot be improved without major changes in production processes. In discrete part manufacturing, the use of some key ideas from the Toyota Production System, which in turn require changes in layouts, process improvements and so on, have helped several firms across the world to improve quality. An exclusive focus on quality tools like SQC and SPC, or on programs like TQM and TPM without some basic changes may not achieve the desired purpose. However, this is currently not a priority, and it is not clear whether this link between quality and other required changes is well understood. Similarly, quality is largely a function of design. Without attention to product design, it is unlikely that improvement can be sustained. The recent interest in Business Process Re-engineering within the manufacturing function is more encouraging since it focuses on making some required fundamental changes.

Figure 2 gives a relative ranking of various manufacturing priorities of Indian firms. At the top of the list is the ability to provide consistent quality with low defects. It is being widely recognized that by reducing defects, firms can improve not only on price but also on delivery and flexibility parameters significantly as lead times reduce drastically. World class firms are now targeting six-sigma quality levels and are measuring defect in parts per million (or ppm). Figure 2 shows that firms are planning to pay attention to several aspects of manufacturing, and this is encouraging.

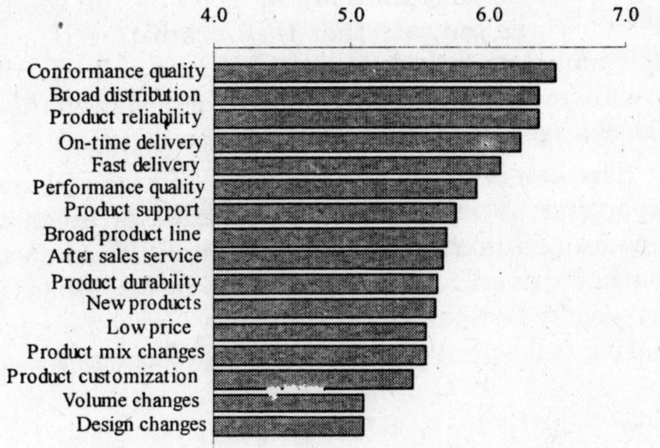

Figure: Competitive priorities of firms (degree of importance over next five years)

Interestingly, firms also perceive quality as their key strength with respect to their primary Indian competitor.

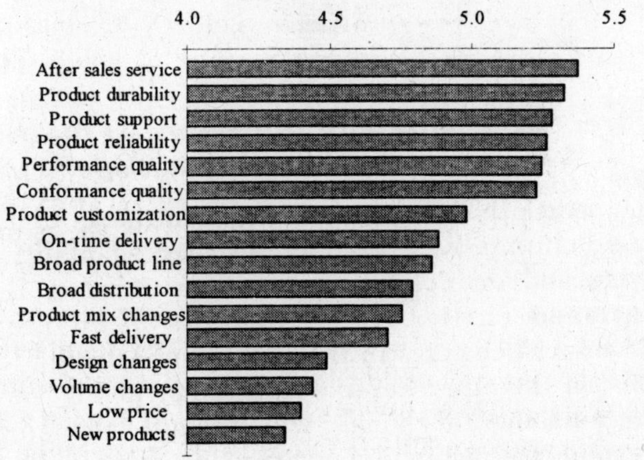

Figure: Perceived competitive strengths of firms (degree of strength relative to Indian competitors)

The Figure shows how firms have rated themselves with respect to domestic competition on a 7 point scale where a score of 4 indicates that they are as good as the competition, and higher scores indicate that they are better. These firms rate their ability to introduce new products and offer flexibility (in terms of managing volume changes or design changes or product mix changes) as being relatively low.

The competitive gap, or the difference between stated importance & strength, gives an idea of areas that require maximum attention in order to make manufacturing more "market driven". The largest gap is for broad distribution, followed by fast and on time delivery, developing new products, offering consistent quality with no defects, and reducing costs.

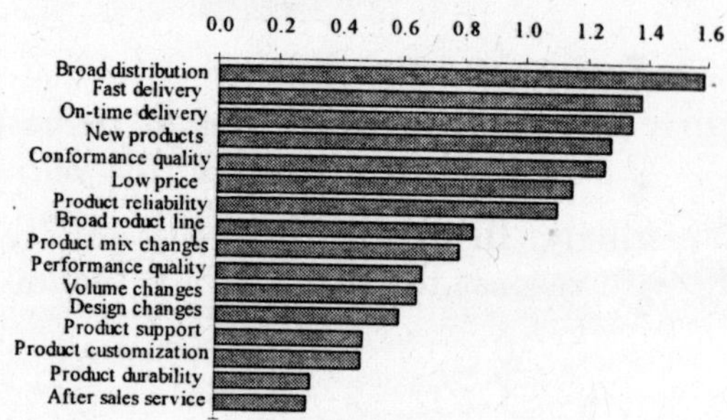

Figure: Competitive gap (difference of future priorities and current strengths)

It seems that the manufacturing strategy of most firms is focused on improving product and process quality, after sales service and on delivering products on-time. However, as mentioned earlier, improvements often require more fundamental changes in the way manufacturing is organised. Firms on the other hand are currently giving low priority to these fundamental changes which require changing processes, developing the ability to change product mix rapidly or investing in R&D to develop new processes and products.

On the other hand, in the United States, Innovation and R&D has the highest priority followed by structural changes. We discuss this issue in greater detail in the Section on International Comparisons. Interestingly, most Indian firms believe that they are at least as good as, or better than their foreign competitors on price, flexibility, quality, service and product design capabilities. This is seen in Figure 5 which has a 5 point scale, and where any score above 3 shows that the firm considers itself to be superior to foreign competitors. It is obvious that the average Indian firm's perception of its abilities differs considerably from its status in the global market place. This perception could be because many firms are not directly competing with MNCs in the same product market segments, or due to an inherent bias when firms are asked to rate themselves.

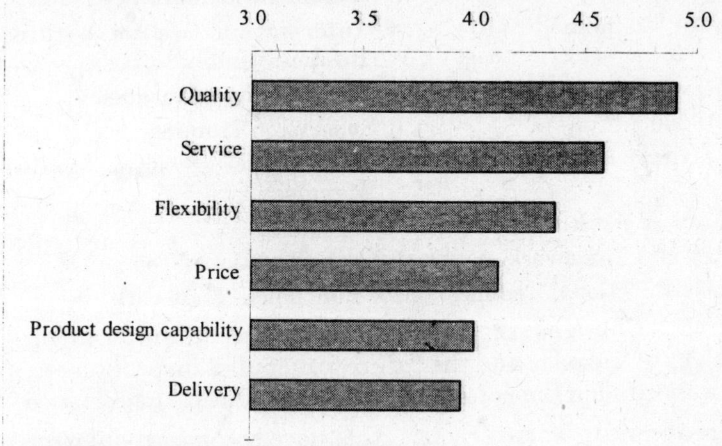

Figure: Comparison with foreign firms on various factors

Manufacturing companies have recently invested in a variety of improvement programmes or activities in order to enhance their competitiveness. Table 1 gives the changes in emphasis on various manufacturing related programmes. It lists the top ten programmes that Indian managers implemented in the last two years and compares them with the top ten initiatives that they will focus on in the next two years. It is evident that firms are investing in training their employees (note: worker training was accorded the eleventh position in terms of future emphasis) and on making their workers cross functional. In addition, firms believe that their investment in information technology (IT) in manufacturing will increase in the future. What is not clear is how they plan to use this information for better decision making. While managers have rated functional teamwork quite high in their list of priorities, they have given low priority to "reconfiguration of plant layouts" - a step necessary for implementing functional teamwork. Perhaps may firms have already made some of these changes. Automation in the form of robots, CIM, CAM, FMS,

Initiatives in the Past	Initiatives in the Future
1. Work Enlargement	1. Continuous Improvement
2. Management Training	2. Management Training
3. Continuous Improvement	3. Manufacturing Strategy
4. Worker Training	4. Information System within Business Unit
5. Supervisor Training	5. Total Quality Management
6. ISO 9000	6. Supervisor Training
7. Manufacturing Strategy	7. Information System within Manufacturing
8. Quality of Work Life	8. ISO 9000
9. Functional Teamwork	9. Cross Functional Teams
10. Cross Functional Teams	10. Functional Teamwork

Table: Changes in emphasis: Top ten manufacturing initiatives of the past and the future automated inspection etc., have been rated in the bottom ten in terms of future importance.

The absence of some practices that have become synonymous with world class manufacturing from the top ten list in Table is noticeable. Just-in-time manufacturing has still not found acceptance in Indian firms.

This could be because of several hurdles encountered while trying to implement such programs, or in some cases, due to poor understanding of JIT or pull production systems in the industry which has led to "unfavourable" myths developing around it. Other practices that have not been given adequate importance include forging customer and supplier partnerships, strategic outsourcing, use of statistical process control (SPC) effectively and continuously, value engineering and product re-design, use of CAD/CAE systems etc. Moreover, inadequate attention from top managers has sometimes not allowed firms to develop manufacturing into a competitive strength. Manufacturing related interventions are sometimes done piece meal, in line with the fads of the time. A well defined strategy with a clear understanding of the sequence of manufacturing programmes that must be implemented is missing.

It must be mentioned that Indian industry have "islands of excellence," i.e., firms that have recognized the need to change and have a well thought out plan of action to become competitive. Such firms have started implementing practices that are employed by world class plants. However, many firms do not seem to have a coherent plan about what needs to be done. For instance, in discrete part manufacturing, one possible route could be to first implement house-keeping and preventive maintenance programs, followed by conversion of manufacturing to flow shops, introduction of quality systems, setup reduction, and ISO certification, with the eventual goal of getting close to just-in-time manufacturing systems.

House Keeping involves maintaining a proper discipline in demarcating parts, tools & equipment locations, cleanliness etc. (including 5S Tools); preventive maintenance of equipments (including TPM) follows a regular schedule for machine & tool checkups instead of doing maintenance during breakdowns; flow manufacturing involves process flow analysis and cellular production layouts to smoothen flows of material on the shop floor and reduce WIP; quality systems include SPC and process capability analyses; setup reduction further enhances process effectiveness by trying to reduce changeover times and thereby increasing the flexibility of firms; and ISO certification helps the firm strengthen its internal systems.

Finally, JIT manufacturing facilitates a pull based production control, reduces investments in inventory, drastically cuts throughput and delivery times, improves quality on a sustained basis, and makes new product introduction much easier.

Similarly, a well thought out plan is required for continuous production or process industries. Establishing a program that implements these practices in a defined sequence allows the development of process discipline that is necessary to become a competitive manufacturer. Moreover, improvements of the nature mentioned above require little capital investment except those in training, instrumentation and calibration, and some changes in tooling and layouts.

Manufacturing Performance

The first question that needs to be asked is, given the above mentioned manufacturing strategy of Indian firms, how well have they performed ? It would also be useful to identify areas where intervention has been most beneficial and where it has not been successful. The 1997 survey shows that, over the last two years, there has been a marked improvement in the performance of firms on a variety of factors. Improvements in quality, especially, within the plant have been significant. In fact, 77 percent of firms that were surveyed reported an increase in profitability while 87 percent of firms claimed to have increased their market share. While these improvements should be viewed in terms of the low base value in many cases, the fact remains that the Indian industry has been changing rapidly for the better.

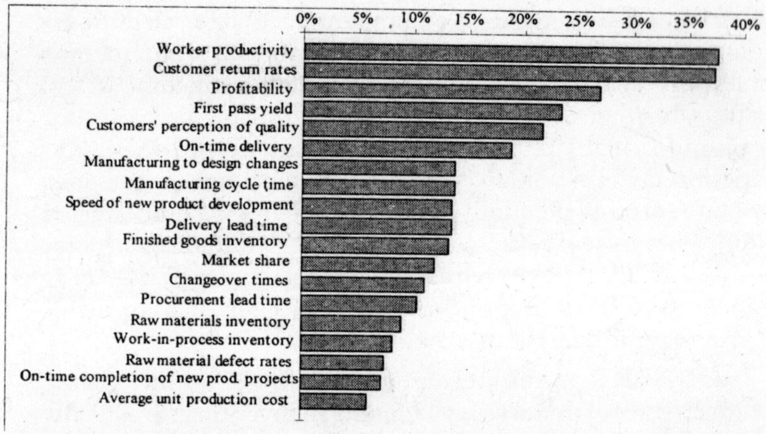

Figure: shows the extent of improvement in Indian manufacturing firms over the last two years.

The maximum improvement has occurred in the productivity of direct production workers (about 38 percent). There could be variety of reasons for the same: improved as well as increased emphasis on training of workers, incorporation of faster machines that also require fewer workers, etc. This has been followed by reduction in customer returns, improvements in first-pass yields and in the overall perception of quality by customers. Other dimensions that are worth mentioning in terms of improvements are on-time delivery, speed of response on the shop floor to design changes and reduction in manufacturing cycle times. It is apparent that shop floor improvement programmes, in many firms, are proving to be beneficial. However, there are three disturbing trends. First, though the mean improvement scores for factors like productivity of direct labour, customer return rates and profitability were the highest, the variance was also very high. Thus many firms have done well on these factors, but several others have not.

In fact, 9 percent of firms have reported a decline in productivity of production workers, 13 percent have seen an increase in return rates and 23 percent of firms have witnessed a loss in profitability in the last two years. Second, there has not been adequate improvement on inventory levels, i.e., raw material, work-in-process (WIP) and finished goods. In this case, 27 percent, 26 percent and 27 percent of sample firms have reported an increase in raw material, WIP and finished goods inventory respectively, over the last two years. This increase is not entirely explained by a corresponding increase in turnover. Third, the pre-occupation with labour productivity is evident although on the average, labour is only 10% of total cost. This is reflected in the fact that improvements in costs are relatively low compared to other improvements. More attention to materials and overheads which comprise 90% of costs is perhaps needed.

Therefore, we may have gained in some areas, but may be losing on others. Many of our firms have not yet been able to tightly control inventories across the supply chain. They still appear to be using inventories to meet demand rather than developing quick response manufacturing to meet changes in market needs. The relationship between batch sizes, WIP and lead times is very close. Increase in batch sizes leads to higher WIP and longer leadtimes. The key is to perform process analysis, de-bottleneck, reduce setup times and synchronize order release with throughput rates. In short, manufacturing has to become process oriented.

It provides a comparison on various indicators across industry types (e.g., automotive, consumer goods, electronics, engineering & machinery, textiles and process industry). We also present averages on these indicators for the entire sample as a whole. Some of this data can be benchmarked against overall industry averages from a similar survey done in the USA in 1994[3]. Performance appears to be varying across industry types.

Interestingly, for the period under study, Indian firms on the whole had a higher growth rate in sales (in unit as well as rupee terms) as compared to firms in the US though the pre-tax profit ratio was lower for the Indian firms. This lower realization of profits might indicate hidden costs due to low first pass yields, low inventory turns, high outstanding accounts, long lead times, etc. in Indian firms.

As can be expected, capacity utilization in the process industry is higher than that in discrete part manufacturing. The consumer goods, electronics, and engineering & machinery industries stand out in terms of low capacity utilization. The inventory turns in the process industry is quite low implying that working capital is tied up in this sector for longer periods of time.

Often process industries feel compelled to operate their plants continuously even when the demand is low thereby building up inventory. Inventory turns across are low - an issue which has been discussed earlier as well. Firms sometimes tend to keep expensive resources like machines busy all the time in order to recover their fixed cost.

This approach, stemming from an accounting view of manufacturing, often adds inventory, schedules production in large batches, and prevents firms from being market driven. Similarly, the first pass yield is relatively low in the automotive, consumer goods and electronics industries.

Many firms in the textile sector seem to be doing well financially but modern manufacturing practices and their benefits are yet to take roots here.

Average cash to cash cycle (i.e., total elapsed time from the date that a firms paid its suppliers for materials to the date it was paid by its customers for the products that were made from the same materials) ranges from over one month in the consumer goods industry to over two and half months in textile and slightly less than four months in the engineering & machinery sector. A similar picture emerges if we look at the value of outstanding accounts. There is scope for improvement on these dimensions.

International Comparisons

The US is paying more attention to several Innovation and R&D type of issues like product customisation, new products, design changes, and to issues which require manufacturing to be more flexible like product mix changes, production volume changes, and finally, low price. Indian industry on the other hand is paying attention to more basic issues like broad distribution, after sales service, product reliability and durability.

Indian industry is also interested in broadening their product line; however, to do that, they would need to invest in R&D, which is currently not a priority. To some extent these differences reflect the current realities and requirements. In the future, the Indian industry might need to change some of its priorities, especially if it wants to compete globally.

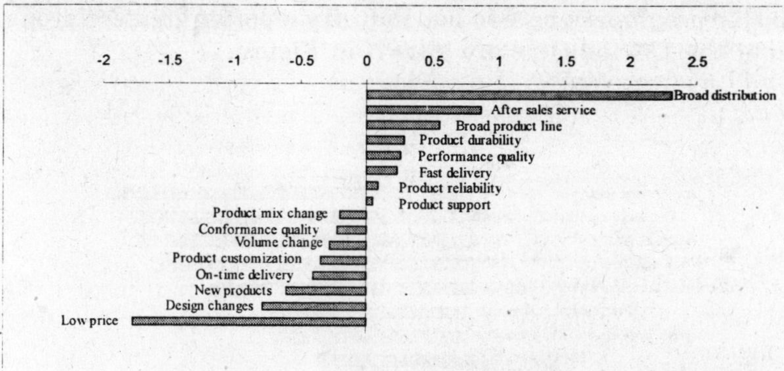

Figure. Comparison of manufacturing priorities between India and the US

Figure 8 shows the ten programs which are most important for US firms and least important for Indian firms. Here there are really significant differences in issues like design for manufacturability (DFM), supplier partnerships which now include global partnerships, worker training, business process re-engineering (BPR), cross functional teams and JIT. The numbers in the figure are the difference between the normalized values of different attributes of US frms and Indian firms.

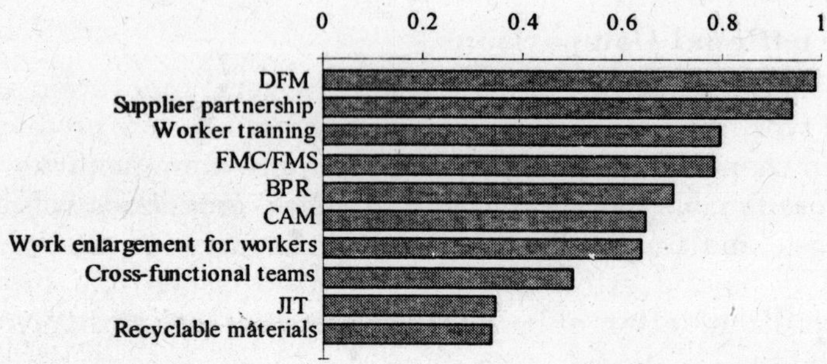

Figure: Programs which are the most important in the US and least important in India.

There are significant differences in terms of payoffs from manufacturing programs carried out in the two countries. The top ten programs where Indian industry reported greater payoffs than the US industry are shown in Figure.

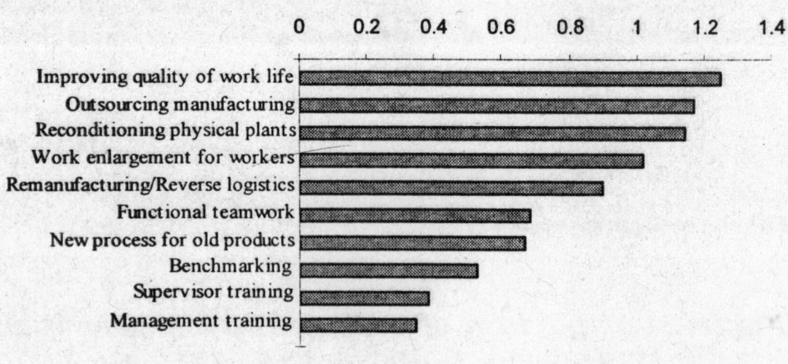

These include improving quality of work life, outsourcing, teamwork, benchmarking, new processes and training. These programs seem to be aimed at bringing manufacturing up to a basic minimum standard. In contrast, Figure shows the programs where the US industry reported greater payoffs. These include programs like JIT, SQC and SPC, CAD/CAE,

DFM (design for manufacturability) and relocation or closing of plants. Although some of these options may not be practical in India at least at this point of time, programs like JIT, SPC and DFM have shown quite clearly that they substantially improve manufacturing costs, quality and flexibility.

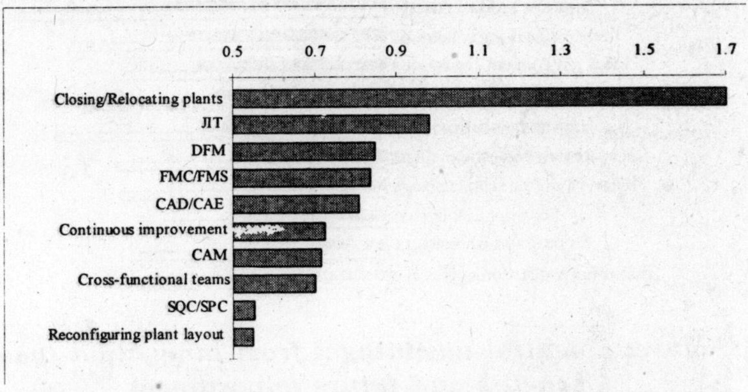

Figure. Programs where US companies got better payoffs than Indian companies

Towards the Future: Innovation

Innovation is widely seen as delivering long term benefits to an organization. In this context, innovation includes any new or substantially improved products that have been commercialized or any new or substantially improved manufacturing processes that have been used for the commercialization of products. Figure 11 shows the nature and extent of benefits that sample firms have enjoyed from innovation in the past with 7 denoting very high benefits and 1 denoting little or no benefits. The firms have also reported the future importance of these benefits via innovation. The top three benefits of innovation in the past have been improvement in product quality, improvement in working conditions & safety and ability to meet government regulations. Interestingly, product quality remains the top focus for innovation even in the future. However, the potential for maximum benefits of innovations are expected to come through product design changes, design for manufacturability, shortening of production cycle times, developing or expanding into foreign markets, and reduction in overhead costs

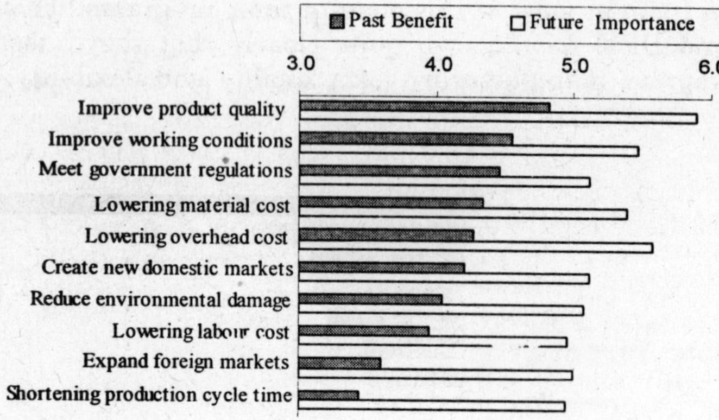

Figure: Potential advantages from innovation (past benefits and future importance)

While almost all the firms recognize the benefits of innovation, very few are investing adequate resources to make such programmes successful.

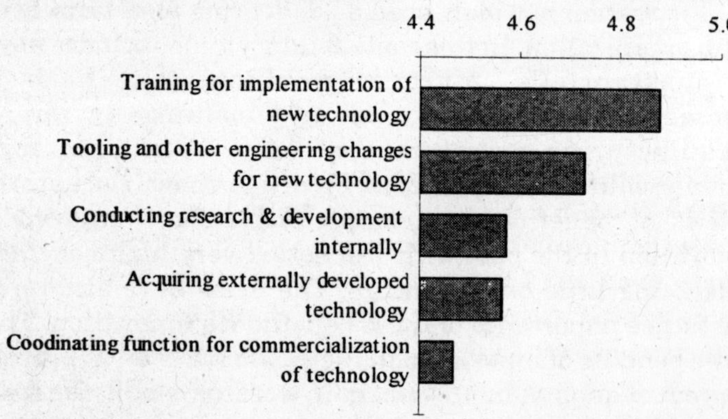

Figure: Projected investments (over next two years) in activities involved in innovation

On the average, the sample firms invested barely 0.84 percent of their sales revenue on internal research & development, 0.15 percent on acquiring externally developed technology, 1.15 percent on training for the implementation of new technology, 2.57 percent on toolings and other engineering changes to start-up new technology and 0.93 percent on coordination for commercializing new technology. These amounts are woefully inadequate given the relatively low turnovers in the Indian industry. As Figure 12 shows, Indian firms do not plan to change these patterns of investment significantly to develop long term capabilities. In this Figure, a score of 4 indicates that firms plan to invest about the same amount in each of the innovation activities as they did in the past two years. The maximum score of 7 represents a plan to invest "much more" in the future.

Supply Chain Management

Supply chain management deals with the process of coordinating the flow of information and goods to customers across a network of suppliers, manufacturers and distributors. Two factors often affect the bottom lines of firms significantly - uncertainty in demand or in availability of men, materials and machines; and long lead times. This is often not well understood in the industry. It has been seen that by improving the flow of information across the supply chain and by reducing cycle times, firms are able to reduce the impact of uncertainty. As we have seen in an earlier section, Indian firms have started paying attention to reducing lead times. However, availability of information on current inventory levels, flow of materials, as well as demand forecasts to different functions within a firm remains poor. As a result, coordination across functions is based either on inaccurate data or personal contacts. This leads to high inventories and delays in most supply chains. There is an absence of a systems approach to planning across the chain.

Most firms in the sample rate the capabilities of their suppliers lower than those of their distributors. Figure 13 shows the difference between the current capabilities of the suppliers of firms and those of their distributors. The key concern that firms have relates to inventories. On a scale of one to seven, the firms on the average rate the ability of their suppliers to optimize inventory levels as 4.18 and those of its distributors as 4.98. Both these figures are not very good, and there is scope for improvement.

The supply chain of an Indian firm has an interesting structure.

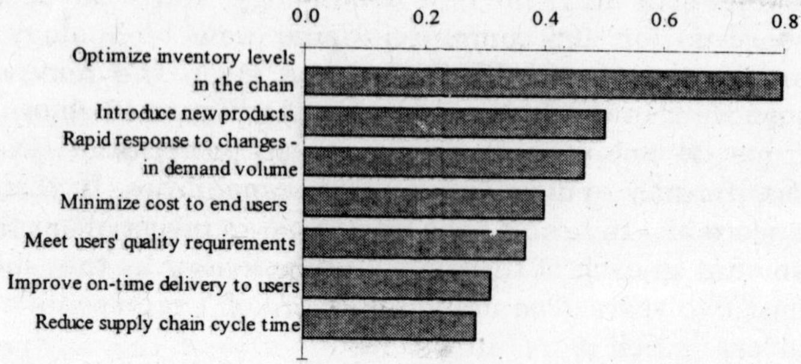

Figure: Difference between current capabilities of suppliers and distributors

The mean (median) values for number of suppliers per firms, number of regional distributors and number of approved retailers were around 436 (112), 210 (15), and 35,077 (200) respectively.

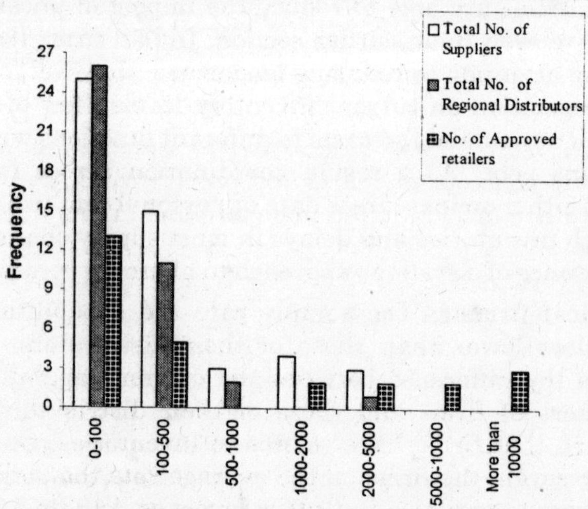

Figure: Distribution of various entities in Indian manufacturing supply chain

By international standards, firms still have far too many suppliers. This adds to problems of coordination, delivery, quality and cost. A smaller supplier base sometimes allows firms to work closely with suppliers and raise the level of the entire operations in terms of product quality, cost and even product design. The data shows that about 43 percent of firms had less than 100 suppliers. Similarly 46 percent firms had less than 100 distributors and 23 percent of firms had less than 100 approved retailers. As the chain progresses from the suppliers to customers, the number of entities increases. While development of capabilities in suppliers becomes crucial, effective coordination of flows & information is the key to successful channel management.

Becoming World Class Manufacturers

The focus of this survey has been to understand how top managers are trying to develop a coherent strategy for improving the manufacturing competitiveness of their firms. We also try to identify factors that these top managers find important in order to enhance the performance of their operations in the future. It can be clearly stated that our firms are going through a "quiet" quality revolution - quality systems are being developed and put in place, measurements are being refined and people are getting trained. The benefits are also obvious. However, the distribution of firms with significant quality programs is highly skewed.

A few firms have progressed by leaps and bounds where workers plot control charts and practice SPC, their managers are trained in TPM (often in Japan) and are implementing the same, process capability of their machines is strictly monitored (with world class cp_k levels above 1.33), in-process defect rates are in the range of 200-700 ppm, and customer return rates are less than one per cent. On the other hand, a large number of firms is struggling with housekeeping, monitoring quality problems, training of managers but not of workers. There are two related observations: first, in a large number of firms the understanding of quality tools is superficial - as a result, progress beyond a certain level is slow; second, many firms are not consistent in their emphasis on quality which results in employees not taking it very seriously.

Some firms have improved their performance on lead time, and have started simplifying the flow of information and material. However, in discrete part manufacturing, most firms have not adequately addressed some difficult issues like drastically cutting lead times by changing the mode of operation from push to pull, reducing setup times, converting job shops to flow shops or using cellular layouts. Very few implementations of JIT are found in our plants - partly due to the fact that we are unable to contain the impact of uncertainty, partly due to high setup times and partly due to the fact that many managers still do not understand the basics of JIT. There is a widespread feeling that JIT simply transfers inventory to suppliers, or that it does not deliver any benefits, especially in India. However, JIT goes far beyond inventory reduction and improves quality, lead times, cuts cost and makes manufacturing more flexible and responsive. Cellular manufacturing is also not a priority for similar reasons. On the positive side, the recent interest in business process re-engineering is encouraging because it is process oriented and helps bring about fundamental changes.

One area of concern is the management of inventories across the supply chain. Most firms have not appreciated the advantage of coordinating various decisions and plans across different entities in the chain - the suppliers are optimizing locally, the plants are optimizing locally and the distribution channels are doing the same. As a result, inventories remain high with working capital being tied up for longer periods of time, there are delays in delivery and the overall cost across the chain remains high. Decisions that seem to be good for one entity turnout to be bad for the entire supply chain. More information has to flow between entities in the supply chain and more decisions have to be made collectively. Many firms are still reluctant to help their suppliers improve their capabilities.

Investments in innovation and R&D activities continue to be very low. Indian manufacturing managers must be aware of the potential dangers of becoming over-dependent on borrowed technology (i.e., products, processes as well as practices). It must be recognized that in the future, firms can stay competitive only through their own innovations. A one time import of technology might be useful, but continuous dependence on borrowed technologies may not be feasible in the future with several multinational corporations themselves entering the Indian market. For firms in the export market, a certain level of strength in manufacturing and R&D is even more important. Put simply, there is no world class company in the manufacturing sector which does not have world class manufacturing and innovation.

One factor that may be partly responsible for the inadequate attention to innovation and continuous improvement is a lack of the right type of training to workers. Whenever firms have paid attention to workforce training, benefits have followed. The authors have documented a number of such cases. Training of workers has been a significant contributor to improvements in several other countries. The automotive sector in India seems to have appreciated the need for worker training. One of the worst training records can be found in the textile sector. As a result the former is quite modern while the latter is very outdated.

Finally, we must get into the habit of benchmarking our performance. The perception of our top managers that their plants are at least as good as their global competitors' plants is a little disturbing. Benchmarking reveals a lot of information on our strengths and weaknesses and several world class manufacturing plants have used this as a starting point in their improvement efforts.

Manufacturing in India is at a critical juncture. Many of our firms are already on the way to becoming world-class, and several others are standing at the threshold. But the average firm is still very far from this threshold. A fundamental issue here is our view of manufacturing. The traditional view that manufacturing is a support activity for marketing or finance, and therefore needs little top management attention is perhaps no longer there in Indian firms. However, a more subtle view still persists. Thus, top managers often want to invest in one large effort to improve manufacturing. After that, they want to go back to their traditional concerns. Meanwhile, international competitors are continuously working on improving manufacturing, bringing in new products, and making manufacturing more flexible and responsive. These firms view manufacturing and R&D in a different way: they recognise it as one of the key sources of their competitive advantage. Therefore, they are continuously honing and perfecting their skills and capabilities in manufacturing. A senior executive of a well known international company, widely acknowledged as the industry leader in manufacturing, said at a conference " it seems we enjoy a good reputation. But internally, we know our weaknesses and are constantly striving to overcome them."

To effectively institutionalise a culture of continuous improvements, top management must have a well thought out manufacturing strategy. Instead, companies often rely on a massive one time effort or a series of piece meal efforts. Top management must understand the strategic dimensions of manufacturing as well as it understands marketing or finance. Very often, top management's involvement in manufacturing is confined to approving capacity expansion plans, approving budgets for equipment purchase, training, or for hiring consultants. But evolving a strategy and carrying it through requires much more than that. Companies that have successfully done this have either become industry leaders worldwide, or have established a secure and profitable niche. They have realised that competitors can quickly imitate marketing or financial strategies, but it takes several years to duplicate a manufacturing advantage.

Bibliography

Angel, Bradley: *Toxic Threat to Indian Lands: A Greenpeace Report*, San Francisco, Greenpeace, 1991.

Bailey, Conner and Charles E. Faupel: *Environmentalism and Civil Rights in Sumter County*, Colorado, Westview Press. 1992.

Burch, William R. Jr.: *Human Ecology: An Environmental Approach*, Belmont, Duxbury Press, 1994.

Chrispeels, Maarten : *Plants, Genes and Crop Biotechnology*, Sudbury MA, Jones and Barlett Publishers, 2003.

Edwards-Rees, D.: *The Service of Youth Book*, Wallington, Religious Education Press, 1943.

Gelobter, Michael: *The Distribution of Air Pollution by Income and Race*, Berkeley, University of California, 1989.

Gitman, Lawrence J.: *Principles of Managerial Finance*, MA: Addison Wesley Longman, 2000.

Johnson, Hazel: *Financial Institutions and Markets: A Global Perspective*, NY, McGraw Hill, 1993.

Martin, Justin: *The Man Behind Money*, Perseus Book Group, 2000.

Milson, F.: *Growing With the Job*, London, National Assocation of Youth Clubs, 1968.

Petty, Keown, Scott, and Martin: *Basic Financial Management*, Prentice Hall, 1993.

Schall and Haley: *Introduction to Financial Management*, McGraw-hill, 1988.

Sontheimer, Sally: *Women and the Environment: Crisis and Development in the Third World*, New York, Monthly Review Press, 1991.

Vallette, J.: *The International Trade in Wastes: A Greenpeace Inventory*, Washington, Greenpeace, 1989.

Index

O

P

S

V

W

□□□